Advanced Brain Training

Simon Wootton
Terry Horne

Hodder Education

338 Euston Road, London NW1 3BH.

Hodder Education is an Hachette UK company

First published in UK 2012 by Hodder Education

This edition published 2012

www.hoddereducation.co.uk

Cover image © Eric Isselée – Fotolia

Typeset by Cenveo Publisher Services.

Printed in Great Britain by CPI Group (UK) Ltd, Croydon, CR0 4YY.

Also available
in ebook

Contents

Dedication

I dedicate this book to my family.

Firstly my wife, Gillian, for tolerating me for writing books, along with a full-time job in the NHS; secondly my eldest daughter, Ellis, who has just commenced her sixth form years having done very well at her GCSEs; thirdly my son, James, who is just starting his GCSEs and wants to go into medicine as a career, and last but not least, my youngest daughter, Holly, who still remains the baby of our family but who is very caring and protective of other people. Thanks for all your support and encouragement and for putting up with a 'grumpy dad' at times!

Simon

I dedicate this book to Carolyn, and Danya.

Carolyn did not live to write her own books. She was hit by a car when training for the London Marathon. She died instantly. A great conceptual thinker, Carolyn constantly demonstrated her capacity for Applied Thinking by maintaining complex networks of close relationships. Her children's party games and reunion trips were legendary. Carolyn's concept of 'The Match' spawned the development of Early Years Education and helped to build the largest single campus Teacher Training Institute in the UK.

My beautiful daughter, Danya, is five years old. She and her baby sister, Tanzeela, were both born between the rock of their mother's tumour and the hard place of their mother's backbone. Only the courage and pain bearing of their mother, Fakhrun Nisa, has enabled them to survive where Brilliana could not. Danya is kind and clever, in mind and brain, as well as beautiful in face and body. She still struggles between a rock and a hard place. My heart hurts everyday that I fail to protect her, and her adopted sister, Yandu.

Terry

Acknowledgements

Dr. Claire Bacha, Psychoanalytic Psychotherapist and Group Analyst. Claire was the prompt, foil and sounding board for much that is original in this edition.

Tony Doherty, Director of Research at the School of African and Oriental Studies, University of London, for his permission to build on *A Thoughtful Approach to the Practice of Management* – the starting point of subsequent research at the University of Central Lancashire, with Roger Armstrong and Gilly McHugh, and later, with Peter Ruddock and Jane Griffiths.

To Professor Peter Stokes at Chester, for his challenge and support.

To Professor Susan Greenfield, former Director of Royal Institute and author of *The Human Brain* (1997) which was the starting point for our neurochemical models of the thinking process.

To Gianni Iaverdino, restaurateur.

To generations of research students including Nickoletta, John, Nadine, Simon, Jay, Marilena, Rachel, Tobyn, Eli, Marcus, Alicia, and James.

First thoughts: Beyond brain training to Advanced Applied Thinking

This book is for people who are, or who wish to become, leading thinkers within their chosen field, or within their wider community.

In every area of endeavour, the gap is wide between followers and leaders. It is necessary to have original ideas. But it is not sufficient. You must be able to think out tactics and plans and put original ideas into practice.

In the twenty-first century, Advanced Applied Thinkers are highly rewarded. The twentieth century has bequeathed many practical problems, e.g. obesity, inequality and young people who are alienated, thoughtless, 'mindless' and unreasonable. Alongside these problems, come opportunities. No longer do we need big muscles, or even machine skills, to earn a good living. Information-based economies need people who can think in ways that turn information into knowledge on which profitable action can be taken. Fortunately the thinking skills required to earn a good living are the same as the thinking skills needed to live a good life.

This book is in three parts.

Part One helps you to understand how to build new and strong connections between different parts of your brain, so that you can use them in concert. You will learn how to increase the cognitive capacity of different parts of your brain, and how to use different parts of your brain in powerful combinations and sequence.

Part Two will help you to develop Advanced Thinking Skills. You will need these Advanced Thinking Skills to take advantage of your increased brain power. It is like doing an Advanced Driving Course when you buy a high-performance car.

Part Three shows you how to develop creative high intelligence with which to deploy your new skills in Advanced Applied Thinking.

Each of the three parts of the book has three sections which will introduce and explain the relevance of recent discoveries by neuroscientists; explain how you can make use of these discoveries; and give you a workout. Different kinds of workouts have been designed to let you practise (and enjoy!) doing puzzles, solving problems and carrying out thought experiments which have been selected and designed by neuroscientists and philosophers.

Finally, the section 'Final Thoughts', *asks,* 'If we do not help our children to think, how can we expect them to be thoughtful? If we don't help them to reason, how can we expect their behaviour to be reasonable?'

This book builds on the success of our series on brain training for Hodder Education, and our best selling books for Kogan Page on *Strategic Planning, Strategic Thinking* and *Strategic Leadership*, the latter nominated as Best Book on Leadership and Management, by the British Institute of Management. This book is based on up-to-date information about how your brain thinks and about the kind of practical problems you need to solve, the decisions you need to take, and plans you need to make, in order to live a good life and earn a good living.

By working your way through puzzles and exercises which are based on twenty-first-century problems, you will develop thinking skills you need.

N.B. As with all lateral thinking or creative thinking puzzles, neural escape paths will only be created by repeated myelination, so do resist looking up answers to any puzzle you cannot solve. A problem you cannot solve is a gift of an opportunity to expand the neural pathways and connections in your brain. Share your struggle with others, but do not give up by looking at the answers in Appendix 1.

Part 1

The make-up of your mind

From brain training to Applied Thinking

1.1

Neuroscience and mental fitness

In this section you will:
- *find out about the neuroscience of mental fitness*
- *learn about the brain and the mind*
- *think about male and female brains.*

1.1.1 Some thoughts about mental fitness

BRAIN RESEARCH AND BRAIN SCANNING: LESSONS AND LIMITATIONS

Recently, ideas on Advanced Applied Thinking (AAT©) have benefited greatly from the ability to watch images of brains, while their owners are thinking about different types of decisions, problems and plans. From the 1970s onwards, we have been trying to imagine what happens inside your brain when you try to think. We were trying to help students, teachers, managers, therapists, social workers and public sector workers to learn to think more effectively about the kinds of decisions they needed to take, the kinds of problems they needed to solve, and the kinds of plans they needed to make.

At first, we were helped by the then prevailing model, or metaphor, of brain-as-computer. This was popular in the 1970s and 1980s, when it was found useful to think of the brain as computer hardware, and the mind as computer software. The idea was beguiling.

However, we kept finding aspects of the ways our students were thinking that the computer model failed to explain. In 1997, Susan Greenfield's model of the brain as a chemical factory liberated us from the straitjacket of our computer model. Suddenly we could better understand the successes and the difficulties we were having with our students. Susan Greenfield's neurochemical approach gave us ways to understand what we already knew.

At last, we could understand why, for many people, learning about almost anything seemed to increase their capacity to learn. For other people, lots of repetitions of relatively simple thinking tasks seemed to produce marked improvements in their capacity to think. This supported our emerging view that Advanced Applied Thinking was a skill, or rather a combination of 15 or so contributory skills (see Figure 1.1).

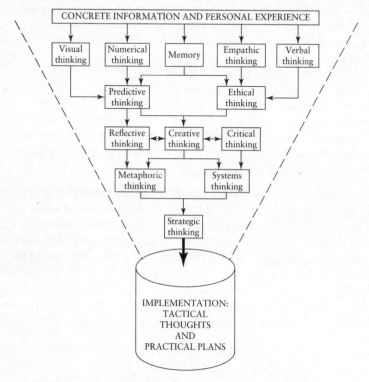

Figure 1.1 Modelling the components: Advanced Applied Thinking

Although logic remains the backbone of good thinking, it is a necessary but not sufficient condition for thinking well. Parts of the brain, other than the frontal cerebral cortex, seem to have a role to play in Advanced Applied Thinking.

In *The Human Brain* (Greenfield, 1997), we found that, for example, the parts of your brain that control visual images, and the parts of your brain that empathize with the likely thoughts and feelings of other people, also work in concert with other parts of your brain that hold different facets of your memory. All these parts of your brain can help the frontal lobe of your cortex to take a more logical decision, or make a more rational plan. We discovered that otherwise matched groups of people who were encouraged to draw, sketch or map problem situations, could think more quickly and more accurately, and produce neater, more elegant solutions, than groups of people who were not directed to do so. Susan Greenfield's work gave us the confidence to extend our ideas on combination thinking, and to devise brain training exercises that involved the simultaneous use of different parts of the brain.

THE STRUCTURE AND COMPOSITION OF THE BRAIN

If you want to develop Advanced Applied Thinking, it can be helpful to find out something about the structure and composition of the brain you are seeking to train. Inside your skull, your brain has the consistency of a sloppy undercooked egg. It has no moving parts. It is surrounded by a colourless circulating fluid. This cerebrospinal fluid contains mainly salt and sugar.

The brain itself is wrinkled and creamy in colour. Although it would fit into the palm of your hand, it is as heavy as three bags of sugar. The brain has two halves and looks rather like a small cauliflower whose stalk tapers to become the top of your spinal cord. The back of the cauliflower overhangs the stalk slightly. The overhang is called the 'cerebellum'. The main part is called the 'cerebrum'.

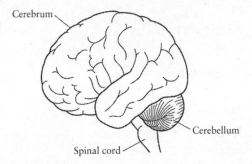

Figure 1.2 The brain

If you turn the brain over, you will see distinct regions that occur in pairs; the underside of the brain appears to be symmetrical about a central line running from the front to the back of the brain. That's its shape. What about its size? And does size really matter?

DIFFERENT JOBS FOR DIFFERENT BITS OF THE BRAIN

Your cerebral cortex is divided into about 50 different areas, many of which have a definite specialized function. In some parts of the cortex, towards the back for instance (the posterior parietal cortex), the distinction between the areas is more blurred. The posterior parietal cortex handles many sensations – sound, sight, touch and movement.

In mature learners, the frontal lobes become active when they are asked to empathize, make predictions or tackle problems that involve planning, complex decisions or creative thinking. Teenagers, or adults under 25, often struggle with these kinds of thinking tasks. This is because the development of the frontal area of their cerebral cortex often lags behind the bushing of their back brain, which is preoccupied with sensation and stimulation. Until the development of their frontal lobes catches up, young people are often reluctant to volunteer verbal information. They can appear to be anti-social.

NEURONS: THE BUILDING BLOCKS OF THE BRAIN

Neurons have a squat, blob-like body, called a 'soma'. The soma sprouts tiny branches called 'dendrites'. Commonly, neurons appear elongated, with dendrites at either end, sometimes on the end of a long thin fibre called an 'axon'. The axon is commonly two to three times longer than the body of the neuron.

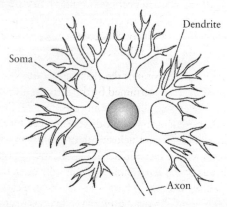

Figure 1.3 The soma

Spinal neurons can trail axons a metre long. So, squat somas, with long thin tails ending in stubby dendrite branches are the building blocks of creative intelligence, and your ability to learn to think.

These are the vessels within which chemical reactions take place, which underpin your Advanced Applied Thinking.

The role of the soma is to ensure the survival of the neuron, but what about the dendrites and the axons. What do they do?

DENDRITES AND AXONS

The dendrites are receiving stations for chemical messages sent out by neighbouring neurons. The chemical messages converge down the dendrites into the neuron body. If the signals are strong enough, the neuron will generate an electrical charge that will be conducted down the axon, towards the dendrites of neighbouring neurons.

The charges are carried by either positively charged sodium, potassium or calcium cations, or by negatively charged chloride anions. The charged anions and cations cannot normally pass through the fatty inter-layers of the neuron wall. However, an accumulation of negative charges on the inside of the wall of the neuron will attract, rather like a magnet, ions and proteins of opposite charge to the outside of the neuron wall, thereby generating a potential difference, or voltage, across the cell wall. When this voltage reaches about 80 milli volts (mV), channels open through the neuron walls to allow positively charged ions (usually sodium) to enter the neuron to neutralize the negative charges on the inside of the neuron. When the charge inside the neuron becomes about 20 mV positive, then potassium ions, positively charged, are allowed out through the wall of the neuron until a negatively charged state is restored inside the neuron. All this happens in a thousandth of a second.

The direction of transmission of the electrical charges, and the speeds of the transmission, are determined by the directions and condition of the axons. If the axon is already connected to a dendrite of another neuron, then that predetermines the direction taken by the charge. If the axon is surrounded by a thick sheath of healthy myelin insulation, the transmission will be fast and accurate. Because we often wish to minimize the delay between one thought and the next, or between thought and action, chemical charges hustle down axons at more than 400 kph, when the myelin insulation of the axon is in good condition.

SYNAPSES: HOW TO BRIDGE THAT GAP

What happens when the electrically charged chemicals hit the gap between the end of the axon and the dendrites of a neighbouring neuron?

With the development of electron microscopes, with magnification factors of over 10,000, chemicals were detected swimming across the synaptic gap. Among the chemicals detected were many differently shaped molecules of acetylcholine. These acetylcholine derivatives belong to a general class of brain chemicals known as 'neurotransmitters'.

The more frequently that electrically charged chemicals were seen arriving at the end of the axon, the more frequently acetylcholine neurotransmitters were seen to be launching themselves into the water in the synaptic gap. The small size of the neurotransmitters enabled them to diffuse very quickly across the salty water that surrounded the axons and dendrites. They crossed the gap in less than a millisecond, but how did they know which dendrite to choose?

Each neurotransmitter swimming across the gap is like a jigsaw piece, looking for a dendrite with a receptor molecule of exactly the right shape to make a perfect fit. Once the neurotransmitter finds and locks on to a correctly fitting receptor, this signals to the channel in the wall of the second neuron to admit a charged chemical. An accumulation of charged chemicals moves down the dendrites of the second neuron into the cell body, and out along the axon of the second neuron, to the edge of the next synaptic gap, where it stares across the water at a third neuron. This is going on inside your chemical brain 24 hours a day, a million times a second!

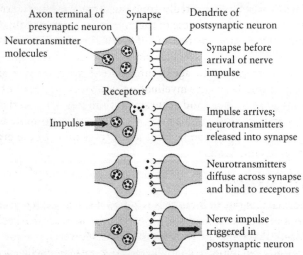

Figure 1.4 Transmitting nerve impulses

YOUR AMAZING BRAIN

It is the quantity (and quality) of neuron connections, not the number of neurons, that appears to determine your mental potential and your mental performance. This changed our view on the way the adult brain develops. Work by Siegler at Carnegie, USA in the late 1990s, on embryos, babies, pre-school infants, teenagers, adults and seniors, indicates that brain development is ongoing throughout adult life and that you need not accept the definite cut-offs that were once expected in the development of adult intelligence and in the Advanced Applied Thinking skills that contribute to it.

WHEN WE WERE YOUNG ... AND LEARNING

The surfeit of synapses makes new learning easy for teenagers and young adults, but the lag in the development of the frontal cortex means that this area of a young person's brain must be engaged explicitly before critical thinking and reflective learning can fully exploit the learning of a young person.

Every year, the young adult brain can lose up to seven in a thousand of its neurons, causing the young adult brain to shrink and lose weight. But, neuron loss can be more than compensated by learning things, almost anything. This is because learning increases the density of the synaptic connections in the neurons that remain. Also, by repeatedly applying what you have learned, you can increase the thickness of the myelin insulation around the axons of the surviving neurons. This thicker myelin insulation results in quicker and clearer electrical transmission through the brain and more secure storage of information, with less risk of it being corrupted. Thicker myelination improves the recall of memories and the speed and accuracy of thinking. The puzzles, exercises and activities in this book are designed to promote both an increase in synaptic connections and a thickening of the myelin insulation in your brain.

AS YOU MATURE

Your normal loss rate of brain cells is between seven and ten neurons a year out of every thousand you have. This can increase markedly if you drink alcohol or use recreational drugs. However, you can preserve and even improve your IQ, and your creative intelligence. This is because many of the thinking skills that contribute to intelligent behaviour improve naturally as you get older, as long as you learn to use them explicitly when you need them.

It is a mistaken belief that memory necessarily deteriorates with age. In fact, your ability to recall early knowledge and experiences may get better. This is because recall benefits from repetition and you are more likely to have repeated the recall the older you get. On the other hand, what is likely to deteriorate, as an adult, is the speed at which you can form new memories. New information processing often does slow down. The brain training exercises in this book can help you avoid this. There are also activities that can help to reverse any decline in processing speed and new memory formation that you may have already suffered. You can learn to use predictive thinking skills, so that you can make an earlier start on thinking tasks that might otherwise be impaired by slower processing.

CAUSES OF DAMAGE AND DECLINE IN THE ADULT BRAIN

It is fortunate that brain training can repair damage, because your brain is susceptible to damage from:

- ▶ alcohol
- ▶ lack of exercise
- ▶ grief, low mood or pessimism
- ▶ raised blood pressure and stress
- ▶ all manner of environmental threats
- ▶ lack of a 'conversational' relationship
- ▶ poor diet and the food additives in processed food.

Overall, mental performance doesn't necessarily decline with age if you stay healthy. Certain illnesses and diseases can directly lower mental performance, but just getting older doesn't necessarily do so. People who do not use their brains productively as they get older tend to drag down the average scores for older adults and so obscure the high scores of those older people who do use their brains actively.

Edward Coffey, of the Henry Ford Foundation, reported that even adults aged from 65 to 90, who used their brains actively, continued to perform well with no signs of loss of memory or reason, despite their MRI scans showing shrinkage in the size of their brains. In 2002, Quartz reported on a famous study of 4,000 nuns. This study was commenced by David Snowdon in Kentucky, USA in 1986. The study is particularly interesting because all the nuns have similar lifestyles but some continue to teach and to be mentally active and some don't. The nuns who continue to be mentally active are currently living, on average, four years longer, and their brain autopsies show, on average, 40 per cent more synapses and thicker myelin insulation on their axons.

Advanced Applied Thinking can help to keep your brain healthier and to keep you alive longer. Advanced Applied Thinking 'adds years to your life and life to your years' (American Society of Gerontologists).

THE ADVANTAGES OF A CHEMICAL BRAIN

Chemicals react to different extents, and at different speeds, depending on the chemical environment in which the reaction takes place. You have the ability to change the chemical environment in which your brain is trying to do its chemical work. As a result, you can affect the extent and speed of the chemical reactions in your brain, and so improve its performance. You can change the chemical environment in your brain through diet, sleep, ergonomics, and stress reduction and by doing the mental and physical exercises and puzzles in this book.

A chemical model of the brain can help you to understand how the frequent practice of separate and combined Advanced Applied Thinking skills can progressively improve the speed and accuracy of your thinking, because each repetitive pass through a neuron increases the thickness of its myelin insulation.

If a problem recurs, a chemical model of the thinking process leaves open the exciting possibility that you won't always come up with the same response, or solution. Because the neurons that are involved the first time are changed by that involvement, the chances are increased of a novel response should the same problem or input be presented a second time. This has important implications for the development of creative thinking. Not only do we think and learn, but the way we think and learn gets better in the process.

Finally, a chemical brain holds out the prospect of improving mental functions during adulthood. Decline is not inevitable. Your brain weight will not decline significantly before you are 90 years of age and, on average, 80 per cent of your brain weight will still be left even at 90. That is more than enough neurons as long as they are well connected. And 80 per cent is an average. If you train your brain, your brain weight is likely to be above the average, like the nuns who are continuing to learn and teach.

Brain chemistry has shown that Alzheimer's and Parkinson's are diseases. Diseases may produce premature ageing, but they are not a necessary consequence of getting older. That is not to say that your neurons will not change at all during your old age. They will. Consequently, you may perform less well on time-constrained problem solving and on tasks that require rapid memorization of new information but, as is shown in *Keep Your Brain Sharp* (Wootton and Horne, 2010b), these disadvantages can be more than compensated by exploiting the many aspects of mental functioning that improve with age, like verbal reasoning, reflective learning, prediction and creativity. In the end, what matters most is not the weight of your brain, but the extent and quality of its interconnectedness, and this is helped by social learning, thoughtful conversation, meaningful relationships, broad experience, and by working through the thought experiments, thinking exercises, perplexing puzzles and devilish dilemmas in sections 1.2, 1.3, 2,1 and 2.3; taking the real world difficult decisions needed in the Case Study in section 2.3; following the ten-day brain boost plan in section 3.1; developing creative high intelligence the 4S© way in section 3.2; and finally by challenging yourself as an Advanced Applied Thinker in the workout at section 3.3 at the end of this book.

1.1.2 The brain and the mind

IS SUPERHUMAN INTELLIGENCE POSSIBLE?

Our neurochemical model of a thinking brain presents no visible limitations to the development of superhuman intelligence. The only prerequisites are an adequate dietary supply for neurochemical building blocks such as myelin, acetylcholine and other hormones and enzymes involved in the thinking process, and enough time to devote to the exercises and activities that increase cell interconnections and myelination and which also promote chemical conditions needed to further the extent, speed and efficiency of the chemical reactions involved in thinking. However, not everyone will agree.

Since confidence and optimism are proven indicators of successful outcomes, you should be prepared to defend yourself against at least three challenges, all of which merit respect. To be forewarned is to be forearmed!

Challenge 1: Is superhuman intelligence possible?

Challenge 1 is a subset of the general challenge to science and to scientists. This can become particularly animated when scientists have the temerity to try to explain the human mind. The thinking of romantic mystics and other irrationalists may not prioritize the logic, and what they perceive as reductionism, of science. The tentative hypothesis and putative theories of neuroscientists are seen as impatient and inferior to those insights that might be gained from longer contemplation.

Challenge 2: Is superhuman intelligence possible?

Challenge 2 comes from dogma. You should take heed of the fate that befell Galileo. He got into serious trouble when his scientific methods of hypothesis and revision threatened truth, as perceived by others. Galileo threatened the livelihoods of the priests and of the then established religions. There are many established belief systems in the field of human behaviour and human consciousness. Beware those priests who offer models that map your own. They are skilled colonialists! They will try to colonize your ideas to control your thinking.

Challenge 3: Is superhuman intelligence possible?

Challenge 3 comes from postmodernists who see all truth as relative and variable with context. Paranoid postmodernists see ulterior motives everywhere. They may see neuroscientists as agents of the free market, or as anarchic liberals, or purveyors of an opiate optimism that helps to sedate resistance to the working of capitalism. Their critiques are valid from within their collective paradigm. But their paradigm is not the one occupied by the authors, or by those readers who would like to use neuroscience to improve how they think at work, at home or in society.

All three of these challenges will come from outside the scientific tradition, and so they will be hard for you to refute. Guard against being drawn onto ground where taken-for-granted assumptions will automatically undermine beliefs that may be useful to you, once you have acted upon them sufficiently to gain confidence and skill in their application.

Critics will seize upon your everyday scientific confusions, in the same way that religious fundamentalists undermined early attempts to understand the movement of the moon. Such challenges will always be mounted by iconoclasts and by defensive 'dropouts from the age of reason' (Calvin, W., 1997)

1.1.3 Male brains and female minds

WHAT'S THE DIFFERENCE?

▶ On average men's brains are 10 per cent bigger than women's.
▶ Women have the same number of brain cells as men.
▶ Women have more lateral cortex connections.

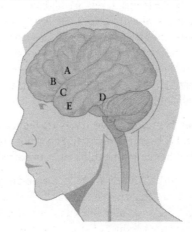

Figure 1.5

Area A is known as the anterior cingulate. It is active while you are evaluating information or evidence, or while you are taking decisions or passing judgments, or while you forming opinions or worrying. This area of the brain is larger in women.

Area B is known as the prefrontal cortex. It is active while you try to control emotions. This area of the brain is larger in women.

Area C is known as the insula. It is active when people are making intuitive assessments or passing intuitive judgements. This area of the brain is larger in women.

Area D is known as the hippocampus. It is active when people are remembering or recalling events, sights and tender moments. This area of the brain is larger in women.

Area E is known as the amygdala. It is active when people act instinctively, often wildly. This area of the brain is larger in men.

Do women think differently because of these differences in their brains, or are the differences in their brains the result of thinking differently? In any event, greater differences are to be found in the waxing and waning of the concentrations of certain chemicals.

As the levels of the following neurochemicals wax and wane they favour, or sometimes impair, the ability of some women to think in certain ways. The chief neurochemicals are:

Oestrogen When the oestrogen levels are high, a woman can feel like an aggressive seductress. She can also think clearly and quickly about business calculations and risk assessment. Oestrogen favours her production of dopamine, serotonin and oxytocin, thereby producing relaxation, trust and creative thinking. Acetylcholine derivatives are produced and these aid the accuracy of her neurotransmission and her speed of thought.

Testosterone When her testosterone levels are high, a woman can think, focus and concentrate quickly. She is not distracted by emotional issues but her empathic thinking is impaired.

Cortisol When her cortisol levels are high, a woman can be as hypersensitive and frazzled as her male counterpart, i.e. impatient, premature in judgement and sometimes unable to think at all. Cortisol is the immediate product of stress. Cortisol kills brain cells and impairs the immune system. Most illnesses, even mild colds or flu viruses, reduce performance on thinking tasks.

Androstenedione When levels of this ovarian chemical are high, a woman can be sassy and spontaneous, displaying high levels of mental energy and creative thinking. Her levels of mental stamina and persistence can be very high – she can create all day and party all night. Her powers of concentration can be so high that she can lose all track of time.

Allopregnenolone When levels of this neurochemical are high, a woman can be a calming influence in the boardroom and the bedroom. If her levels fall remarkably (normally three or four days before her monthly period) she can be testy, irrational and unable to think.

Do these neurochemical differences cause different behaviours that eventually modify women's brains, or do the different social roles and expectations of women produce different behaviours that modify, in turn, a woman's neurochemistry? The 30,000 genes that are different have the potential to account for more differences than we actually experience.

THE FOUR G SPOTS

The wonder is that we do not experience greater differences between the way men and women think, given that the way we think is affected by the differences we have detected in the Genes, Genitals, Gonads and Gender.

Under Gender we include the differentiated effects of social expectation, politics and economics. The way Genes, Genitals, Gonads and Gender may interact to cause different chemicals and different ways of thinking in male and female brain is shown in Figure 1.6.

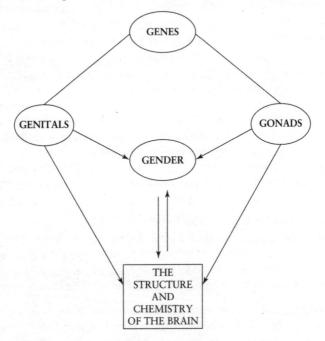

Figure 1.6 The Four G Spots – Modelling the difference between men and women (Bacha, Horne and Wootton, 2011)

Because the interactive effects on the brain are complex, no two genitally determined males will be the same as each other and no two genitally determined females will be the same as each other. However, the variations between genitally determined males and genitally determined females are greater than the variations within the two groups, so it is possible to arrive at stereotypical scores for genitally determined men and women. If you want to see where your own way of thinking lies between the two poles of stereotypical male and stereotypical female ways of thinking, complete our test in Appendix 2. Since high performance in some professions correlates with extreme stereotypical thinking models, you might want to work on those components of Advanced Applied Thinking that would help to move your overall thinking style in the direction you desire. For example, higher scores on stereotypical female thinking correlates with superior performance in senior management. The test can also be a way of thinking about sexual preference and orientation.

Group Thinking: Why do men fancy each other's wives?
Brain scans show that when you watch others, mirror neurons in your brain spring into action. Initially, this gives you the capacity to think empathically. If exposure to what you are seeing is sustained or repeated, the neuronal responses in your brain become rehearsed and myelinated. This may explain why many people are best able to learn through observation, or through periods of working as an assistant, or deputy. Alvaro Pascual-Leone (2007) showed the effect on their brains when people learned the piano by watching a self-created image (imagined) of themselves practising a new piece of music (see Figure 1.7). They learned just as much as the central group who did daily physical practice.

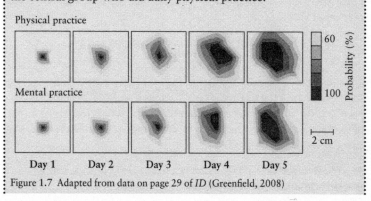

Figure 1.7 Adapted from data on page 29 of *ID* (Greenfield, 2008)

Train Your Brain (Wootton and Horne, 2010a) reports similar effects (e.g. gains in physical strength and fitness) when people only imagined themselves working out in the gym. This is thought to bring new insights to group thinking. Dr. Jamil Zaki in the *British Journal of Psychology* (December 2010), found that when men were estimating the attractiveness of women in 201 photographs, they changed their ratings of particular women markedly upwards if they were given information that the woman was highly rated by other men in the group. Beauty, it would appear, is just not in the eye of the beholder, but also in the eye of their friends, colleagues or work group. Functional NMR scans revealed that the men were not lying to appear to conform to the group's assessment. Activity in the parts of the brain processing pleasure indicated that the group's opinion did actually change each man's mind. Each man actually did fancy more the women most desired by others. Each man experienced more pleasure on beholding her face, after he found out that other men in the group also fancied her.

THINKING LIKE A WOMAN

A stereotypical female brain displays:

- ▶ Outstanding verbal thinking.
- ▶ Empathic thinking that pre-empts and defuses conflict.
- ▶ Visual thinking that delivers near psychic ability to read faces and to detect deception.

These abilities appear to be hardwired into many women's brains. These are talents that many women have and many men do not. Men have other skills...

HOW TO THINK LIKE A MAN – STEREOTYPICAL MALE FILTERS

If you have used our test in Appendix 2 to discover where you lie between thinking like a stereotypical man and thinking like a stereotypical woman, it may be useful to think about the way a stereotypical male can filter his world through:

- ▶ Who he is.
- ▶ What he does.
- ▶ How much he gains from either.

MATING A MAN

A useful strategy for a would-be mate might be to help a man to get clear about who he is, what he wants to do and the rewards that lie ahead, and to create an emotionally charged image of yourself as part of that plan. In this way, you can increase your chances that you will be with him during his journey and at his destination.

LOVING LIKE A WOMAN

The unique thinking strengths of a stereotypical female brain (visual, empathic and verbal) mean that she is able to verbally express a love that is generous, nurturing and compassionate. A stereotypical male brain may be unable to reciprocate readily.

LOVING LIKE A MAN

A man who is on the stereotypically male end of the thinking spectrum is unlikely to be smart, sensitive and supportive. He will not cry when he is hurt. If you expect him to love like a stereotypical woman, he won't. His love is likely to be different. But it is still love. It is hard when you discover that he does not keep texting you when you are away from him and that he does not scratch your back, massage your head or stroke your feet for half an hour at the end of each day. He is unlikely to ply you with herbal tea and chicken soup when you feel unwell. But he does love you. It's just that his stereotypical love is different from that of a stereotypical woman. It is as good as it gets. You can learn to think more like a man, or you may choose to befriend a man who thinks more like a woman.

THE EXTREME MALE – THE EXTREME FEMALE

An extreme stereotypical male may not love like an extreme woman, but he does love. In return he asks for gratitude, loyalty and sex. If you cease to say thank you, badmouth him to others, or leave his bed, your relationship with him is in its death throes. You need to know, and remember, that an extreme male is validated by who he is, what he does and by what he gains from being and doing these things. Extreme females who flaunt their own career and house and financial independence to cut male egos down to size may turn their men into people they can no longer love.

These extreme poles reflect stereotypical ways of masculine and feminine thinking. You can use your brain and knowledge of the components of Advanced Applied Thinking to navigate yourself away from these stereotypical extremes and around the rocks on which an intimate loving relationship will otherwise founder. Although the stereotypical male thinks well of your ability to handle money, admires your success, and is turned on by your self sufficiency, if you have your own money you don't need his, and if you work out and do martial arts, you don't need his protection either. If you undermine your man and don't help him to fulfil who he is, and what he does, he will likely sleep with you and then leave when adversity strikes:

- ▶ e.g. in sickness and in health – sooner or later someone will get sick
- ▶ e.g. for richer for poorer – sooner or later someone will get broke
- ▶ e.g. for better or for worse – sooner or later hard times will come.

What matters is not what happens, but how each of you thinks about what happens.

SEXUAL MYTHS AND WHY THEY MATTER

Neuroscience challenges some feminist orthodoxy. We prefer the evidence of neuroscience to the dogma of political correctness. We offer models and exercises based on neuroscience, which enable you to do two things. Firstly, to see where you lie on a spectrum between two stereotypical polarities representing how typical men think and how typical women think; secondly, if you see advantages in changing your position, for example, you may be a man who wishes to think more like a woman to improve your performance in senior management, or maybe you are a woman who wishes to think more like a man to improve your prospects as an architect, then the models and exercises in this book will enable you to develop the prerequisite components of Advanced Applied Thinking.

Another myth is that men and women communicate in what they think is a different language, implying that the internal dialogue component of their thinking is different. We challenge this belief. Our evidence, over 32 years, from teaching males and females of all ages and nationalities, points in a different direction.

Challenging myths is important, because people hide behind myths. People use myths to explain away their bad behaviour or to misrepresent their motives, or to justify the unproductive lives they lead. Whether or not myths have validity is more than an academic spat. Myths have consequences. Myths and beliefs influence actions, like convictions for rape. The myth that male–female misunderstandings are inevitable has led women to be advised to be firm (often brutally direct) in giving feedback to sexually interested males, yet Susan Ehrlich's (2006) research indicates that brutally direct feedback may put women at increased risk of violence.

The myth about female verbal ability has led to widespread discrimination against men in many growing areas of employment, such as call centres. This bias against men will become increasingly prejudicial in economies with growing service sectors.

Stereotypical female capacities for empathy have pointed women towards careers in, for example, nursing, whereas we would say that nurses need stereotypically male thinking skills in numeracy, quantification and system analysis, if they are to keep their patients alive on a modern medical ward.

Do the differences in the neurochemistry of men and women affect, or reflect, the different ways in which they think? Are these differences in neurochemistry caused by power differences in social groups? Women often also serve because they are treated as second class, i.e. women are not 'different but equal', they are treated as different and unequal.

As is argued in *Managing Public Services* (Horne and Doherty, 2003) male managers with power are usually very anxious, and rarely give power up voluntarily. Many men in society seem reluctant to relinquish power to women. It is, however, wrong to judge individual men or individual women against the myths and stereotypes of the groups to which they belong. That is why we aim to give you a map of relevant knowledge, a compass of direction, and practical ways of developing the skill and confidence that you will need if you are to navigate your way around myths and stereotypes that you may find restrictive.

SUMMARY

▶ Female brains are smaller but their IQs average about 3 per cent higher than men on many tests. Men are more highly represented in the very high bands (IQs of 130/140 plus).
▶ Differences are detectable in babies as young as eight weeks.
▶ There are 30 per cent more connections between the left-hand side and the right-hand side of Typical Female Brains (TFBs), enabling them more easily to switch between parallel tasks. They cannot multi-task; that is a myth.

- TFBs are generally better at tasks involving conversation.
- Most TFBs can sense more, and in more detail, than most men.
- A resting TFB is 30 per cent more active than a Typical Male Brain (TMB).
- A TFB constantly senses what is going on.
- Most TFBs' eyes have more cone-shaped colour detectors.
- Male peripheral vision is generally inferior but it improves in combat or under threat.
- The 30 per cent greater inter-linkages of the lobes of TFBs enable most women more rapidly to detect inconsistencies or incongruence. They are better at detecting lying and cheating and affairs than men.
- Brain scans show that TMBs have specific sites dedicated to solving 3D spatial problems. Few TFBs have such sites. Men often are better than women at visualizing in three dimensions.
- TFBs' superior ability in manipulating symbols gives them advantages in conversational thinking, learning languages, music and mathemtatics.
- Men frequently 'um' and 'ah'. Unless trained, they have less than half the tonal range of their sisters. Men use monosyllabic grunts and incomplete sentences more often than their sisters.
- Rising testosterone levels during a woman's menstrual cycle partly disable TFBs, making a woman think more like a man.
- Research has found that mothers talk to baby boys in a systematically different way than they talk to baby girls.
- Mothers talking to baby sons generally do not get the same encouraging facial responses that they get from their daughters.
- To keep all the information she acquires filed and sorted, on average a woman will use about 6,500 words a day. On a busy day, a man will need at most 4,000 words, often less than 2,000.
- Among women who seek counselling with UK Relate, 30 per cent say that their man can't talk about things.
- Relationship-building requires the ability simultaneously to think about physical, visual, tonal, behavioural and emotional information. TFBs are better wired for this kind of work.
- Oestrogen helps with recollection. Some women have memory problems when their oestrogen level drops.
- While TMBs can only recognize and process emotional information in the right hemisphere, TFBs have a number

of specific sites in both hemispheres. This makes emotional information harder for TFBs to side step.

▶ Testosterone activates the hypothalamus, causing it to release chemicals that stimulate the genitals. Men have 15 times more testosterone than women, acting on a larger hypothalamus, so it is not surprising that men have a higher sex drive than women. Size does matter after all!

▶ Most men find it easier to get a second erection with a different partner, than with a partner they have just impregnated.

▶ 80 per cent of men would like to be promiscuous or polygamous.

1.2

···

A mental laboratory: Some thoughtful things to think about

In this section you will:
- *explore how to make your mind fit to think*
- *learn about the neuroscience versus philosophy debate*
- *think about the role of reason and imagination in supporting creative intelligence.*

1.2.1 How to make your mind fit to think

Once touted as the fastest way to tone your mental powers, get promoted and delay dementia, most brain training software and games have now been researched and evaluated. In 2011, Adrian Owen of Cambridge University organized 100,000 volunteers to test on-line brain training systems, with a control group surfing the web. All groups got better at the tasks assigned, but none retained improvement in cognitive capacity.

Pencil and paper puzzles, children's games and lifestyle activities of the kind described in *Train Your Brain* (Wootton and Horne, 2010a) and *Keep Your Brain Sharp* (Wootton and Horne, 2010b) are not only cheaper, but their beneficial effects are accumulative and enduring, while the effects of electronic brain training starts to fade within three weeks, and is largely extinguished after six, except with stroke victims for whom there often appears to be residual benefit.

Many of the practical suggestions and exercises for improving, retaining, protecting and restoring cognitive capacity that are found in *Train Your Brain* or *Keep Your Brain Sharp* are based on up-to-date neuroscience and have been subject to research evaluation. They go beyond brain training and aspirational self help. Researchers, for example, have reported that after 15 months of learning a musical instrument, as suggested in *Train Your Brain*, children have residual physical developments in their brains that their untutored peers do not. It has since been confirmed that the brains of professional musicians have more grey and white matter. This is a measure of their brain's interconnected neurons.

Musical training has now been shown to improve performance in reading tests and to improve scores on IQ tests. According to Patrick Rogert at Ruhr University, musically trained brains also recover better from trauma and learn new things faster. The suggestion in *Train Your Brain* to learn a second language has also been evaluated. Learning a second language has been found to enhance the ability to learn generally and also to refine empathic thinking. *Train Your Brain* offered a model of the thinking brain which indicated the need to interconnect separate areas of the brain involved in different kinds of thinking.

Using transcranial direct current stimulation (tDCS), Roi Kaolosh from Oxford University has targeted the parts of the brain involved in mathematics and numerical thinking and discovered the central role of the brain's parietal lobe. By targeting this area for tDCS, Roi's students have shown improvements in mathematical thinking that have been retained for ten months and more.

Richard Chi at the University of Sydney has also used tDCS to identify a region of the brain near the right temple that is involved in the ability to remember visual information. He has reported a 110 per cent improvement in his subjects.

Train Your Brain and *Keep Your Brain Sharp* also advocated the use of light, especially in the mornings, to switch brains on. This has now been shown to increase blood flow to those parts of the brain involved in visual information, and to affect mental alertness and speed of thought.

Train Your Brain and *Keep Your Brain Sharp* also recommend the eating of flavonoids (found in such foods as blueberries). This has since been found to raise the level of brain derived neurotrophic factor (BDNF), which is important in memory and learning. It stimulates growth in the axons that link one neuron in the brain to the next. These flavonoids appear to stimulate the growth of new brain cells near the hippocampus, which is central to the neural pathways in the brain that connect the memory to most of the brain's activities.

The books also identified the advantages of physical exercise on the brain. Research at the University of Illinois has now confirmed that a daily walk improves the quality of decisions taken by management executives and the quality of abstract reasoning in young adults. More sedentary readers will be relieved by some evidence that exhausting or excessive exercise has a detrimental effect on performance of mental tasks and actually decreases the levels of BDNF available to support the growth of new human brain cells and new connections between them.

But all this scientific Information is only a starting point. It needs to be thought about in a way that produces reasonable Inferences and then thought about some more, to see if Implications for useful practical action can be found. These are the 3Is of Applied Thinking. Applied Thinking takes you beyond brain training.

APPLIED THINKING

Applied Thinking involves the use of higher order thinking skills like critical, creative and reflective thinking to assess the truth of Information, and the reasonableness of Inferences on which Implications for useful action can be based. The 3Is (the way you move from Information, via Inferences, to Implied action), and the roles played by your critical, creative and reflective thinking are shown in Figure 1.8.

APPLIED THINKING – THE 3IS

The 3 'I's of Applied Thinking are: Information, Inference and Implication.

Information You need to use critical thinking to assess the extent to which you justifiably believe in the accuracy, completeness and relevance of the information you have about the problem, decision or proposal. (Is it 'the truth, the whole truth and nothing but the truth'?) This will involve surfacing implicit assumptions, being sceptical about the motives of sources, and finally cross-checking your perceptions with those of other people.

Inferences You will need to use creative and reflective thinking to generate a long list of the possible insights, interpretations, principles, opinions, lessons, ideas and even conclusions that you might reasonably infer from information that you justifiably believe to be true.

Implications You will again need to think creatively and reflectively in order to formulate feasible and practical plans of action soundly based on reasonable inferences you have drawn and soundly based on justifiably believable information you have assessed. You will need

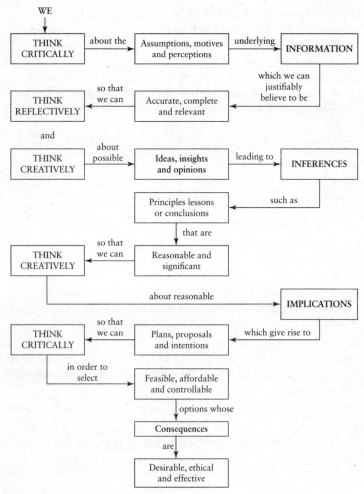

Figure 1.8 Information, Inferences and Implications – the 3Is

critical thinking again before you move to implement your plans or proposals – are these plans affordable, ethical and likely to be effective, and will you be able to control their implementation?

APPLIED THINKING: TEN QUESTIONS TO ASK

Concerning the believability of information

1 Which words or phrases are ambiguous or imprecise?
2 What assumptions are not admitted?

3 What assumptions are admitted?
4 Why is this being said or written?
5 What statistics are offered?
6 Are the statistics skewed?
7 What is omitted?
8 Who might construe this information differently?
9 What concepts underpin the collection, or analysis, of this information?
10 Is the use of these concepts valid?

Concerning the reasonableness of inferences
1 What internal contradictions can we see?
2 What counter-examples can we think of?
3 What opinions are being offered as facts?
4 What evidence is offered?
5 How authoritative, or biased, are the sources of evidence?
6 What conflicting evidence is offered?
7 What flaws are there in the reasoning?
8 Have counter-arguments been considered?
9 Is the evaluation fair and the rebuttal convincing?
10 Does the conclusion over-stretch the evidence available?

Concerning the practicality of implications
1 If the implied action were taken, would it so change the situation that it would invalidate the assumptions on which the argument for action is based?
2 How controllable is the behaviour of the key actors?
3 Do we have the skills needed to take the implied action?
4 Are all the consequences beneficial? Judged by what criteria?
5 Are there unwanted side-effects?
6 Does the implied action confer the greatest benefit to the greatest number of people?
7 Does the implied action waste the least resources?
8 Does the implied action do least harm?
9 Thinking about resources, how feasible is the implied action?
10 What risks are associated with the implied action? What is the probability of the risk and the extent of the consequence? Is the worst case acceptable, and by what criteria is acceptability judged?

Ten questions to ask as a critical friend
1 Can you distinguish what you know from what you believe?
2 Are you open to the possibility that you may be wrong?

3 Who might disagree with you and what would they say?
4 Can you understand why they might think this way?
5 Can you see any connection between these things?
6 What do you personally have to gain if people agree with you?
7 Are you offering me opinions or facts?
8 Have you considered this counter-example?
9 How will you stand up to the ridicule of others?
10 Do you accept this because it seems hard to question it?

Ten rules for everyday critical thinking

1 Ask yourself what assumptions you are making.
2 Articulate as clearly as possible criteria you use to make judgements.
3 Remember to own what you feel, as well as what you think.
4 Treat initial reactions, your own and other people's, only as tentative positions.
5 Enquire whether other people share your perceptions.
6 Empathize with the feelings and thoughts of other people.
7 Decide whether you have enough justifiably believable information to support a tentative conclusion. Could more information be gathered easily? What kind of information is needed? Is there a reliable source that is readily available? What credibility would the source have and why?
8 Recognize that all interpretations, including your own, are subjective.
9 Admit the limitations of your information.
10 Contextualize your conclusions. Don't claim universal truths.

It can been seen from the model of Applied Thinking in Figure 1.1 that the quality of your planned actions and your intended consequences depends on the quality of your critical, creative and reflective thinking. These cannot be improved by exhortation. They must be analysed into their constituent basic thinking skills. These must be improved through exercise and practice. You must learn how to combine your improved basic thinking skills to form more powerful thinking combinations. This needs repeated practice so that myelinated neural pathways are built in your brain that enable you to rely your neural network. The types of exercises in this book will give you the kind of practice your brain needs to myelinate your development. The way the basic, higher order and more advanced components of Applied Thinking link together, is shown in Figure 1.1. The way in which the basic skills link together to support creative, critical and reflective thinking is shown in Figures 1.9, 1.10 and 1.11.

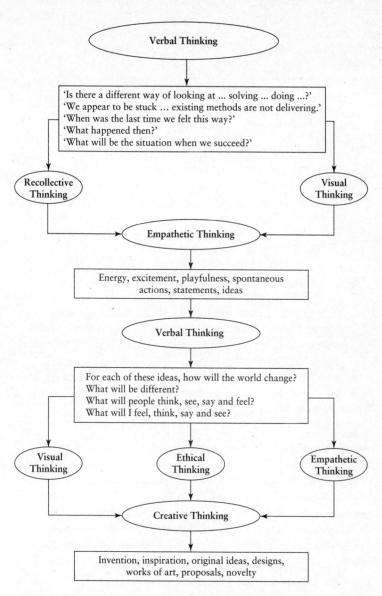

Figure 1.9 A Model of Creative Thinking (Horne and Wootten, 2003)

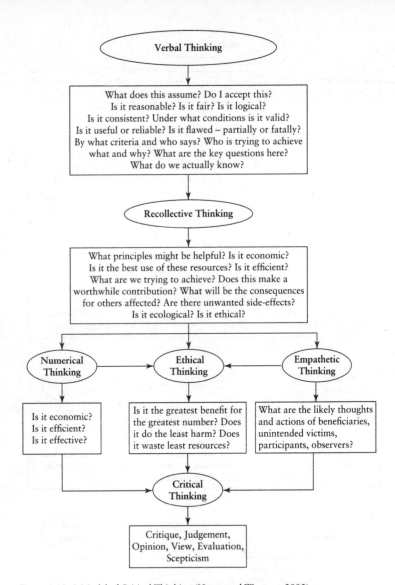

Figure 1.10 A Model of Critical Thinking (Horne and Wootten, 2003)

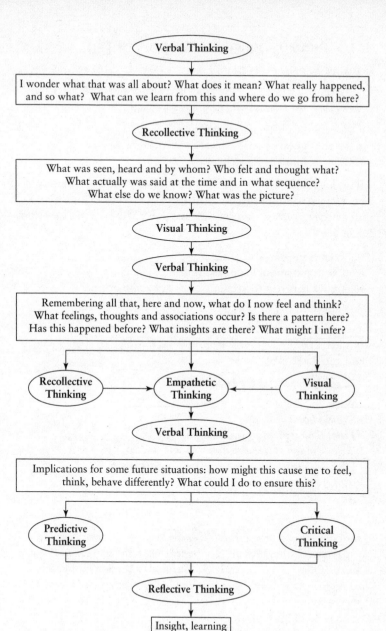

Figure 1.11 A Model of Reflective Thinking (Horne and Wootten, 2003)

1.2.2 Neuroscience versus philosophy

WHAT IS PHILOSOPHY?

Philosophy is classified by the types of questions philosophers are considering, for example:

- ▶ What is beautiful? Aesthetic
- ▶ What is good or evil? Ethics
- ▶ What is known? Epistemology.

All philosophers believe that they should give good reason, proof or evidence, to support their answers to questions. (This is one difference between philosophy and religion.) More specific questions might be:

- ▶ What is the purpose of life?
- ▶ Is your pursuit of happiness futile?
- ▶ Are we here just to help ourselves or to help others?

Such questions have been puzzled over by priests and philosophers down the centuries. But there are many issues on which evidence is still silent and these provide fruitful fields in which to stretch your mind and make it fit.

Carpe Diem (Seize the Day)

When life is short,
Should hope be long?
From the moment of your waking,
When envious tides ebb away
Oh seize me now, let not envious anchors sway
And trust the morrow
As you may

(Terry Horne, 2011 – after Horace)

If the concept of *Carpe Diem* (Seize the Day) is not clear from the poem, watch Robin Williams as the teacher in the film *Dead Poets Society*. Williams is constantly quoting and exhorting his pupils to 'live deep and suck out the marrow of life'. At the core of *Carpe Diem* is the notion that enacted experience is of the essence. Action is to be distilled and refluxed back as eau de vie.

Overwhelmed in a powerful present tense experience, it is possible to lose all track of time and then suddenly see a necessary link between the joy of the moment and the pain of it passing. This sense of

Carpe Diem keeps you well grounded in times past, through the present to future.

The *Carpe Diem* lesson is that life's time is short. Shakespeare warns that 'there is a tide in the affairs of men, which, taken at the flood, leads on to fortune, but which missed can leave you stranded on a mud bank'. While the thinking lessons of philosophy may be old, the thinking lessons of neuroscience are not all new.

NEUROSCIENCE IS NOT ALL NEW

Poets, actors, singers and playwrights all seem to have been prescient about the working of the brain. When you look farther you will find writers, painters and composers who discovered tangible truths about the human mind that neuroscientists have only found out in the last 15 years. Artists like Virginia Woolf, Igor Stravinsky, Paul Cézanne, Marcel Proust, George Eliot, Walt Whitman and Leonardo da Vinci. Artists had an advantage over neuroscientists in that they have often been able to communicate their ideas to a wide audience. Until recently, neuroscientists have struggled to communicate well or widely. The mould was broken by professors like Susan Greenfield, Colin Blakemore and Richard Dawkins. Professors like Robert Winston, Steven Pinker and Peter Checkland have done important research and learned to write about it in elegant prose, but McEwan's fictional *Saturday* demonstrates that the voice of the artist is still important, while you wait for neurosciences to catch up.

But neurotruth is not the only truth. That is why we join neuroscience with art and philosophy to improve our Applied Thinking. Such an endeavour is inevitably flawed with the bias, hopes and dreams of artists and authors. This book will not be beyond the reach of your criticism, which will rein in and counterbalance excessive claims of neuroscience, by testing them against the real world of your human experience.

1.2.3 Reason and imagination – creative intelligence

Reason without imagination is not fertile. For intelligence to be creative, its reasoning power must be fertilized by imagination. Philosophers have always sharpened their thinking by posing imaginary challenges to their energy and ideas. Now they are joined by neuroscientists who have also designed thought experiments to stretch the brain and sharpen the mind. A well-designed thought experiment will strip away irrelevance, allowing the thinker to isolate variables relevant to the problem. Imaginary thought experiments help to isolate the key issues on which an argument turns, and the relative valency of the issues which the experiment has helped to isolate. For hints on how to approach the following thought experiments, see Appendix 1 at the back of the book.

Thought experiment 1: Should you eat meat?

In real life, the issue is complicated and contingent, for example, some animals are factory farmed, others are shot as wildlife, while the grazing of others displaces the rainforest. Some meat is organic, while other meat has been genetically modified. Some meat eating will support the local economy and small-holders, while other meat eating will help to make millions for food processing giants, who, you may think, are frying the planet with animal air miles. However, if you are concerned about whether the rearing of animals for consumption is inherently wrong you will need to design a thought experiment that temporarily removes the impacts and consequences brainstormed alone. You need to begin an 'all other things being equal' thought. A thought experiment is a tool. The purpose of a thought experiment is to give you practice in thinking. Sometimes your thought experiment will help you to resolve a real world problem that seems intractable to other people. Often new lines of thought are opened, rarely are any closed down. Have a go at more thought experiments.

Thought experiment 2: The feathering of Café Nest

You are at your favourite café, Café Nest. One reason you like it is because it is very cheap. Prices are set at only four times the cost of the coffee beans, not 20 times, as in the international chain of coffee houses on the high street. One day, you learn from the café owner that all the Café Nest staff are illegal immigrants who are allowed to sleep in one room at the back in return for their labour. They are given food and a little cash in return for working up to ten hours per day, six days a week. 'With such a low wage bill,' the manager confides, 'you get low prices and I make a handsome profit. Everybody wins.'

Will you boycott Café Nest in future, or will you continue to feather your own nest?

Thought experiment 3: Lose–Lose

You are a soldier. You have been ordered to do a terrible thing. You are in no doubt it is a war crime. You have been ordered to rape a prisoner and then murder her. The prisoner is an innocent woman who happens to belong to the wrong ethnic group. You feel you have no choice. You can try to make it bearable for the woman and to minimize her suffering. If you refuse you feel sure you will be shot and the victim would suffer eventually at the hands of your fellow soldiers. What will you do?

Thought experiment 4: Till pre-nup do us part

During your marriage ceremony, you will be asked to vow to put your collective interests as a couple before your own interests as an individual. Your marriage would be better if you both could make and keep this vow. In practice, you have discussed with your partner your fears that this is an unrealistic burden to lay on each other – even if the outcome would result in a better union. Both of you thought that the risk of failure, the likelihood of deceit and fear of shame and betrayal were too great. Should you ask for the vow to be removed from the ceremony?

Thought experiment 5: Finders keepers – the self-serving bias

You go to a cash machine and request $10 with a receipt. Out of the machine comes $100,000 with a receipt for $10. You take the $100,000 home and hide it. You wait a week for your bank statement. It arrives and your balance shows you have only withdrawn $10. Is the $100,000 now yours to do with as you please?

Thought experiment 6: You play, they pay

You have found that your computer can access your neighbour's Wi-Fi network. You are enjoying rapid surfing, live streaming and fast downloads – and it's free! Your neighbour has paid for the network already and you are only using up spare bandwidth. Your 'magpie minimize' software ensures that your use is not detected and that any slowing of your neighbour's service is negligible. Are you a thief?

Thought experiment 7: It's not my fault!

Philosopher Jean-Paul Sartre told a story similar to this.

Three accused, Peter, Paul and Mary, confess to the judge: 'I did it, your honour, but it was not my fault.' Peter explained that he had acted on expert advice. Paul had followed the advice of his doctor.

Mary had consulted her priest. Giving sentence, the judge said that, based on the advice from colleagues on the bench, he would sentence them each to the maximum possible sentence. Is the judge's judgment unjust?

Thought experiment 8: Hypocrisy – do as I say
You fly around the world talking to influential people about the urgency of global warming. Among other things, you present evidence that flying pumps out more carbon dioxide in a year than the whole of Africa. Yet you are flying! Are you a hypocrite?

Thought experiment 9: The case for sustainable development
This thought experiment was inspired by Bjorn Lomborg.

A few years ago, you purchased an old stone mill and after some restoration work you moved your family's injection moulding business into it. You got lots of grant aid. People were pleased that a use had been found for the old heritage mill and with the tasteful restoration and repair work you were able to fund from your business (this also reduced your business tax bill). Recently you realized that to stay competitive you needed to increase production and buy a bigger machine. The increased vibration would undo the restoration work and damage the structure of the mill. You made the decision to cut back on production, rather than expand and damage your building. This proved uneconomic; the business failed and the mill deteriorated. There was no money left to repair and maintain the mill or even to remove all the waste left over from the business. Should you have increased production (and the damage) in the short term, so that you would have had funds to restore the mill and move to purpose-built premises, and make donations to the Green Party?

Thought experiment 10: Unequal treatment is better
This thought experiment was inspired by John Rawls.

You try scrupulously to treat each of your three children equally. They are aged 10, 11 and 12. You determine to spend $100 in total on all three of them at Eid. You will buy them each a phone. The phones cost $30 each. You will donate the $10 remaining in your budget to an orphanage. At the last minute your partner spots that a superior phone, costing $60, is available on a 2-for-1 promotion. Your partner wants two of your children to each have a $60 phone and the third child to have the $30 phone originally decided upon. Is this unequal treatment better than equality?

Thought experiment 11: Affairs are okay
You are away at a conference. During a long, lonely walk on a long, sandy beach, you can feel a warm breeze on your bare arms. It is very arousing. The solitary walker coming towards you looks tanned, and toned and attractive. The walker offers you a drink at a nearby bar. You get on well together. Your companion turns out to be a conference celebrity and probes to see if you could be discreet about spending just one night together. You are married. Your marriage is good and your partner loving. But your partner is at home and would never know. What is not known can't hurt. It would be one night of fantasy. What a buzz. You would go home on such a high everyone would benefit. No one would suffer. With so much to enjoy and nothing to lose, will you resist those come to bed eyes?

Thought experiment 12: Heads you do, hearts you don't – which rules?
Christine and Michael both shelter fugitives from an evil dictator. Christine's kindness is spontaneous. She doesn't have to think about what to do. It is instantly self evident to her. The needs of others speak directly to her heart. Her friends are in awe of her generous nature, but fear the road to hell is paved with her goodness. Michael on the other hand, can appear aloof, cold to some. He finds friendships difficult, but he has a few old friends to whom he is obsessively loyal. He thinks about the plight of the fugitives and the standards of conduct he sets for himself and others and he decides it is his duty to help them. He feels no warm glow but is easy in his conscience. Is Christine or Michael the more moral? Why?

Thought experiment 13: It can be good to torture?
You are the officer in charge of interrogation. Your suspect looks resolute, but you are sure you can break him. And break him you must. Many hundreds of present and future lives depend on it. You know that suspect A knows the whereabouts of the remote control to the hidden nuclear device. You know that suspect A is a loving father and you have his two young daughters held captive. Even though the girls do not know anything, you will torture them in front of their father. He will tell you what you need to know to prevent further pain for his daughters. You only need to learn enough to disable the bomb, but there is no time to lose. If you do not give the order to torture the

girls in front of suspect A, you will condemn hundreds of thousands of innocent men, women and children and future babies to death and mutilation. Surely you will not let personal qualms stand in your way? Do you have the moral courage to order the torture?

Thought experiment 14: It is always cash for honours

You are the Prime Minister. An unscrupulous businesswoman (who has always narrowly escaped conviction for criminal misbehaviour) has offered to donate 100 million Euros to provide clean water, seeds and breeding goats, sheep and cows to hundreds of thousands of families in Africa. All she wants in return is for you to nominate her for one of your country's highest honorary titles. It will cost you nothing and the gain for sick and needy children in Africa will transform their lives and prospects. Do you agree to nominate her?

Thought experiment 15: Crime – let's chemically cosh repeat offenders

You are the Minister for Justice. You have been informed of nine successful long-term trials and evaluation of a chemical treatment affecting the brain of repeat-offending life-long criminals. A 100 per cent success rate over a large sample covering all types of offences, all ages, sex, ethnicity and social economic groups has been reported. The chemicals have shown no undesirable side-effects. The chemicals are cheap, readily available and tasteless, and easily introduced into a prisoner's normal diet or drinking water. The treatment leaves prisoners so repulsed and fearful of repeat imprisonment that 100 per cent of the sample has never reoffended during the long-term follow up. What can you lose? Will you sign the permissive letter to prison governors?

Thought experiment 16: Could you become a bad bomber?

You are a leader of a resistance movement. Your beloved country is controlled by a foreign dictator. The dictator's occupying forces are vicious and vindictive. The slightest transgression of the dictator's rules is punished with overwhelming force. Vengeance is exacted on your women and young girls. Open resistance is futile. You have volunteer resistance fighters who have sworn preparedness to die for their country. A campaign of suicide bombing against the occupying regime and its collaborators will persuade the dictator that occupation of your country is more trouble than it is worth. You know that the suicide bomb is a risky and imprecise weapon that will inevitably injure some of your countrymen and women. You have no other weapon at your disposal. Will you sanction suicide bombing?

Thought experiment 17: Giving peace a chance is too costly
You are the President. Your country is besieged by a dictator. You
know you cannot resist the overwhelming superiority of the dictator's
power and force. You and the dictator both know that continuing
conflict between your two countries will cost millions of lives. This
can be averted. The dictator promises you that once he has purged
evil dissident insurrectionists from the countries he has already
overrun, he will not order further offensives against other counties,
especially yours. All you have to do is not get in his way and he will
leave your country free, saving the lives and mutilation of millions of
his countrymen and yours. Do you agree terms?

Thought experiment 18: How to think about an abortion
This thought experiment is based on work on abortion by Judith
Thompson in the 1970s.

It is the year 2015 and you have volunteered for a scheme that gives
you paid leave if you agree to be connected, for up to nine months, to
someone, a writer, who will share your organs, until a donor can be found
or you can be replaced with another volunteer at the end of the nine
months. It is proving more difficult than you expected. Being connected
in this way is making you nauseous and sweaty and giving you cramps.

Thought experiment 19: Free speech – to whom, where and when?
This thought experiment is based on Alan Haworth's examples.

You have been leading a campaign for greater free speech in your
country. You are reading the government's latest bulletin on the
street riots, which you have been helping to organize. The bulletin
explains it will still be necessary, for the foreseeable future, to outlaw
public talk which stirs dissent or which brings the country into
disrepute, but that, as of Monday, people will not be prosecuted for
doing things they say in private to no more than one other person,
even if they are things critical of the government. Repeat or pyramid
communications will, however, be illegal. Otherwise, all citizens are
free to say whatever they wish. Free speech has been restored. Do
you think it has? Do you have any reservations about the bulletin?
If so, why?

Thought experiment 20: Should you put family first?
You are a trained life guard and lifeboat crew member. On an off-
duty day, sailing a large cruiser, you pick up a distress call about

people floundering in cold sea following a ferry accident. You immediately set course towards them. A second call from your partner who is out sailing with your two children, says they are taking in water in heavy swell and about to capsize. Your family is behind you. No one else can get to the ferry passengers before they die of hypothermia. Whoever you decide to leave till last will be dead by the time you get there. Will you turn back to help your family and leave the ferry passengers to drown?

Thought experiment 21: Would you turn off the life support?
This thought experiment is based on work in the 1970s by Jonathan Glover.

The cleaner has left the ventilator unplugged. The doctor has said it is your decision and only yours. He has shown you the plug and socket. Your grandmother is terminally ill. Every time she regains consciousness, she asks you repeatedly to stop them resuscitating her. She has been unconscious now for several days. The hospital policy is that it is wrong to take any action that shortens life. Yet lack of such action is prolonging the agony of your grandmother against her will. Will you put the plug back in? Will you report it? Will you just wait and hope she dies peacefully before anyone notices.

Thought experiment 22: When would you eat a friend (or a pet dog)?
This thought experiment is based on various articles that appeared in volume 65 of the *Journal of Personalized Social Psychology* in 1973.

The population of the world is 6 billion and rising, soon to be 9 billion. How to feed them all? Waste not, want not – every year we waste the food value of around 90 million human corpses. There will be even more dead pets, as pets do not live as long as humans. The authors' generation lived in wartimes and warzones where adults and children alike learned to skin rabbits to make rabbit pie. Skinning a dog or a cat cannot be technically more difficult. Of course, there will be regrets and sad memories, but also the need for practical thinking. Do you tell the children lest sentimentally spoil their appetite? Would you eat your pet (or your friend)?

THOUGHT EXPERIMENTS – TIME TO REFLECT

If you have found the thought experiments in the mental laboratory easy, then you are well warmed up to go into the philosophical gymnasium which comes next. If you have found a particular experiment difficult, try consulting the references and recommended reading list in Appendix 3 (where you may find an in-depth analysis of the particular thought experiment). If you found the thought experiments difficult, or just very interesting, the books which we recommend are by Julian Baggini and are excellent and easy to read, often with amusing approaches to similar issues, and contain many more examples of this particular route to getting your mind fit and your brain's neural networks more extensively connected.

In the philosophical gymnasium that comes next, perplexing paradoxical puzzles will not be so easy. This is because, unlike the thought experiments you have just undertaken, these paradoxical puzzles have not been stripped of real world practical complications. Unlike the thought experiments, they have not been simplified to one or two variables. In the philosophical gymnasium, there will be many more issues and variables to consider and balance. In the hints, your hand will be less tightly held. The more complex philosophical gymnasium is an important preparation for Part Two, which will consider the routes to Creative Intelligence and Advanced Applied Thinking.

1.3

....

Workout: A mental gymnasium

In this section you will:
- *learn how to keep your mind fit*
- *do some mental circuits and try physical exercises*
- *test your self against perplexing paradoxical puzzles and devilish dilemmas.*

1.3.1 How to keep your mind fit to think

As soon as your brain senses any information input, an MRI scanner will show your brain immediately going into action to try to make sense of it. Your brain compares each piece of information by size, shape, colour, texture and emotional content with information that is already mentally categorized in your memory. This might explain the popularity of puzzles. Your brain traces each of your neural pathways seeking similarities between bits of information stored in your long-term memory and aspects of the problem situation, now temporarily stored in your working memory. You are puzzling things out. Mental flexibility and cognitive capacity are extended by pushing against hard puzzles, because puzzles create a cognitive dissonance between what we know now – details of the puzzle – and what we desire to know – the solution to the puzzle. When dissonance is resolved your brain releases neurochemicals such as dopamine, which are associated with pleasure (and addiction!).

Puzzles can be found in every culture, as far back as an Iranian paper puzzle dated at 2000 BC (the earliest evidence of writing is only 2500 BC). Puzzles were semi-engineered in stone by Pharaoh Amenemhet III of Ancient Egypt, who designed a labyrinth to protect his treasure. In Greece, there was a craze for lateral thinking puzzles and logical dilemmas in the 5th century BC. At the same time, the Chinese were playing their mathematical puzzle – The River Map (Lo Shu). The Chinese game 'Go' dates from 500 BC arriving in Japan in 500 AD. It is still popular in Japan today. At this time chess appeared in India – known as Chaturanga. Snakes and Ladders followed in China in 700 AD. Playing cards, as they are known in the West, appeared in Iran between the and eleventh and twelfth centuries. The Industrial Revolution resulted in the burgeoning of puzzles with jigsaws in 1766 and poker in 1830. The first crossword appeared in New York in 1913. Rubik invented his Cube around 1975 and Howard Gains invented Sudoku around 1980, though it had a different name at that time.

The puzzles in this book involve interconnecting many parts of your brain in ways that strongly myelinate the connections between different parts of your brain, so that those neural connections will be available to you for subsequent intellectual use. Working on puzzles like the ones in this book can sometimes route connections round the physical damage caused by mini-strokes, blows to your head or protein deposits. At autopsy there is very little physical difference between your brain at age 25 and your brain at age 75. As you mature, your brain adapts to your lifestyle. Circuits rarely used can be brought back into regular use and become more efficient. Just like the muscles of your body, your mind can respond to exercise making it more sensitive and mentally fitter.

THE PUZZLES AND HOW TO GROW YOUR BRAIN

Adults do not lose significant swathes of brain cells as they mature. Mental muscles that have been allowed to atrophy can be made strong again. Research reported in 2007 by Mensa – the high IQ society – identified correlates with venerable lucidity. The correlates included:

- ▶ life long learning
- ▶ major life changes
- ▶ a physical lifestyle
- ▶ a thoughtful, conversation-liking partner.

These are not genetic determinants – they are lifestyle choices. Also correlated with an intelligence that increased with age was:

- ▶ travel
- ▶ social activities
- ▶ reading stimulating books
- ▶ awareness of current affairs
- ▶ playing games (see Section 2.2 and Appendix 4)
- ▶ and, importantly, solving puzzles.

But they must be the right kind of puzzles. The design of the puzzles must be informed by neuroscience. The puzzles in this book are based on neuroscience. (Sources are referenced in Appendix 3.)

The Mensa research also reported that watching TV impedes mental development in children and hastens mental decay in adults. Your brain is also switched off by a social life replete with texts and emails, but short of face-to-face contact.

PUZZLES AND THE PROTECTION OF YOUR BRAIN

Dr. Stern's US study of nearly 2,000 pensioners, over a period of seven years, found that, even after controlling for the effect of ethnicity, education and social and economic background, pensioners were protected from Alzheimer's Disease, or the effects of Alzheimer's, by physical, social and intellectual activities. The cumulative contribution of each category was around 10 per cent. For people engaged in all three categories of activity the reduction in Alzheimer's risk was nearly 40 per cent, and the greatest contribution was from intellectual activities like solving puzzles. The comparable figure in a study of 50,000 people in Australia by Michael Venegas was a 46 per cent reduced likelihood of Alzheimer's. (For a detailed exploration of how to protect your brain from degenerative disease read *Keep your Brain Sharp*, Horne and Wootton 2010b). In this study you can read about 'the busy nuns'. The busy nuns research has since been supported by Dr. David Bennet's autopsy of the donated brains of people who showed no dementia. More than 35 per cent were found to have extensive brain tissue damage. Prior to death, this group had shown normal scores on cognitive function and reasoning tests. They had engaged in the kinds of social and physical activities described in sections 2.2 and 3.2 and Appendix 4, and in solving the kinds of intellectual puzzles and problems that you will find throughout the book. Here are some hard examples.

1.3.2 Mental circuits and physical exercises

If you have ever asked yourself questions like:

▶ Where might the universe have come from?
▶ How could I make a machine think?
▶ If I could design a child how would I do it?

then you probably already use your head as a mental gymnasium. Perhaps you already use your brain to tease out possible consequences to 'what if scenarios'. If your important habits of mind had been universal, the world might never have seen Auschwitz, Srebrenica and Rwanda. Working out in a mental gymnasium can increase your resistance to false ideology. The thinking skills involved are transferable. A mental gymnasium, like the mental laboratory, is intended to be diagnostic. If you find you need to further develop particular thinking skills, you will find them treated separately in *Train Your Brain* (Wootton and Horne, 2010a). In Part 2 you will advance your use of Advanced Applied Thinking Skills and in Part 3 you will increase your Creative Intelligence.

MENTAL GYMNASIUM – WARM-UP

Warm-up 1: Homosexuality
Even if you reject homosexuality on religious grounds, consider the following:

▶ Is homosexuality unnatural?
▶ Is homosexuality unhealthy?
▶ Does homosexuality corrupt the young?
▶ Are male homosexuals more promiscuous than male heterosexuals?
▶ Doesn't homosexuality really undermine the role of the family?

Warm-up 2: Separating Siamese twins
The twins are joined at the lower abdomen. Both will die if they are not surgically separated. One will die if they are surgically separated. One may live if they are separated. Is it acceptable to kill one twin by surgical separation?

Warm-up 3: Organ transplants
Patient 1 has terminal cancer and will die shortly. Patient 2 has a heart condition that will soon be fatal. Should you kill Patient 1 and transplant her heart into Patient 2, so that Patient 2 may live?

MENTAL GYMNASIUM – HEAVY LIFTING

Heavy lift 1: Travelling though time – Superman and Terminator

▶ Is a time travelling machine possible?
▶ Could you ever visit your future to find out what will happen to you?

- ► Could you ever go back in time and change things then so that life would have better consequences for you now?
- ► See Appendix 1 for hints on how to approach this.

Heavy lift 2: The conscious conundrum

- ► How might that giant walnut-shaped cauliflower between your ears, produce the rich experience of your inner world?
- ► Given that people can observe you experiencing a beautiful red and black sky sunset, can they ever enter your mind and know and share what that experience is?
- ► Even if you understand the science of radar or eco-location, can you know or experience what it is like to be a bat?
- ► See Appendix 1 for hints on how to approach this.

Heavy lift 3: True or false?

A fallacy is an error in reasoning. Reason is a tool of philosophy. Reasoning is also what you need to use in everyday life if you are to be gainfully employed in a brain-based knowledge economy. Is reasoning a capacity you must develop in children before you can reasonably expect them to be reasonable teenagers and young adults? Surely they will not be reasonable if they cannot reason?

Heavy lift 4: The non-caused correlation

When local taxes went up local crime figures came down, so if we want to eliminate crime, we should keep raising taxes until crime is eliminated. True or false? Why?

Heavy lift 5: Vulnerable authority

A: Boots No. 7 cream removes wrinkles from my face.
B: How do you know?
A: Mrs X says it does and she's an expert.

True or false? Why?

Heavy lift 6: The slippery slope

If you allow one person to select the sex of this baby today, tomorrow you will have to consider selection by eye colour, hair type and IQ. Pretty soon you will have to allow people to discard babies that are not to their liking. True or false? Why?

Heavy lift 7: The false choice
If we do not cut public spending, government finances will go into the red. We cannot allow government finances to go into the red so we must make cuts in public spending. True or false? Why?

Heavy lift 8: The failure to disconfirm
A politician believes that crime will fall if taxes are cut. He asks his researcher to find 100 supporting cases and she does. The politician is justified in announcing a programme of tax cuts in order to reduce crime. True or false? Why?

Heavy lift 9: The gambler's fallacy
She: Doing the lottery this week?
He: Yes, but I'm not choosing 4, 8, and 28.
She: Why not?
He: Because 4, 8, and 28 have come up a lot recently – well above what you would expect on random chance – so they are less likely to come up for a while.

True or false? Why?

Heavy lift 10: The circular argument
A: Jim is honest.
B: How do you know?
A: Tom told me.
B: How do you know Tom is honest?
A: Jan told me, and Jim told me I could trust her.

True or false? Why?

Heavy lift 11: The false inference
If you are taller than Sally, then Sally is short. Sally is short, therefore you are taller than Sally. True or false? Why?

PHILOSOPHICAL GYMNASIUM – GENTLE STRETCHING

Stretch 1: Nuclear submarine out of control
You are the President. Owing to a computer malfunction one of your nuclear submarines is about to launch its missiles, which will kill millions of people. The only way to avert this disaster is to launch a land-based missile to destroy your own submarine and its crew. Is it acceptable to do this, Mr. President?

Stretch 2: Miracles and superstition
Given and accepting the wealth of evidence supporting the occurrences of supernatural events, it is acceptable to believe in miracles?

Stretch 3: The origin of the universe
Given and accepting scientific evidence that the universe was created during a colossal explosion about 12,000 million years ago, why do you think the explosion might have happened?

Saints, sin and suicide
Amelia was brought up in a Quaker household. She was not a rebellious teenager. She worships in silence. From time to time, she hears the voice of God, prompting her to do acts of social justice. She acts on her promptings. She also finds inspiration from stories in the Bible and the Qur'an. She tries to let her life speak for her, preferring to leave religious labelling to others.

Danya was adopted by a devout Muslim mother who taught her to pray to Allah five times a day. She finds this very comforting. She finds inspiration from the great books which include the Bible and the Qur'an. She acts on her inspiration. She believes that Islam is a practical way of living, through which she deepens her understanding of the Qur'an. Jesus is one of her messengers from God but she thinks that the teachings of Mohammed are more up to date.

If Amelia and Danya had been identical twins and had been swapped at birth, then it is likely that Amelia would have been Muslim and Danya would have been Quaker. The religious beliefs which influence them both so strongly are the arbitrary result of upbringings over which they had little control. Amelia and Danya are highly intelligent, creative, modern-day 'saints', who seek peace, value kindness and both seem vulnerable to an upbringing that might have venerated violence and the suicide bombing of a school bus? What do you think?

1.3.3 Paradoxical puzzles and devilish dilemmas

Any instructor in a physical gymnasium will tell you that muscle growth or increased fitness only comes from doing the 10 per cent of the exercise when you are straining against your limit. The rest is warm-up and warm-down. The same is true in a mental gymnasium. When you find a puzzle you cannot solve, rejoice! Do not give up and turn to the back of the book for the answer! You have a rare opportunity to let your mind churn against your difficulty. The churning is the learning. Try again the next day or after a break or a nap. Preferably try after discussing the problem with someone else. Following are 32 examples of very hard puzzles with which you can struggle for a long time. That is what makes them good for developing your brain. Keep going until you find one you can't do, then rejoice – and struggle some more!

SOME PERPLEXING PUZZLES

Puzzle 1: Where to put 5?

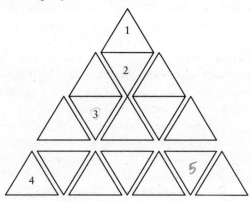

Hint: Start from the top triangle and count left to right from one number to the next, 1, 2, 3, 4, and finally 5.

Puzzle 2: Insert a shape

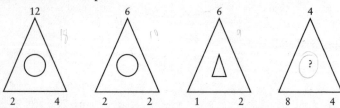

Hint: If the total of the numbers is even...

Puzzle 3: Next number

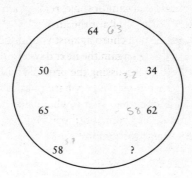

Hint: Work clockwise. Subtract 1, 2, 4, 8, etc. and place the answer in the circle.

Puzzle 4: What are B & G?

If Y = 14 and the total value of the segments = 114, what does B = and G =?

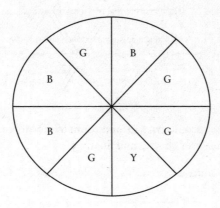

Hint: Trial and error

Puzzle 5: Which is the odd one out?

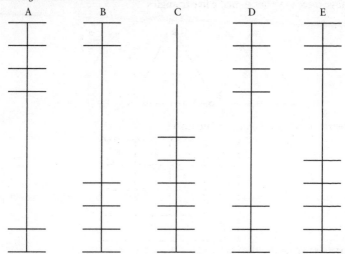

A   B   C   D   E

Hint: In A, B, C & D, the number of horizontal bars at the top of the figure multiplied by the number at the bottom equals...

Puzzle 6: What time will the next digital watch show?

16:15:02   13:19:01   09:27:59   04:43:56   ?:?:?

Hint: Move the seconds back, 1, 2, etc. Move the minutes forward 4, 8, etc. Move the hours back 3, 4, etc.

Puzzle 7: What is the missing value '?', if the values of O, G, R and P are each less than 10?

G	P	O	R	=	?
O	R	R	P	=	32
O	R	R	G	=	35
G	P	P	G	=	36
38	39	31	35		

Hint: The total of rows must = the total of...

Puzzle 8: Lay matches or similar out in three triangles as shown. Now move three matches to make five triangles

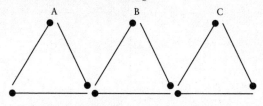

Puzzle 9: What's the missing number?

6	6	18	6
10	16	4	2
8	6	16	2
16	4	2	?

Hint: In each row, one number is the total of...

Puzzle 10: How many sachets?

Customs officers suspect that one of a group of men is carrying sachets of powdered cocaine. Stick man is their prime suspect. The scanner reveals that he has concealed cocaine in the five places marked X. On searching him, sure enough, they find two sachets in his mouth, three in his right hand, five in his left hand and seven in his right shoe. After they have checked his left shoe, how many sachets will they have recovered altogether from their prime suspect?

Hint: The finds on the body of their prime suspect are a rising sequence of...

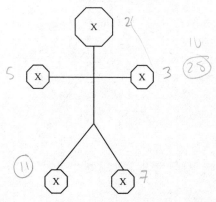

Puzzle 11: Which number is the odd one out?

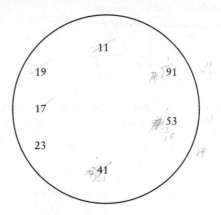

Hint: Strange that it should be this, given that all the other numbers would be prime suspects.

Puzzle 12: What is the weight?
This diver's helmet weighs 25. He has weights around his waist, and in his shoes as shown. What is the weight around his left wrist?

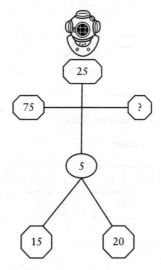

Hint: Divide right foot by waist and multiply by helmet.

Puzzle 13: What is the missing number?

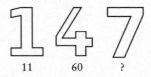

11   60   ?

Hint: The number is multiplied by the number of straight lines needed to construct it. E.g. four is constructed of 15 lines × 4 = 60.

Puzzle 14: A is to B as C is to …?

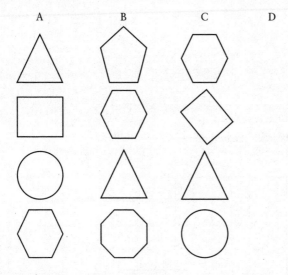

Hint: Each shape adds two extra lines.

Puzzle 15: What's the number?

12	8
128	

18	14
336	

24	12
384	

6	28
?	

Hint: Two-thirds of left × ? = bottom.

Puzzle 16: What's the number?

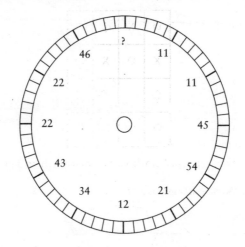

Hint: Clockwise the numbers are pairs formed by...

Puzzle 17: Which is the odd one out?

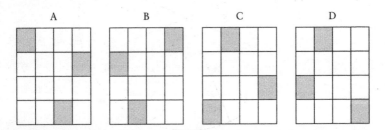

Hint: Which does not have a mirror image?

Puzzle 18: What's the number?

12	4
72	

16	14
336	

24	8
?	

Hint: Half the top left × ? = bottom.

Puzzle 19: What's the missing symbol?

O	X	◇	O
X	O	X	◇
◇	?	◇	X
O	◇	X	O

Hint: Follow spiral sequence clockwise from top-left corner.

Puzzle 20: What's the missing number?

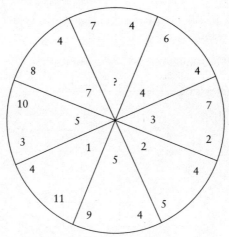

Hint: Proceeding clockwise, subtract the two figures at the circumference of the pie slice and place it...

Puzzle 21: What's the missing number?

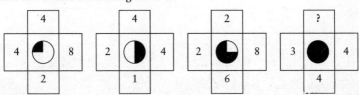

Hint: The bottom number is the shaded pie fraction of the circle in the middle and ... divided by the ...

Puzzle 22: Where to place the X?

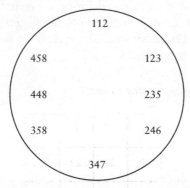

Hint: Move in a clockwise spiral starting top left and each time you move, rotate the X anticlockwise to the...

Puzzle 23: Which number is the odd one out?

112

458 123

448 235

358 246

347

Hint: Add the first two digits and compare with the third digit.

Puzzle 24: Which is the odd one out?

A		
	90	
4	7	5
	6	

B		
	24	
1	4	2
	3	

C		
	45	
2	5	3
	4	

D		
	72	
3	6	4
	5	

Hint: Left plus right plus bottom × ? = ?

Puzzle 25: What is the time on the clock?

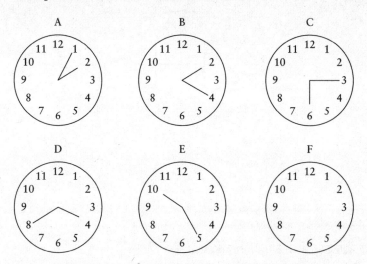

Hint: All clocks show one finger pointing to a number double the number at which the other finger points. The fingers are moving clockwise around the clock face. With each move, the big finger and the small finger change places.

Puzzle 26: What is the missing number?

6	12	6	10
8	24	22	2
6	?	30	10
2	12	14	4

Hint: Move clockwise round the square, in a spiral, starting top left. Add three digits, and then place the total as close as you can to...

Puzzle 27: What is the next number?

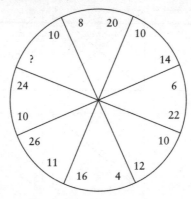

Hint: Proceed clockwise, add the digits and then place the sum of the digits in your answer in the next segment.

Puzzle 28: What is the missing number?

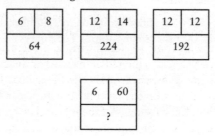

Hint: Two-thirds left × right and double = bottom.

Puzzle 29: What is the missing number?

24	38		10	14
22	?		9	12

32	9		9	28
22	18		6	20

Hint: Add the digits of the total of...

Puzzle 30: Where do A and B go next?

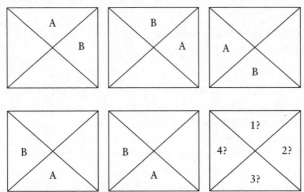

Hint: A moves clockwise, B moves anticlockwise.

Mr Nice and Mr Nasty

Mr Nice is British. He left school with few qualifications but he has been a good husband and has raised his family decently by working as a gas fitter, with some weekend work as a security guard. Mr Nasty is German, also limited in the work available as a camp guard and gas fitter at Auschwitz. He helps the camp to kill hundreds of thousands of men, women and children who are brought there from Poland and Russia – many of them Jews. Is their moral status only the product of their circumstances and are these not within their control? Is Mr Nice praiseworthy and Mr Nasty to be condemned?

PHILOSOPHICAL PROBLEMS AND MORAL DILEMMAS – THORNS IN YOUR BRAIN

If you have found the neuroscientifically designed puzzles in the last section difficult – good. There will be more like them in the ensuing sections. If you found them relatively easy, you may find the following paradoxical dilemmas more demanding and more developmental for your brain. It is again a question of neuroscience versus philosophy. Some of these matters do matter. Many are matters of life and death, policies and penury, logic and epistemology. There are distinctions between what we think and what we would like to think. The puzzles are the equivalent of circuit training that is now demanded by all coaches of top sports people, whereas the thoughtful provocations and moral dilemmas that follow will better suit those for whom the game is the best coach.

> *'When I'm good, I'm very very good.*
> *But when I'm bad, I'm better.'*

Mae West

Mae West's ordinary life wit gives rise to thoughts that are good and bad, but by what criteria? And from whose perspective? How are goodness and badness to be judged? Philosophical games generate ambiguity and contradiction. You will be driven to resolve the resulting cognitive dissonance. You want to find the false assumptions or the faulty reasoning that have led to the ambiguity or contradiction that you experience as you consider the following philosophical problems and moral dilemmas. If you are lucky, you will remain perplexed, with your dissonance unresolved. Those of you who have ever had a thorn in your thumb will know how often, over a period of days, you were reminded of the thorn. Almost every physical task seems to involve hurting your sore thumb. Good philosophical dilemmas work the same way on your brain, repeatedly prompting you to think again and again about the same thing. This is the philosophical equivalent of the neuromyelination caused by puzzles that involve the repeated running of the same neural pathways. Your mind's abhorrence of dissonance means that your brain is constantly taxed to make sense of what your senses sense. Philosophy feeds your senses with apparent contradictions and invites your brain to play mind games that keep your neural pathways active over long periods, often years. Do we have free will when many things we do are driven by genes, unconscious motives and events outside our control? Does plausibility equal truth? Whose truth? When you reason accurately from a true premise or assumption, you can reach conclusions that are also true.

When your newly concluded truth flies in the face of your experience, or is counter intuitive, or is manifestly false, or just does not seem plausible, something has to give. For example, you cannot, at this moment, be both reading these words and not reading these words. You can try to make sense of this apparent contradiction by realizing that you may be doing something else as you read or by arguing that it all depends on what you mean by reading. You cannot just accept to be doing something and not doing it at the same time. Here's another example…

Play 'Open the Box'

There are three boxes; A, B and C. One has the key to the treasure inside it. The other two each have snakes in them. Only the keeper knows what is in which box. You get the key and choose Box A.

Before you can open Box A, the keeper opens Box B to show you a snake inside. The keeper then asks you if you wish to swap from Box A to Box B. Would you swap to Box B? The question is whether, over a sequence of games of 'open the box', you would increase your chances of winning by taking up the option to swap? (You may wish to read the discussion of this in Appendix 1.)

Go now to the Devilish Dilemmas that follow.

DEVILISH DILEMMAS

....

DD1   Under what circumstances would you kill one person to save the lives of others?

DD2   Is it right that extra people die when spending on health and social care is cut to fund spending on Arts and prestigious sports?

DD3   In what circumstances is letting people die (e.g. for want of food, continued life support or agreement to take organs) better than murder?

DD4   In what circumstances is it not right for you to allow the notion of 'the greatest good to the greatest number' (utilitarianism), to drive your decision making.

DD5   Is taxation theft? If not, why not?

DD6   Is the unintended killing and maiming of children justified in a just war?

DD7   Is the unintended killing and maiming of children through acts of terrorism ever justifiable?

DD8   Is it right to judge actions only by their consequences, regardless of their intentions?

DD9   If it is wrong for you to kill (or let die) is it also wrong for you to deny life through celibacy or assisted suicide or abortions? Are chaste nuns and monks no better than murderers? Is contraception wrong?

....

(continued)

DD10   Are you right to create more lives when there are insufficient resources to support them (resulting in increased poverty, poor health and an increased risk of war)?

DD11   Is it right for you to exercise a right to take your own life (voluntary euthanasia) or to take the life of a willing victim (assisted suicide), if to do so creates distress for other people (e.g. the public, the wider family or the helping professions)?

DD12   Does the golden rule 'do unto others as you would have them do unto you' always apply? What exceptions can you think of? How do you justify these exceptions?

DD13   Given that experimenting on children is not morally permissible, would it be morally permissible to experiment on animals? (An adult chimp has the same emotional chemistry and about the same intellectual development and life perspective as a four-year-old child.)

DD14   If it is not right to discriminate on racial grounds, is it right to discriminate on grounds of species?

DD15   Given there is no reason to believe that sheep have future plans, hopes and intentions, is it acceptable to kill them for food?

DD16   If a girl has an incurable illness or injury, such that she has no adult development potential, is it acceptable to kill her or to experiment on her?

DD17   Is having greater affection for one's own children, or black-haired beauties, or men with beards, unfair?

DD18   When experiments on an individual are intended to benefit a wider group, should they be conducted on human adults who can value the hoped-for outcomes?

DD19   If there is risk to the future life quality of the adults on whom such experiments are made, should not the experiments be confined to the elderly, or those suffering from dementia as they have less of a future to jeopardize?

DD20   If it is acceptable to treat a butcher as a meat-giving object, a baker as a bread-giving object and a candlestick maker as a source of candlesticks, what is wrong with treating someone of the opposite (or same) sex as a sex object?

DD21 Given that the Christian marriage contract gives a partner equal access to life-long reciprocal use of the other's genitals and sexual capacities, good will and affection, is a general concern to elevate the mood of the other the essence of contract?

DD22 Given that in many forms of human contact we use others as a means to achieve our own objectives, is it especially reprehensible to see another as a sex object?

DD23 Given that builders are called on in part because of their physical strengths, and taxi drivers are whistled at to gain their services, why do you think some women object so strongly to the wolf whistle?

DD24 Given that some men, as well as some women, like to be whistled at, when is flirtation or sexual innuendo inappropriate?

DD25 Given, that neither men nor women typically seek out unresponsive objects as sexual partners, does intercourse involve the domination, penetration and occupation of a surrendered female, or the enveloping, smothering and devouring of a surrendered male?

DD26 Is the statement, 'When a woman says 'No' she means 'No' any more likely to be right than the statement, 'When a woman says 'Yes' she means 'Yes'?

DD27 Do you agree that what people do consensually between themselves is permitted so long as it harms no one without their consent.

DD28 What is it that you love, when you love someone?

DD29 When considering an actual or potential lover would you love them just for their money? (If they had a lot, why not?) Would you love them just because they were sexually arousing? If not, why not? Will you love them when they are old and grey? Why? Will you love them if they become paralysed or lose their mind? Why or why not?

DD30 Is marriage a word, or a sentence?

DD31 Who is the who that is wanting to love?

DD32 Who is the you that you want to be loved?

(continued)

DD33   If you can have any organ transplants, new brain tissue and implants, and if all your body's molecules and cells replace themselves over time, are you still you? And who are you? If someone else had the same memories, desires, hopes, fears and intentions as you, would they be you? If you have amnesia, are you still you?

DD34   Some things you do, or don't do, don't appear to have significant or noticeable consequences, so should you vote? Would you better spend your time visiting a sick neighbour? What if everybody thought the same?

DD35   Can knowingly wealthy champagne socialists sincerely campaign for a more equal society? Whatever they donate or give away, will it make any significant difference to the divide between rich and poor?

DD36   Should some rich people have their wealth forcibly taken from them (e.g. by taxation) and given in benefits to the poor? Does it matter how the wealth was acquired, for example by drugs, trade, bonuses, gambling, fraud, arms trade or inheritance?

DD37   Should you be praised or blamed for things not in your control, for example genes or inheritance?

DD38   Are religious believers rational (and does it matter?)

DD39   Are religiously motivated actions the result of social, political and economic forces (e.g. burning witches, the slaughter of infidels, the persecution of Jews) rather than spiritual beliefs?

Unconscious decisions – irrational thoughts

Cell by cell the foetus grows, or the terrorist plot. At what point does abortion become murder? At what point should the security forces arrest and detain without trial? At what point do accumulating molecular neurochemical reactions produce conscious awareness? Imperceptible changes will have started well before you have conscious awareness – is this the basis of 'unconscious' thoughts and feelings that nevertheless drive decisions that sometimes seem irrational?

Sally's teeny bikini

One grain of sand blown off a sand castle still leaves a sandcastle. Teeny changes make no difference. Removing one pebble still leaves a heap of pebbles. Not all incremental change is beneficial. Consider Sally in her tiny polka dot bikini…

Sally noticed the man staring at her. Her bikini is slowly, indiscernibly slipping south. Neither she nor the man can see the teeny movements of the skimpy material over her breasts until they both see the cumulative effect. Sally is excited by what she imagines the man might be thinking. Then she notices that he is wearing a dark uniform. He has a notepad and asks her questions and talks of public indecency. She clutches her towel to her breasts as she rolls to get her bag to get the cash to pay the fine. Looking up into the man's eyes, she realizes that she may have an alternative to paying the fine…

Summary

In Part 1, you have done a lot of thinking. You have watched yourself thinking, like you were a football coach watching one of your players playing. You decided to work on particular skills. The skills you need to think and the way they can be combined have been modelled for you in Figure 1.1. Most of the skills shown there can be improved by referring to *Train Your Brain* (Wootton and Horne, 2010a). Part 2, coming next, deals with more Advanced Applied Thinking skills, in particular with Mathematical Thinking, Creative Thinking, Metaphoric, Systemic and Strategic Thinking.

Part 2
Advanced Applied Thinking skills

Introduction: The world's most advanced models of how the brain thinks

Train Your Brain (Wootton and Horne, 2010a) and *Keep Your Brain Sharp* (Wootton and Horne, 2010b) led to recognition that these books were based on 'some of the world's most advanced models of how thinking takes place' and of the way different parts of the brain were involved in each component of Applied Thinking. That is why exercises and activities based on these models lead to faster, more accurate thinking, and to more intelligent solutions, decisions and plans.

Advanced Applied Thinking – a new model

Part 1 looked at the way neuroscience-based training puzzles can be used to leave better connected neural networks in your brain. Part 1 also looked at the use of 'thought experiments' that generate extra neural connections by getting you to think in repetitive depth about real world problems that have been simplified to focus on only one or two variables. Finally, you were encouraged to use 'the game as coach' and to improve your thinking by doing just that, i.e. thinking. You were asked to think about a wide range of real world problems.

Figure 2.1 is 'the world's most advanced model of the way the brain thinks'. It shows the way Basic Thinking Skills can be combined to deliver Higher Order and Advanced Thinking Skills. It has been developed during 15 years of research by the authors, starting with Gillie Meltugh and Roger Armstrong at Lancashire Business School.

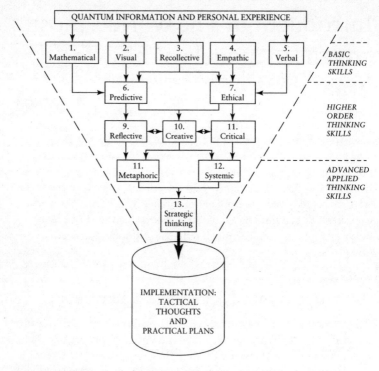

Figure 2.1 Modelling the components of Advanced Applied Thinking (© Wootton & Horne, 2011)

This is the world's most advanced model of the way the brain thinks. It shows how Basic Thinking Skills can be combined to deliver Advanced Applied Thinking and to support the development of Creative Intelligence.

BASIC THINKING SKILLS

The development of Basic Thinking Skills and High Order Thinking Skills is dealt with in *Train Your Brain* (Wootton and Horne, 2010a) and *Keep Your Brain Sharp* (Wootton and Horne, 2010b). Here, Part 2 will look at a more advanced role for Mathematical Thinking in section 2.1; Creative and 'Lateral Thinking' in section 2.2; and the practical application of more Advanced Thinking Skills – metaphoric, systemic and strategic – in section 2.3, where the workshop invites you to apply these skills to 'taking difficult decisions in difficult times'.

In section 2.1, Mathematical and Numerical Thinking has been selected for more advanced treatment for two reasons:

1 Advances in neuroscience reveal how information is held in your brain as a nearly infinite matrix of neuron connections. Mathematicians learned long ago how to think about the properties of infinite sets of data and so Mathematical Thinking will be recruited to help you better understand how millions of neuron connections could become words, feelings and thoughts.

2 Mathematics and numeracy underpin physical sciences like physics, chemistry and biology, without advances in which economies will collapse and the planet will not be rescued from the worst legacies of twentieth-century science and technology – like nuclear pollution and carbon emissions.

In section 2.2, Creativity has been selected for further development and practice because:

1 Neuroscientists have discovered which parts of your brain must be active when you solve problems creatively and when you plan innovations.

2 Twenty-first-century problems like the North–South divide; poverty; bankers' bonuses; debt crises; nuclear proliferation; cuts in public services; youth alienation; failing schools and rising urban crime, will require creative solutions.

3 When managers in organizations have access to the same databases and use the same tools to analyse the same data, they will come up with similar decisions and plans. This will result in over capacity, over provision, collapses in pricing, bankruptcies and wasted resources. Organizations need decisions that are distinctive and plans that give them comparative advantage.

A QUANTUM LEAP IN THINKING ABOUT THINKING – QUANTUM THINKING

The Mathematical Thinking normally associated with the quantum mechanics of atomic and sub-atomic particles may be just the sort of thinking that will help you to think about how we think.

David Hilbert developed the Mathematical Thinking now used by theoretical chemists and physicists, well before the theoretical chemists and physicists needed it. Fortunately, quantum mathematicians are quite used to counter-intuitive, illogical solutions, for example particles that need to be in more than one place at the same time. This makes quantum mathematics well suited to human thinking, since human thinking is also often illogical. Advanced Applied thinkers often appear to make leaps of imagination and free association to experience the gap-jumping sparks of ideas. Quantum Thinking and quantum ideas can help us to map the jumps and leaps in human thinking. Search algorithms based on quantum logic will help to discern meanings in voluminous quantities of information much more efficiently than the logic that normally underpins traditional academic education. Quantum Thinking may better enable you to capture the flexible and plastic way that neuroscientists now observe the brain to be working when you are thinking.

Thought experiment 1
Imagine that you sent a spray of ideas through a narrow slit of perception P1, and that you obtained result R1, as shown in Figure 2.2.

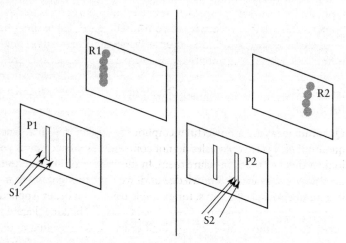

Figure 2.2

Imagine next that you sent the same or different sprays of ideas through another slit of perception, P2, and then you obtain result R2. If you now spray S1 and S2 simultaneously through Slits P1 and P2, then R1 and R2 will interact. They will interfere with each other to produce totally new results that have never been seen before, as shown in Figure 2.3.

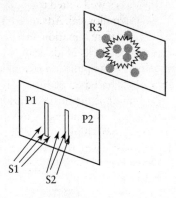

Figure 2.3

The Thinking processes in this book increase the probability that you will make 'quantum leaps' in your thinking and produce R3 type results. You will be able to use the thinking processes in this book to enhance the creativity of your intelligence. These ideas have been tested by Tversky and Shafter at Princeton University. They found that when two probable outcomes of putative actions are combined, people's behaviour in practice does not follow what you might predict by thinking logically about them, or empathically for them.

Quantum ideas are a powerful metaphor for human thinking. One quantum idea is that particles do not come into existence unless you look at them or try to measure them. In the same way, information does not exist as usable knowledge until we have thought about it in a number of specific ways, for example using high order Applied Thinking Skills like Reflective, Critical and Creative Thinking (Figure 1.1, Section 1.1). Among other things, high order thinking evaluates the utility or novelty of sensed, remembered or imagined words. During the contextual evaluation and construction of their meanings, the behaviour of words is quantum like, e.g. the co-joined meaning of a word changes in arbitrary and unequal steps.

Thought experiment 2

Write down the meaning of the word 'white' in each of the following conjunctions:

No	White...	Means.........
1.	White skin	
2.	White wine	
3.	White hair	
4.	White horse	
5.	White flag	

Keith Rijsbergen at Glasgow University thinks that Google search language has a strong quantum feel because it tries to double guess the conjunctions that will be in the searcher's mind – this is likely to include illogical, subjective and associative conjunctions.

A pressing need for action characterizes the intent of Advanced Applied Thinking. Yet there is often too much, too complex information to calculate a decision or to compute a rational plan. Quantum Thinking enables you to feel relaxed about producing creatively intelligent ideas that involve arbitrary, unexplained jumps. (You will not have to push yourself forward as a leader in times of crisis or economic downturn. Others will step back from difficult decisions in difficult times, thus leaving you in the front (section 2.3).)

LOGIC B – THE BIRTH OF SPECIFICITY?

Advanced Applied Thinking stresses the importance of Mathematical and Numerical Thinking. There is good reason for this. Mathematicians have form. This section makes the point that mathematicians developed mathematics that predicted the need for Quantum Thinking long before Einstein had his dream about Relativity. The same is true of climate change – early mathematical models correctly predicted the weather patterns that were subsequently confirmed by scientists drilling core samples through the Arctic ice cap. Thinking metaphorically about Quantum Mathematics and Quantum Theory produces insights and explanations that are relevant to Creative Thinking and Creative Intelligence. Mathematical Thinking about infinity and set theory can help to free your thinking from the limitations of logic – or at least from the limitations of Logic A, the kind that underpinned most of the industrial advances of the twentieth century. Given its productive track record, Logic A currently underpins the education curricula in most western countries. However, mathematical thinking about infinity and set theory offers the possibility of liberation from some of the limitations of Logic A and creates the possibility of a replacement system of logic – Logic B.

Thought experiment 1

Start counting now 1, 2, 3 … How far can you go? Infinity, of course. Logically there is no biggest number, it depends only on how much time you and your computer have, and is that infinite? This is a 'countable infinity'. The question occurs – are there other kinds, or levels, of infinity? Can they too be counted? Are there infinite levels of 'countable' infinities?

Thought experiment 2

Consider a continuous straight line without holes or gaps. How many points compose it? Logically an infinite number – 'a continuous infinity' – as there is no logical limit to mathematical powers of subdivision.

But this 'continuous infinity' is clearly different in nature to the 'countable infinity' you thought about in Thought experiment 1, in which you were bounding ever upwards in a series of separated steps – steps that followed patterns and rules. Whereas this new 'continuous infinity', which you discovered in Thought experiment 2, is not, for example, characterized by whole numbers or integers. 'Continuous infinity' uses integers plus all the fractions or decimal points that can possibly exist between one integer and the next – which is, of course, another 'countable infinity' of decimal points. So, logically, there is an infinite series of infinities. This idea cannot be readily accommodated by Logic A. Logic A requires you to try to disprove the hypothesis that 'there exists an infinite set of countable, and or continuous, and or other, infinities'. This is proving difficult, but it is not yet possible to know that it is not possible. Countable sets of whole numbers have subsets – even infinite countable sets can be mentally split into at least two subsets – one of even numbers and another of odd numbers, Continuous sets offer no easy route to subsetting, at least not following Logic A. Suppose there were other systems of logical Thinking, including, say, Logic B. By 1901, British philosopher Bertrand Russell was already struggling with these ideas.

By 1922, German mathematicians were trying to find ways of comparing the size of different infinite sets. They were already struggling with the limitations of Logic A!

Thought experiment 3
Imagine you have several collections of sets of cooking ingredients. It is not hard to imagine how you can select one set out of each collection and, by merging the selected sets, create a completely new set of tastes that may never have existed before.

Consider the surface of a sphere. The infinite number of points on its surface can be divided into an infinite number of lines. These are subsets of an infinity. By 1930, the Polish mathematician Alfred Tarski had used the kind of thinking you used in Thought experiment 3 to divide the sets of points of a spherical surface or into six subsets, which he could then merge to create two balls, each of the same size as the original. Logic B thus provides a mathematical metaphor which you can use in conjunction with the Quantum Thinking, to understand how finite but very large sets of neuronal data in your brain can double your brain power, or create new thoughts that have never been thought before. There may exist, for example, an infinite set of logics that we can learn to use to help us think about an infinite range of problems, and if none of the known systems of logic is helpful, we can select from the infinite sets of systems of logic, two or more, and merge them to form a system of logic that best helps you, as a 'specific' individual, to think about a 'specific' problem, under a 'specific' set of conditions. Logic B enables you to plunder the diversity of the mathematical multiverse to come up with metaphors that will help you under 'specific' conditions. Logic B supports the idea of 'specificity'.

2.1

Numeracy and mathematical thinking

In this section you will:
- *test yourself*
- *take the Mensa challenge*
- *do a Numerical Thinking workout.*

2.1.1 Some diagnostic questions

If you find them easy, move on. If you find them difficult, move back to *Train Your Brain* (Wootton and Horne, 2010a). Answers are in Appendix 1 at the back of the book.

If you want more questions, move to Appendix 3.

DIAGNOSTIC TEST

Attempt all questions. The questions carry equal marks.

A1: You have done something very bad for your brain. You have drunk alcohol at the Canal Inn.

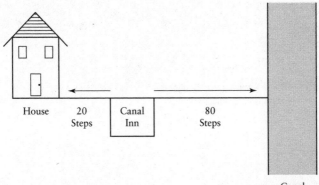

You have drunk so much that when you come out of the Inn and the cold night air hits you, you can only stagger to the left or the right. After each stagger, there is an equal probability that you will stagger left or right. What is the chance that you will end up in the canal rather than at home? What chance does your younger brother stand? He has drunk as much as you, but his steps are half as long as yours?

A2: You need a cube-shaped tank with a capacity of 125 cubic metres. What size sheets do you need to weld together?

A3: How do you find the reciprocal of a number?

A4: Is 161 a prime number?

A5: Is a set of data comprising all possible observations of an event called?

  a the population
  b the sample
  c the range
  d none of the above

A6: Is the sum of the integers from 110 to 630 greater or less than 190,000?

A7: A stepladder rests on the ground against a wall, so that its base is 3 feet from the bottom of the wall. The ladder is 8 feet long. Does the ladder touch the wall more or less than 7 feet from the ground?

A8: When you make a forecast, is the term you use to indicate the relative importance you attach to a factor?

  a the value
  b the weight
  c the outcome

A9: Your flight closes 1 hour and 47 minutes before take off. What else do you need to know?

A10: The top and bottom of this silo are circles, each of diameter 14 metres. You are required to spray the silo on the inside and the outside. Each canister will spray 100 square metres. How many canisters will you need?

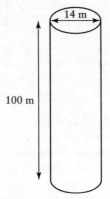

100 m

A11: Assuming all the angles in this L-shaped seat are right angles, what volume of foam will you need to fill it?

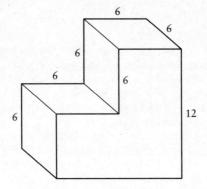

A12: Which of these quadrilaterals does not have two pairs of equal sides?

a kite
b rectangle
c rhombus
d square
e trapezium
f parallelogram

A13: What is the perimeter of this field?

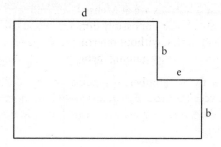

A14: PRIMNEXT fashions is having a clearance sale. Week 1 is 50 per cent off; week 3 a further 10 per cent off the original price; Week 6 another 20 per cent off the original price. You buy a dress for £12.50 at week 6. How much have you saved compared with the original price?

A15: You throw two dice. What is the probability that the sum of the faces is 5?

A16: Your floor is 4m × 4.5m. How many tiles of 20cm × 30cm will you need?

A17: If an event occurs 23 times out of 50 samples, how many times would you estimate it would occur altogether, if you take another 100 samples?

A18: A fruit juice recipe is 3 parts sugar to 2 parts fruit. How much sugar is there in a 750ml bottle?

If you did not get 16 correct, you need more practice to be sure to get a senior job or a place on a high level course using numerical aptitude testing such as GMAT, Fast Stream or SHI. Turn to Appendix 3 and find the Kogan Page series on *numeracy tests* by Mike Bryon. Alternatively, revise using *Train Your Brain* (Wootton and Horne, 2010a).

2.1.2 The Mensa challenge

The next ten test questions are at Mensa level, followed by several questions that are almost impossibly difficult. If you can do six of the following M puzzles, without referring to Appendix 1, you will probably have no difficulty gaining membership of Mensa!

M19: Complete the six numbers beginning 451 by adding a three-digit number exceeding 100. By what two-digit number must you divide each of the numbers you have created to yield the following answers (dividends)?

156; 339; 461; 644; 400; 949

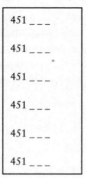

```
451 _ _ _

451 _ _ _

451 _ _ _

451 _ _ _

451 _ _ _

451 _ _ _
```

M20: On what rules is this matrix based? Which two-digit number is missing from the shaded square?

B	C	D	E	F
18	0	12	18	12
16	2	12	18	14
14	4	12	18	16
14	2	10	16	
6	2	2	8	4

M21: Arrange these tiles into a square made up of ten-digit numbers such that each ten-digit number occurs twice – once horizontally and once vertically.

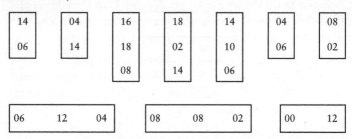

M22: The treasure is buried at T. You can start anywhere (except T!). By counting the number of spaces shown in the direction indicated, you must land exactly on T to dig for the treasure. (You may find that you walk over the spot where the treasure is buried many times before you land exactly on the spot marked T.)

Key: S = towards the sea, R = to your right, L = to your left, T = towards the trees

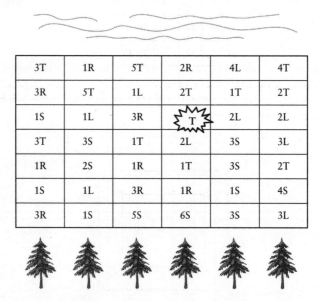

Where must you start looking in order to finally land exactly on T, which marks the spot where you must dig for the treasure?

86

M23: What three numbers, each used as often as you wish, would help you to complete the matrix, such that each row, column and diagonal adds to 80?

24	6	24	6	20
12	20			4
	28		4	
			12	38
12		8	36	8

M24: Move from square to square, from start to finish, collecting nine numbers that total 108. Moves can be in any direction, including diagonally.

18	16	10	18	10	← Finish
12	10	16	12	18
16	18	14	10	12
14	18	8	16	14
8	12	8	10	8

Start → (bottom left)

M25: What is the lowest total penalty you can incur? You can start at any corner and you must collect at least another four penalties by following any of the paths shown.

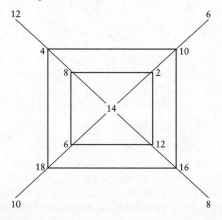

M26: What is the missing number?

10	8	6	2	12
16	14	12	10	24
6	6	?	8	12

M27: What is the missing number?

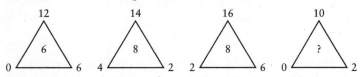

M28: Add numbers so that each segment totals are the same as each other segment, and so that each concentric circle totals the same as each other concentric circle:

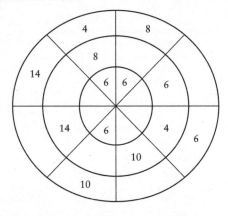

If you solved more than six of the M numerical puzzles correctly, then consider applying for membership of MENSA. If you need more practice, consult Appendix 3.

DIFFICULT NUMERICALLY

You have had a look at some of the implications of quantum mathematics for a model of Quantum Thinking. You have tested yourself against the most advanced numerical aptitude tests currently in use in employment selection and course admissions, and you have rated yourself against MENSA Numerical IQ standards.

There follows a Numerical Thinking Skill workout that has been specifically designed to connect up many parts of your brain simultaneously, and which are difficult enough to require a great deal of reiteration to solve them. This will ensure that your new connections are well myelinated and left in place to help you with more demanding work in later sections. Many of these problems are very difficult.

2.1.3 Workout: Numerical Thinking

D29: What are the missing numbers from series A and B?

A: 8163264128.

B: 193876152.

D30: 975949=634536=182018= ?

D31: What's the missing number?

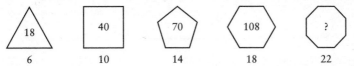

D32: What are the letter values?

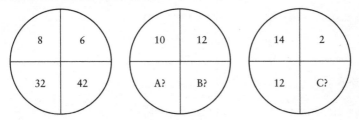

D33: What are A and B in the following sequence?

22262429263228353A?3B?

D34: What are A and B?

21	2			12	2
42	1764	1	2	24	576
		A?	B?		

D35: What's the value?

After a furniture auction, you approach the dealer who outbid you for the lot you wanted (well, it was only the antique chess set you wanted, not the complete lot). The dealer had bid £624. The dealer does not want the chess set and is willing to split the lot, and let you have the chess set at a proportion of his bid. The lot contains a valise, a table and pitcher jugs, besides the chess set you want. The dealer thinks the relative values are: chess set 30 times the value of the valise, and six times the value of the pitchers, but one quarter the value of the table. How much will you need to pay him for the chess set?

D36: What is the missing number?

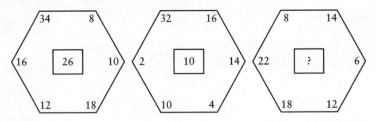

D37: What is the missing number?

30	4
66	2
54	2
72	8
64	?
36	18
44	22
24	6

D38: In a five horse race, the winning jockey wore red, the second placed horse orange, and the third yellow. What colour did the losing jockey wear?

D39: How many squares are there on a Chess Board?

D40: You are sitting in the rear most seat of a train that is 250 metres long. The train is travelling at 120 kph. It has just entered a tunnel that is 4000 metres long. For how long might you be in darkness?

D41: What's the missing number?

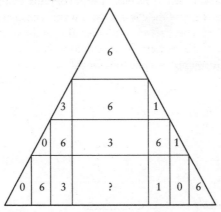

D42: The London to Glasgow express only stops at Watford, Crewe, Preston, Lancaster and Carlisle. How many tickets need to be printed so that passengers may travel from any station to any other?

D43: By what fraction does 38/72 exceed one-quarter?

D44: What weights of product (between 2kg and 28kg) could you not weigh with the weights you have available?

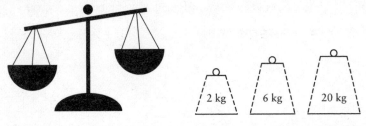

D45: Insert one of the following operators +, −, ÷ or × into the empty circles such that, starting with 5, and proceeding clockwise, produces the total 90.

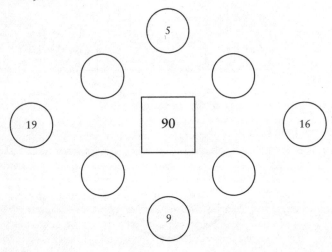

D46: Insert the same number the same number of times as itself to balance the equation:

2 ÷ 2 = I

D47: The numbers on the three concealed faces of spinning tops A and B continue in the same pattern sequence as the sequence on the three revealed faces. Spinner B spins 50 per cent faster than Spinner A and in the opposite rotation to Spinner A, which spins clockwise.

A and B start spinning simultaneously. After A spins 6×2 moves (and therefore B 6×3 moves), what will be the product of the faces that will face each other (the way that A face 10 and B face 4, currently face each other?)

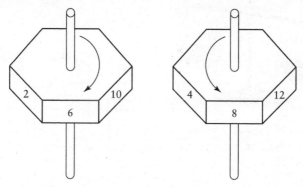

D48: The clock shows that the time is 5 hours, 50 minutes and 6 seconds. What time exactly will it show in 3½ hours, if the clock is running slow by 4 seconds in every hour.

D49: What is the product of the square root of the highest perfect square and the square of the lowest prime in the series:

3, 4, 5, 6, 7, 8, 9, 10, 64, 144, 152, 158, 168, 169, 171, 175

D50: 30 per cent of your students have failed an assignment. You have received 200 marked scripts, marked by three tutors. You will need to moderate the marking by three tutors. You pick ten scripts at random. Then you pick out two out of the sample randomly to second mark. What are the chances that they are both failures?

D51: You go to the station at random times every day to get a train to the shopping mall. You get on the first train that arrives and seem to end up shopping at North Mall nine times more often than South Mall. Why might that be?

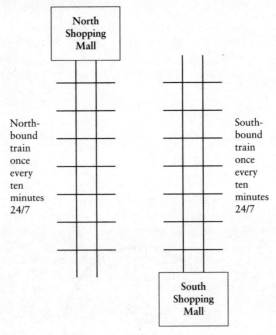

D52: If the points add up to the centre, what is probably the missing letter?

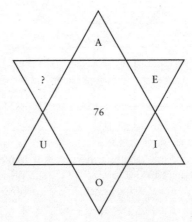

D53: What is the sum of the prime numbers and the perfect squares?

7, 12, 15, 23, 31, 36, 50, 56, 64, 81

D54: What is the next number?

111, 315, 171, 921, 232 ???

D55. You are playing Bridge. You are examining the hand you have been dealt. You have twice as many diamonds as spades and twice as many hearts as diamonds. You have one more black card than red cards. How many clubs do you have?

D56: What is the missing number?

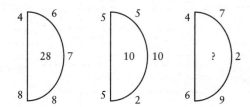

D57: Which two numbers have been transposed between the rows?

5	7	53	64
3	8	50	82

D58: In how many years' time will the combined age of three brothers and two sisters be half what it will be in 11 years' time, if their combined age in 11 years' time will be 100?

D59: How many squares are there?

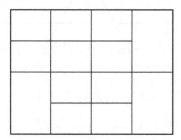

D60: You are trying to disable the bomb. All eight sensors must be disabled and in the strict sequence shown. If you disturb a sensor square twice, the bomb will explode. Decode the instructions in each sensor box and work out with which box you must start to avoid triggering the bomb.

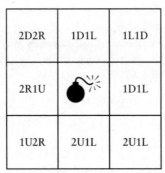

2D2R	1D1L	1L1D
2R1U	💣	1D1L
1U2R	2U1L	2U1L

D61: What are the missing letters and numbers?

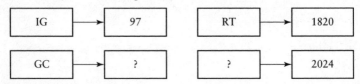

| IG | → | 97 |

| RT | → | 1820 |

| GC | → | ? |

| ? | → | 2024 |

D62: What is needed to balance the scale?

| 12 | | | | | | | ? |

8   8   6   6

D63: Supermarket complaints.

The supermarket has complained that 10 per cent of the apples you sent in your last delivery were bruised. They have returned them. You take out two to check. If the manager is right, what is the chance that you will pick out two bruised apples?

D64: What's the missing number?

2   5   4   6   5   3   3   5   3   ?

D65: The dice is rolled from stations A–F in the directions shown. It takes a one face roll only from one station to the next. What number will be uppermost in station F?

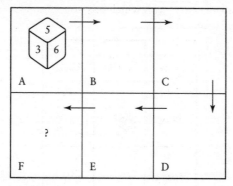

D66: What is the missing number?

35 36 38 39 40 42 44 45 46 ? 49 50 51

D67: What is the next number?

2 4 5 10 12 24 27 54 58 116 ?

D68: Going swimming

Terry can swim faster than John but slower than Sam. Henry swims faster than John and even Terry (sometimes), but cannot swim faster than Sam. Who is the slowest swimmer?

D69: Weather forecasts

The rainfall this month is 115ml which is 15 per cent up on the same month last year. What was the rainfall in the same month last year?

D70: Playing card games

How many different three-card combinations can be made from a standard pack of 52 playing cards?

D71: Saving raw materials

You are a potter and you find a way to save one-sixth of the clay you use to make one pot. The clay saved from six pots enables you to make one new pot. You normally make 40 pots per day. You make pots on five days per week. How many extra pots will you make in a week?

D72: What is the missing number?

16					
2	14				
6	2	?			
2	4	6	4		
4	4	2	2	4	
4	2	2	4	2	2

D73: Average speed speeding checks

The milometer in your car shows 15951. Two hours later your milometer is palindrome. At what average speed have you been driving for the last two hours?

D74: Journey planning

Your car travels an 80-mile journey in the same time as your friend's car covers 120 miles, with your friend on average driving 40 mph faster than you. How long will your journey take?

D75: What is the missing number?

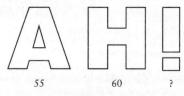

55   60   ?

D76: The answer is 66, what is the question?

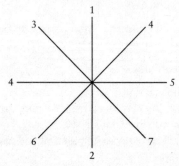

D77: What is five times one-third of three-fifths of 128976.73?

D78: Days out with the kids

It costs you $21 per day to enter the museum. You go the museum four days in succession. During the day, you spend half the money you have in your pocket on coffee and cakes. When you leave you pay $1 to get out of the car park. When you get home at the end of the fourth day, you have only $1 in your pocket. How much did you have at the start of the first day?

D79: When you lose your bath plug

You have lost the plug to your bath but it doesn't matter as the drain is very slow – it takes 40 minutes to empty the bath, so there is still time for a bath if you fill it to the top. The hot tap will fill the bath to the top in 10 minutes. The cold tap will fill it to the top in 8 minutes. You will need a ratio of 5 parts hot to 4 parts cold water for your bath to be safe and warm enough. How long will it take you to fill the bath? What is the maximum time you can stay in the water?

D80: Playing snooker

It is your turn to play. You chalk your cue as you come to the table and contemplate the ten reds that remain on the snooker table. The six colours have descending value from 7 for black to 2 for yellow. (Potting a red ball counts as 1 point.) At this stage, you must precede potting any colour by potting a red. You manage to pot each colour in turn, but your break ends when you miss your seventh red. What is your break score?

D81: Make three squares by moving four matches.

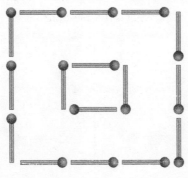

D82: Reduce these five connected squares to only four connected squares by moving only two matches.

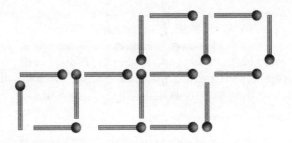

D83: Make this west-swimming fish swim north by moving only two matches.

D84: Reduce this five-square arch to four connected squares, by moving only three matches.

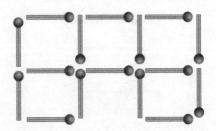

D85: Turn this noughts and crosses field into three connected squares by moving three matches.

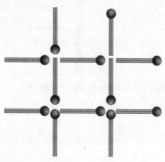

D86: Change the hexagon of six connected triangles into three connected equilateral triangles by moving (not removing!) only four matches.

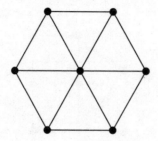

D87: Convert this stack of three triangles into four connected equilateral triangles by moving only three matches.

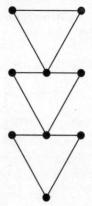

D88: Make a square by moving one match only.

D89: Make four triangles by moving only one match.

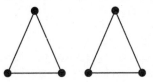

D90: Reduce these five squares to two squares by removing only two matches.

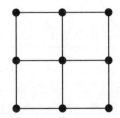

Thought experiment

Would you worry more or less if you were told cancer kills 20 people out of 100, or 200 in 1000 people? Most people think 200 people in 1000 is riskier. They react to the bigger number even though the actual risk is the same. Useful to know if you are writing attention-grabbing headlines, advertisements or book titles. The bigger the number, the riskier it is perceived to be. Fox News, for example, is fond of reporting big number percentage changes in very small absolute levels of risk. For example: 'Throat cancer up 400 per cent in 30 years' (Fox News, 27 May 2008). Actual figures supplied in the *Journal of US National Cancer Institute* were more circumspect, showing that the risk of adenocarcinoma in 1975 was 0.00101 per cent and 29 years later in 2004, it was still only 0.00569 per cent!

You have broadened your mind generally by thinking about quantum thinking. You have been introduced to metaphoric thinking, which will be developed in section 2.3. You have assessed your numerical aptitude in the way it is assessed for top jobs and top course admissions and have a plan if you are not happy with your self-assessment. You have rated your numerical intelligence against MENSA IQ standards and may be thinking of joining. You have worked out your brain and warmed it up for the next section on Creative Intelligence and Creative Thinking.

2.2

The neuroscience: Creativity and creative thinking

In this section you will:
* *learn about the neuroscience of creativity and creative thinking*
* *learn about ethical thinking*
* *do a lateral thinking workout.*

2.2.1 Creative Thinking

It is not necessary either to be born a genius or to drive yourself 'mad' in order to think creatively. Professor Martindale studied the brain scans of people writing creatively and, in *Psychology* in August 2007, he reported that the most creative writing was done by people who could deliberately shift their brain activity from their rear brain parietal sensory cortex to the front brain lobes of their cerebral cortex. Although it was true that the right-hand sides of their brains were involved, so were the left-hand sides of their brains. The myth that creative people are those who are naturally 'right brained' is mistaken. You can train your brain to shift from back to front, and from left to right.

COMMON BLOCKS TO CREATIVE THINKING

▶ Aversion to risk.
▶ Inability to relax.
▶ Obsessive tidiness.
▶ Prevalent pessimism.
▶ A tendency to be cynical.
▶ A preoccupation with control.
▶ A tendency to be judgemental.
▶ Fear of reverie or daydreaming.
▶ Excessive need for quick success.

- A fear of failure or of making mistakes.
- A limited capacity for delayed gratification.
- An inability to tolerate uncertainty or ambiguity.
- A strong preference for reality rather than fantasy.
- Unwillingness to deal with hypothesis or conjecture.
- A propensity to be 'laid back', unexcited by challenge.

REMOVING BLOCKS TO CREATIVE THINKING

If the block is…

1	Habit	Do one different thing every day.
2	Firm beliefs	Ask 'If I didn't believe this, what might happen?'
3	Familiarity	Ask 'How will I feel when I have solved this problem?'
4	Adult behaviour	Indulge in one piece of 'child-like' behaviour each day.
5	Lack of language	Mix with creative people. Join an art or drama group.
6	Not my area	Say 'Good, most breakthroughs come from non-specialists.'
7	Fear of mistakes	Ask 'What's the worst thing that could happen?'
8	Existing models	Ask 'What if you had arrived from Mars?'
9	I'm too old	Realize that creative Thinking involves bringing lots of knowledge and experience together and that the older you are, the more you have.
10	Lack of time	Accept that you have all the time there is. (Deadlines aid creativity so long as you don't get anxious.)

20 WAYS TO DEVELOP CREATIVITY

1. Don't forget

Keep pocket Dictaphones or pads and pencils on desks, by phones, in cars, by beds. Jot down or record key words. You will forget them quickly, especially after waking or getting involved in an activity.

2. A move with a view

Move your chair, your desk, your room, your house or your country periodically – anything to gain a new perspective.

3. Make a date
Julia Cameron suggests that you make a 'date' with your creative self once a week. Take time out to meet your creative self for at least a couple of hours at a bookshop, art shop, a fabric shop, a gallery, a café or just a coffee bar where you can be alone with a magazine or a notepad.

4. Catch the worm (before it turns)
The early bird can catch the creative worm. If it is fiction you want to write, start straight out of bed – some writers do not even turn on the light. Write in long hand, double-line spaced. Edit and re-edit until it is no longer decipherable. Write it out again. Keep going for your allotted time, 30 minutes or an hour at the most. Then stop and clean your teeth. Surprisingly, fixed deadlines seem to aid creativity in the morning, perhaps raising anxiety just enough to sharpen your waking mind.

If you are writing non-fiction, or designing something, your routine will be different. You need lots of light to switch off your pineal gland (*Train Your Brain*, Wootton and Horne, 2010a). Clean your teeth using minty toothpaste and the hand you do not normally use. Do the head in hand, and eye switch exercises, and finish with the 60 second hand rub (see section 3.2). You will then be well oxygenated for a dawn raid on your neurons. For more eye exercises, see section 3.2 in *Train your Brain* (Woottend and Horne, 2010a).

5. Signal your creative intent
Creative Thinking requires a deliberate shift to a new zone. Sometimes it helps to signal your intent to others and to yourself. Victor Hugo signalled his intent by taking off all his clothes. Alexandre Dumas ate an apple every day at 7 a.m. under the Arc de Triomphe and then wrote for an hour at a streetside café. Mark Twain lay on the floor. Ernest Hemingway sharpened pencils. Thomas Huxley wrote with his nose.

6. The long march
Like William Wordsworth, A. E.Houseman and Bertrand Russell, go for a walk! Professor Clayton recommends at least 20 minutes a day. Down the long march of history, aborigines have gone 'walkabout', Native Americans went on 'vision quests', Christians on pilgrimages and Muslims on the Hajj.

7. Become a private eye
In your total immersion phase, you may need to become a private investigator. Thinking metaphorically (see section 2.3), what style of undercover detective will you become? Hercule Poirot collects all the

'facts' and then sits down and thinks about them. Miss Marple often just sits behind her net curtain and watches the world; she has a great eye for detail – she doesn't miss a thing. Columbo acts dumb but asks good questions. Sherlock Holmes thinks aloud with Watson. Who can be your role model when you become a private eye?

8. Time's up
Surprisingly, tight deadlines often produce creative solutions, especially in the last ten minutes.

9. Bin the best and keep the rest
The exhortation to 'bin the best' recognizes the blocking effect on your creativity when you become so attached to the good bits of your work that you are reluctant to surrender space to new ideas.

10. First the good news
Know your creative style before you invite others to comment on your work. Problems arise, especially if your style is predominantly 'N' for needy. You need approval, admiration, attention and applause, so always say 'Okay, give me the good news first', and ask 'What do you like about any work?' Next ask 'What do you find interesting about my work?', 'What are its potential growth points?' and 'What would you like to see less of?' (steel yourself). Then, finally, 'What would you like to see more of?', 'What is the best thing you liked about my work?' Start and finish with the good news.

11. Girls and boys come out to play
On an 'I-need-to-be-creative' day, think of life as a game (even if you don't know the rules). Adopt a playful disposition in meetings and encourage it in others. Ignore put-downs like 'Don't be facetious' or 'Don't be childish'. As a child, you probably had no problem thinking creatively.

12. Get a brainwave
Before a task that requires creative thinking, do relaxation exercises (Chapters 1 and 5 in *Train your Brain* (Wootton and Horne, 2010a)). These slow down the electrical activity in your brain and literally produce bigger brainwaves. Favour deep-breathing exercises that involve visualizing objects, colours, stories or good memories.

13. Pass it on
To get up to 80 ideas from eight people, give them each a blank sheet of paper and ask them to write down three ideas working alone.

They pass their sheets to the right. Each person reads the ideas on the sheet in front of them and adds one more and again passes the sheet to the person on their right.

14. Love me, love my dog
If you get stuck, try using analogies to help you become unstuck (see section 2.3). Ask yourself what connection this situation has with the problems facing a particular animal such as a dog, an owl, an elephant, etc. Alternatively, try comparing the situation with, for example, using a photocopier, learning to drive, cooking a meal, etc.

15. Travel is in the telling
Reading, travelling and talking are proactive, unlike watching television which is passive. Find bantering partners who do not evaluate or judge what you say. The greater the variety of subjects you talk about, the better. Never miss a chance to talk to anyone who is an expert on anything. Try to take holidays in a culture that is very different from your own.

16. Surprise, surprise!
If you are looking for inspiration from a group of people, do something surprising. Meet them at a theme park, a zoo or on a beach, and then give them the situation about which you want them to think creatively. Then play rounders, five-a-side football or go bowling. Collect and record as many ideas as possible as you mingle with individuals but do not comment, even positively, on any of the ideas. Quantity of ideas is more important than the quality of ideas at this stage.

17. Make piles
Piles not files – if you file information away in filing cabinets or, even worse, boxes, you will rapidly forget it exists and so you will be unable to combine it with any information in a nearby pile. By making piles, preferably on a horizontal surface like a large table, you are creating a three-dimensional map of information that might be relevant to this or your next creative project. Extract all the creative tension and creative connections you can from the information in competing piles, and then remove yourself to a large empty table somewhere you can do your writing, painting, building or designing without further distraction. Immersion profits from piles, but incubation, insight and implementation excel in empty spaces. Interruption is the enemy of inspiration.

18. Talk to yourself – put on your Thinking cap
By all means talk to other people as well – the more perspectives you can get on the situation the better for your immersion and also for

checking your Implementation plans make sense. But if they won't listen to you, let alone talk to you, you can always talk to yourself. Edward de Bono has some good ways of orchestrating conversations between different aspects of yourself:

- ▶ optimist ('What's good about this is …')
- ▶ grower ('We could extend this by …')
- ▶ cardinal ('Ethically, we need to be concerned that …')
- ▶ pessimist ('The problem might be …')
- ▶ logician ('Let's just check if that necessarily follows …')
- ▶ factual ('What do we know and how can we find …')
- ▶ emotional ('This is exciting, passionate, frightening …').

19. Do it to music
If you can think with music playing, find out which music most favours your Creative Thinking (section 3.2).

20. Madness in the method
Creative solutions can sometimes be found by borrowing method acting techniques. List the key roles or objects. Take it in turn to be each of the key roles or objects. In each role, imagine what you would feel and what you would think. Record it. If you have a partner you can work with, ask them to interview you about your experience in each role and make the notes for you.

CREATIVITY – THE ROLE OF HUMOUR

Creating humour, or enjoying humour, predisposes your brain to be open to sudden mental shifts, to the sudden 'Aha!' as you see things from a new and unexpected perspective. It raises your tolerance for surprises. The side-effects of the laughter – relaxation and distraction – help to change your brainwave pattern from high frequency, shorter beta waves, to the slower, longer alpha waves that Bagely (Heilman, 2005) has strongly correlated with Creative Thinking and invention.

Not everyone is a natural humorist, but you can choose to mix with people who are. They will raise your mental energy and maybe your creativity. Children are great; they laugh an average of 450 times a day (compared to about 15 times a day for the average adult).

CREATIVE PLACES

Winnicott discovered that Creative Thinking was more likely to take place in some places than in others. He found that creative ideas flowed better in places where the questioning of authority and the challenging of received wisdom were welcomed and where people were encouraged to joke and be playful. Kanter argued for the creation of autonomous 'play areas'. She recognized the close relationship between playfulness, humour and creativity. Hurst reported that people were more likely to produce new ideas when they laughed, felt comfortable and trusted the people around them.

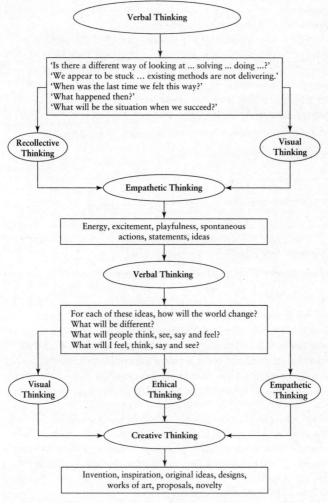

Figure 2.4 The Model of Creative Thinking from *Train your Brain* (Wootten and Horne, 2010a)

THE NEUROCHEMISTRY OF CREATIVE MOODS

The chemical conditions in your brain that are optimal for Creative Thinking are when you are in a state of BLISS (Body-based pleasure, Laughter, Involvement, Satisfaction and Sex), not happiness (the pursuit of which is argued to be futile (Wootton and Horne, 2010b)).

Ignorance can be BLISS

Information rich, question poor. Digi-disease, (see Final Thoughts at the end of the book) discusses the adverse impact of technology on the cognitive capacity of the human brain.

There is also an adverse impact on your prevailing mood, plus the creation of a chemical regime in your head that is a barrier to quick, accurate, creative Thinking.

An appropriate mood-related chemical regime in your head is an important prerequisite to your being able to exercise Creative Intelligence. There appears to be some virtue in saying, 'I don't want to know, thank you' or 'Enough! Too much information.' Knowing less certainly helps you to be a better teacher and a better learner.

Also, an overly erudite mind can often be a block to making money. Pamela Hinds of Stanford University has found that ignorant novices often make judgements, estimates and predictions that are better than those made by experts who are knowledgeable.

Perhaps knowing less, and thinking more, produces a better outcome. It is certainly more likely to produce a more creative outcome and, in a world where competitive advantage lies with inventors and innovators, a new thoughtful outcome will be better than one that is already known about. Advanced Applied Thinking is a way of thinking about Information as 'capta' (sought after and captured) rather than data (enough given information to drown in). Capta is then thought about using combinations of basic and higher order thinking skills, in order to turn it into usable knowledge on which beneficial action can be based. Advanced Applied Thinking involves devising a way of thinking, and sets of criteria to evaluate that thinking, that are person and situation specific. This is a far cry from the one-size-fits-all heuristics of knowledgeable 'experts' and management consultants. Tetlock's work at Berkeley over a period of 20 years showed that you are better off thinking things out for yourself. All the more reason to develop your Advanced Applied Thinking skills.

Here are five creative mood boosters to try:

....

Creative Mood Booster 1	Keep a diary. The mood benefits remain, on average, for two weeks.
Creative Mood Booster 2	Confront a negative thought immediately, before it takes root. Try to reframe it in a more positive way.
Creative Mood Booster 3	Learn to meditate. This has been shown to assist in Creative Thinking.
Creative Mood Booster 4	Nurture your relationships with friends and family. Living in isolation inhibits your will to live healthily, as well as your ability to think creatively.
Creative Mood Booster 5	Give up consumerism and retail therapy to enhance chemical conditions in your brain that favour creative Thinking. Spend some of the money you save on social activities, new experiences, or travel to different cultures and places not visited before.

....

CREATIVITY AND THE CULT OF OPTIMISM

Martin Seligman's lifelong research on health and economic success related them to optimism and positive thinking. Currently the UK Government is discussing using some of these measures of perceived wellbeing alongside economic measures, like per capita GDP, as measures of national or governmental success. Certainly there are strong correlates between optimistic expectation, by yourself and others, and success in mental tasks, especially those requiring creative thinking.

CREATING WHAT'S RIGHT – AVOIDING EVIL GENIUS

Part 3, section 3.1, will deal with the notion of creative genius and evil genius in particular. Creative Thinking has a role to play in thinking what is right. The model of Creative Thinking (Figure 2.4) includes Ethical Thinking as one of its components.

2.2.2 Ethical Thinking

When I do good things, I feel good.
When I do bad things, I feel bad.
That is my religion.

Abraham Lincoln

Neuroscientists have discovered that chemical activity, in the dendrite gaps between your neurons, chemically constructs your thoughts and chemically expresses your feelings. It is this chemical construction that will drive your decisions, plans and actions. You have little control over certain kinds of feelings, like jealousy, lust, greed and fear, some of which can be present when thinking strategically about rewards, fame, ambition, power and competitive rivalry. Unless you learn to mobilize the 'thought' component of your beliefs very quickly, your decisions may bypass your cerebral cortex and lead to consequences you may later regret (or not).

Baggini has pointed out that there is nothing wrong with Abraham Lincoln's Thinking above. Action does not have to hurt to be ethical. Altruism need not involve self-sacrifice. The Chinese character for thinking incorporates the Chinese character for 'heart' as well as the Chinese character for 'head'. The heart reminds you to rethink the issue 'empathically' from the point of view of the intended beneficiaries, or potential victims.

Unless creative thinkers specifically and explicitly introduce an ethical Thinking component into their Creative Thinking process, they will be biased toward self-serving conclusions. In 2003, *Managing Public Services: A Thoughtful Approach to the Practice of Management* (Horne and Doherty, 2003)) argued that adults not trained in moral reasoning could only be prevented from acting against their own interest by legal or regulatory restraint. We had already warned that 'high principles were not compatible with high bonuses'. Our concerns unfortunately proved prophetic in the present turmoil, about which we must now learn to think more clearly. We need to use Ethical Thinking and moral reasoning deliberately and explicitly.

As a creative thinker, you are unlikely to behave reasonably if you cannot reason, or if you do not value intellectual virtues, like the need to ask for and give good reasons to support a case for implementing your creative ideas.

If you would like your moral reasoning to be stronger, you could practise on more of the Thinking dilemmas and perplexing puzzles in sections 1.2 and 1.3. This will help you to realize what your personal values are, and which of them are more important to you than others. By repeatedly carrying out thought experiments that involve moral dilemmas, a ranking of your personal values will emerge. Particular rankings of personal values may then become your moral principles. You can use these moral principles to take ethical decisions quickly, before neurochemicals from the deeper parts of your brain bypass the frontal lobes of your cerebral cortex.

Ethical Thinking relies on the development of skills in verbal thinking, visual thinking, recollection and empathy. The sequence in which these can be deployed to help you decide what is right, is shown in Figure 2.5.

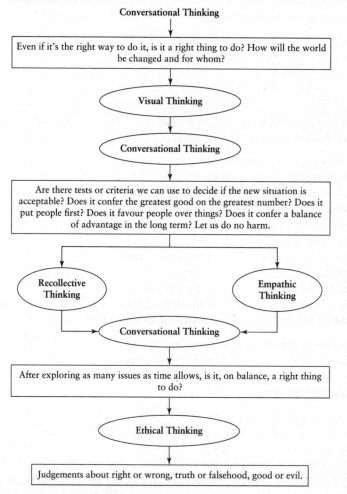

Conversational Thinking

Even if it's the right way to do it, is it a right thing to do? How will the world be changed and for whom?

Visual Thinking

Conversational Thinking

Are there tests or criteria we can use to decide if the new situation is acceptable? Does it confer the greatest good on the greatest number? Does it put people first? Does it favour people over things? Does it confer a balance of advantage in the long term? Let us do no harm.

Recollective Thinking

Empathic Thinking

Conversational Thinking

After exploring as many issues as time allows, is it, on balance, a right thing to do?

Ethical Thinking

Judgements about right or wrong, truth or falsehood, good or evil.

Figure 2.5 How to think ethically (*Train your Brain*, Wootten and Horne, 2010a)

CRAMPER'S CREATIVE CHECKLIST

C is for Combine	Try combining customers, units, purposes, appeals, products, features and offers.
R is for Rearrange	Try rearranging components, advertising messages, team membership, layouts, schedules.
A is for Adapt	Try adapting someone else's idea, experience, copy, success, product, sales promotion.
M is for Modify	Try maximizing/minimizing size, price, colour, taste, smell, frequency, strength, weight, value.
P is for Put	Try putting things to other use. What else could it be used for if it was cramped?
E is for Eliminate	Try eliminating weight, cost, distance, customers, middle people, prejudice, delays.
R is for Reverse	Try reversing polarity, image, opportunities, direction, inside out, upside down, roles.
S is for Substitute	Try substituting who else, what else, ingredients, materials, colours, power source, place.

(This is an amplified 'adapted' version of Osborn's idea (Osborn, 1953).)

CREATIVE GAMES TO PLAY

You were almost certainly highly creative and highly imaginative as a child. It is no coincidence then that as a child you almost certainly loved to play. Playing games – with yourself, with other adults and with children – is an excellent way to rediscover what you always were: a highly imaginative, creative human being. Try these three creative games: Challenging Chess, Hopeful Hexes and Tantalizing Tanagrams.

Creative game 1: Challenging Chess
This could include:

a High Speed Chess – you are allowed five seconds a move against an opponent or computer.

b Capitulation Chess – you must be the first to lose all your pieces (in this version the King can be taken). On your turn you must take an opponent's piece, if you can.

c Refusal Chess – as normal chess but each player has the right, once only every turn, to ask their opponent to take their move back and make a different move.

d Double Knights Chess – as normal chess, but each player has an extra knight up their sleeve which they can bring into play at any point in the game. After the knight has been introduced, the game continues as normal.

e Double Move Chess – normal rules except players take two moves on their turn. (Only one if you check with your first move – your opponent must then move out of check with the first of their two moves).

f Randomized Chess – normal rules apply except the starting positions on the back row are randomized (but identical for each player).

g Genius Chess – first turn one move each; second turn two moves each; third turn three moves each, etc. A player giving check forfeits the rest of their moves. The player in check must use the first of their moves to get out of check.

h Creative Chess – create your own version. Well, go on then …

Creative game 2: Hopeful hexes
Create one hex board (11 hexagons per side, the play area is diamond shaped). You can do it by ruling lines, or by photocopying and magnifying the diagram below.

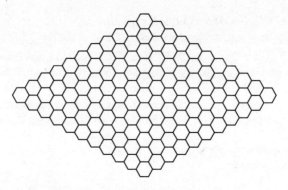

Two opposite sides of the board belong to white.

Two opposites sides of the board belong to black.

The four corners are each jointly owned.

You will also need a supply of pieces or markers in two different colours. Each player chooses a colour of markers and a pair of opposite sides.

Choose which player will go first. If you wish to be fair, flip a coin.

Take turns placing one piece on the board per move. Once a piece is played, it stays there for the rest of the game. Either player may play a piece in any hexagon that is not yet occupied.

Win by connecting a row of adjacent hexagons between your two opposite sides. Any continuous path will do, and the pieces need not have been placed in any order.

Creative game 3 –Tantalizing tanagrams
First create the seven Tanagram pieces. On a piece of card, e.g. an A4 pad:

1 Draw a large square.
2 Draw a diagonal.
3 Draw an equilateral triangle in one of the corners not dissected by the diagonal.
4 Draw in the other diagonal until it meets the base of the isosceles triangle (at 90°).
5 Construct a small square using as one side the line between the diagonal and the point of the intersection 'P' with the base of the isosceles triangle.
6 This will also generate another equilateral triangle.

7 On the opposite side of the line to the square you have just created, create a triangle and a parallelograms using one line.

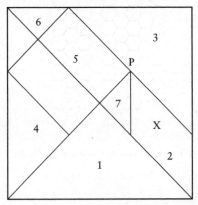

When you have done this, carefully cut out the seven shapes. Now you have the pieces, you can issue creative challenges to your opponent as to what to make. Most shapes can be made by using these Tantalizing Tanagrams.

2.2.3 Workout: Lateral Thinking

Brain scans show how your brain can go into predetermined (well myelinated) sequences of neuron firings. If you want to come up with something new and unique, it may be necessary to break your predetermined neuron firing sequences. That is the role of Lateral Thinking – to create random surprising neural escape paths in your brain. The importance of this is illustrated by the activity below:

Complete the following calculations
1+5 =
7−1 =
4+2 =
8−2 =
3+3 =
0+6 =
Now repeat out loud for 15 seconds the word 'six'.
Look at the panel below.
Name a vegetable
Now look at Answer to 'Name a vegetable' in Appendix 1.

LATERAL TRAINING WORKSHOP

LT1: What do the following animals have in common?

a Koala bear
b Prairie dog
c Guinea pig
d Silkworm
e Firefly

LT2: At 9 p.m. one night in August 2011, three men and two women entered a large casino in Las Vegas. They played together until 3 a.m. the next day. Nobody left and nobody joined them. By the time they left they each had more money than they came with. How might that be possible?

LT3: The vessel entered the sea although there was no water at the time. It completed its journey and the crew were home in time for Christmas. What was the name of the vessel? What was the name of the sea?

LT4: An Olympic athlete had always fancied throwing eggs or tomatoes at a particular male politician and one day he got his chance. The tomatoes struck a direct hit. The athlete was delighted at first, then appalled when the politician collapsed and was pronounced dead. Why did the politician die? (The politician was not allergic to tomatoes.)

LT5: Task 1: A, B and C are three islands. There is a woman on island A and a man on each of islands B and C. Each person has a plank that is not quite long enough to reach another island. How can they get together to give each other a hug?

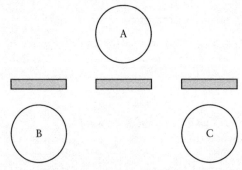

LT5: Task 2: There is one man and one woman on island A. They still have three planks. They wish to separate and take a break, each on a different island. How might they do that?

LT6: One large circle containing 11 crosses. Divide the circle using only four straight lines, making cords from circumference to circumference. In any space you enclose there must be one and only one cross.

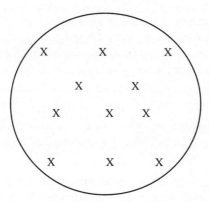

LT7: Use 16 matches to form five squares as shown below. Move two matches to make one square disappear – even though all the squares are still of the same size as before, and you have used all the matches to make the four squares.

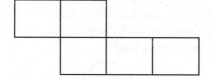

LT8: Using a cork (or coin) arrange for four matches to lie on a flat table, such that none of the heads of the matches touch the table, or another match, or the cork (or coin). The cork (or coin) must not touch the match heads or the table either.

LT9: An act of sacrilege?

A woman bought a square antique table very cheaply at an auction. When she got it home she realized why it was so cheap. A vase of flowers in the auction room had concealed a circular hole through the centre of the table. Perhaps it had been for a lamp or a parasol pole? Undeterred, she cut up the table and rejoined the top, and eliminated the hole, wasting none of the beautiful antique wood. It looked very good. Once she had covered it in thick dark antique wax, you would never have guessed it once had a big hole, nor what she had done. What had she done?

LT10: Prince Masoky was captured by Princess Sadie. She gagged and tortured him by saying, 'I will take off your gag so that you can make one last statement and one only. If your statement is true, I will burn you. If your statement is not true, I will feed you to my pet lions.' After a while the Prince confidently indicated that he was ready to utter his last statement. He is still alive today, so what did he say?

LT11: Draw the following diagram without taking your pen off the page or crossing any line, or retracing any part of your route.

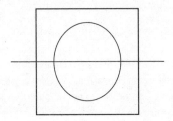

LT12: Rearrange the coins into six rows with four coins in each (=24!) without lifting any coin from the table.

LT13: What is the missing number?

1									
1	1								
2	1								
1	2	1	1						
1	1	1	2	2	1				
3	1	2	2	1	1				
1	3	1	1	2	2	2	1		
1	1	1	3	2	1	2	2	1	1
?	?	?	?	?	?				

Hint: Each row is a description of the rows above.

LT14: Draw this 100 kph speed limit sign without taking your pen off the paper.

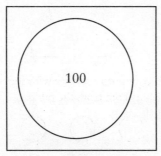

LT15: Tear a strip of paper (fold and press the fold to do so neatly) about 3 cm × 25 cm – from an A4 sheet, for example. Simultaneously draw lines down through the centre (roughly) of the both sides of the strip using only one pen or pencil.

LT16: Arrange five coins so that each coin touches every other coin, simultaneously.

LT17: Using digits 1, 2, 3, 4, 5, 6, 7, 8, 9, place them at the vertices and along the sides as shown so that the total on each side is 20.

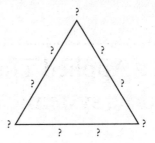

LT18: Take a teacup, some string and scissors. Tie the teacup to a door handle using the string. Cut the string in two places without letting the cup fall to the ground.

LT19: There are ten stools in a room. How can you rearrange them so that there are three on each side of the room?

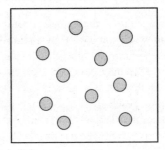

LT20: Put a cloth into a glass. Immerse the glass in a bowl of water. Make sure you keep the cloth dry.

LT21: Rearrange these 11 letters to form just one word.

W U T S R O O N J E D

If you got most of these puzzles correct your brain is already well prepared for Part 3, which is based on the development of creative high intelligence.

2.3

Advanced Applied Thinking: Metaphoric, systemic and strategic

In this section you will:
- *learn about metaphoric mapping*
- *find out about Systems Thinking.*
- *apply your thinking to real-life difficult decisions.*

Writing in the *Harvard Business Review*, Professor Ikyiyero Nonaka explains the way in which comparatively diminutive competitor Honda strategically outflanked the might of the Detroit-based automotive industry, and how Canon moved on from cameras to dominate the world market for office equipment, strategically outmanoeuvring the mighty Xerox Corporation. In each company, managers and market strategists had developed a figurative language that enabled them to think about complex concepts in a way that everyone in their organizations could understand. Nonaka's subsequent research found that similar high level thinking languages lay behind the strategic successes of other Asian companies like Matsushita, Sharp, NEX and Mazda.

Strategic Thinking involves turning information about the past into present knowledge on which changes in future action can profitably be based. But sometimes that knowledge is tacit, not explicit, vague not clear, voluminous and not precise. In such situations, successful companies may be at an advantage if they operate in countries where it comes naturally to think metaphorically, as well as scientifically. Even in the West, great scientific discoveries like the structure of benzene, or the genome, or the theory of relativity, owed as much to metaphor as they did to science or mathematics. By using a beer can as a metaphor for the aluminum drum in a photocopier, Hiroshi Tanaka at Canon was able to come up with a way of making a disposable copier drum.

2.3.1 Metaphoric mapping – Metaphoric Thinking

Sometimes Metaphoric Thinking, using analogies, not only inspires or sparks some new ideas, or inventions, it often suggests enduring principles that can be applied in a new situation. These principles can be represented as a model.

Using the idea of a biological system as a metaphor

Most problems do not exist in isolation and so most problems are best not solved in isolation. Individual issues need to be seen as part of a whole. In 1996, Aronson illustrated this by looking at the problem of an insect 'A' that was damaging crops. When insects are attacking a crop, the conventional response would be to spray the crop with a pesticide that has been designed to kill the insect 'A'. However, that can turn out not to solve the problem. What can happen is that the crop damage gets worse, because insect 'A' may be controlling the population of another insect 'B' by competing with it. When spraying depletes the population of insect 'A', the population of insect 'B' may rise dramatically. The total insect population may be greater than before and so will be the crop damage. Systems Thinking could have come up with better solutions – such as introducing another insect that would compete with insect 'A'. 'Normal' Thinking would not normally come up with the idea of introducing more insects as a way of solving the problem of insect damage. In 1994, Richmond expressed frustration that although Systems Thinking had obvious appeal to those faced with complex problems it was more written about than used. In fact, a great deal of excellent work had been done since the early 1980s by Peter Checkland (1981) and his co-workers to develop a methodology whereby Systems Thinking could be applied and practical experience obtained in its use. From 1995 to 1999, Horne and Doherty built on Checkland's work, developing a 'conversational approach' to using soft Systems Thinking in public service organizations (Horne and Doherty, 2003).

Many years of using this model has produced 'systems thinking' – a way of thinking metaphorically about the world as though it can be usefully viewed as a hierarchy of systems. Through repeated and successful application, systems thinking methodology has been developed. It has 15 systematic steps and you can follow these in order to think clearly and precisely about complex, complicated, turbulent situations, in which many of the variables are interconnected, and in which some are unknown or are the product of the interactions between other variables. You can learn to think clearly and precisely even when some information is murky or vague. You learn to be precisely vague.

2.3.2 Systems Thinking

The 15 'precise' steps, when you think systemically, are:

1 Assume that any problem or decision can usefully be considered to be situated in part of a system that is part of a wider system.

2 Try drawing a 'map', on one side of A4, which shows all the areas relevant to the decision. Create 'bubbles' by drawing a boundary around each of the areas on your map. Imagine that each area within a boundary can be thought of as a system. Insert arrows to show which systems interconnect and affect each other. Give each 'system' a name that contains an action word describing what the system does, or what its output is (for example, a 'knowing' system, a 'finding-out' system, a 'checking-the-cash' system).

3 Along the arrows, write a label for the output that is leaving each system. Each output will become the input to another system, or it will be an output into the system's environment. List the people who are affected by the outputs into the environment. These are your clients, customers, victims or stakeholders.

4 Inside your systems bubbles draw matchstick men and women to represent the key players – the key actors who play an essential part in getting done the work that you have described in the name you have given to the system. Key actors are often experienced or technically knowledgeable people. Find out who 'owns' the whole system, or particular parts of it. Draw them in with a big hat. Draw in the people who are responsible for checking whether what comes out of each system is what is meant to come out. You could draw a magnifying glass in their hands. Who sets the measures of performance (MOPs), and compares them, with what actually happens? Draw in a feedback loop to show how (if at all) this information is used to modify what happens.

5 By now your A4 sheet should be getting quite messy. If it is, re-draw your map to minimize the number of arrows that cross each other. This is a good opportunity to make your labels more succinct and to expand the size of the bubbles that represent the systems on which you have most information. Name your

owners, key actors and the key decision-makers. These will be the people who should be re-allocating resources in the light of the feedback they should be receiving. They are also people who apply constraints. For each system, find out what the resources are – financial, technological and material. Include as resources people with knowledge, experience and expertise. Sketch in little pictures to represent the resources.

6 For each system, consider the impact on it of things that are changing in its environment. Show each impact as an incoming dotted arrow and label the arrows. Consider changes in technology, economics, markets, politics, law, ethics and society (see *Strategic Thinking*, Horne and Wootten, 2010) for a full list of questions to ask).

7 Take your emerging map around with you and show it to people whose names appear on it. Ask them for comments and feedback. Encourage them to draw on your map. Ask them what would threaten the system's survival and what changes they would like to see and why?

8 Ask what information they need to receive, from whom, by when, in order to do their job. How frequently does it need to be updated and how accurately?

9 Ask each person who else you should talk to.

10 Then find a quiet spot. On a separate sheet, for each system, list the 'minimum activities' that someone will need to carry out if the system is to achieve its purpose – to live up to the name you have given it. By now each system's 'purpose' should be clearer. If a system's purpose is not clear enough, talk to the people whose names you have on your maps.

11 Take your list of 'minimum activities' for each system and talk to the people whose names appear on your map of the system. Ask, 'Is anyone doing this? If so, who?' Try to establish how well the activity is being carried out.

12 Retire to a quiet place with your list of 'minimum activities' and consider the ones that no one appears to be carrying out satisfactorily. For each activity that is not being carried out satisfactorily ask yourself, 'How important is this activity to the system?' If the activity is essential for the system's purpose, give it an 'A'. If it is inconsequential, give it a 'C'. Otherwise rate it 'B'. Next consider how easy it would be to rectify the deficiency.

If it would appear to be easy, give it an 'A'. If difficult, give it a 'C'. Otherwise give it a 'B'. Next consider the risks associated with intervening to try to rectify the deficiency. If there is a low chance of a small adverse consequence, give it an 'A'. If there is a big chance of a serious adverse consequence, give it a 'C'. Otherwise give it a 'B' for risk. If you need help with assessing the desirability, feasibility and risk of possible changes (see *Strategic Thinking*, Horne and Wootten, 2010).

13 Take the list of possible changes that you have now rated A, B, or C, for desirability, feasibility or risk, and ask the key actors or stakeholders whether or not they agree with your ratings. Get them to help you choose a triple 'A' change that would make a good starting point. Get their help with planning how to implement it.

14 Implement the selected triple 'A' change and collect reactions to the change from your emerging list of key stakeholders.

15 Revise your systems map in the light of any new information gained.

DESIGNING A NEW ORGANIZATION

If you need to design a new organization, the same Systems Thinking can be used. The main difference will be that when you come to compare your list of minimum activities with the existing situation, there won't be any existing situation. Start to create the new organization by introducing the triple 'A' rated activities first.

SUMMARY

▶ It is possible to use a pen and one sheet of A4 paper to think about turbulent situations.

▶ It is possible to think about complex situations in which almost everything will start to change almost as soon as you make even a small change in any part of it.

▶ It is possible to foresee the future consequences of decisions you make now or that you have made in the past.

▶ It is possible to decide what changes would improve the performance of an existing product, organization, team, group, society or social group.

The steps are represented diagrammatically in Figure 2.6:

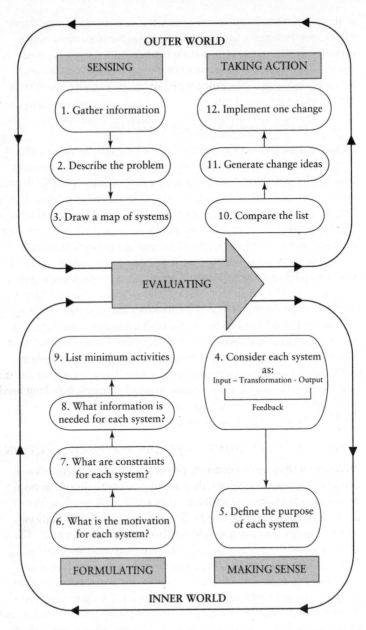

Figure 2.6 Systems Thinking

Systems Thinking is fundamentally different from traditional forms of analysis. Systems Thinking focuses on the whole situation, not on individual pieces of information relevant to the decision. The situation is described using a map of the interconnected systems. Systems Thinking is concerned with how change in any one system affects all the other systems.

METAPHORIC THINKING AND PRACTICE

Metaphors as a source of learning have a long history. Over time, they have been used by teachers to explain ideas that they thought would otherwise have been too abstract for their disciples (Williams, 1986). Metaphors help to make abstract ideas more concrete. Metaphors involve thinking about one thing in terms of another. Metaphors make it possible to think about things that we cannot see or touch. For example, you cannot see or touch 'cheering-up-ness' as a quality of a person. But you can talk about a friend as 'a ray of sunshine'. When you sing 'You are my sunshine, my only sunshine', you are conveying the idea that they have a quality like sunshine – that makes you 'happy when skies are grey'. Because you are using this idea metaphorically, you can find other possible meanings. Do we, for example, find them warm or warming? Do you like to know that they are always shining somewhere in the world? Metaphors help you to understand not only 'how' you feel, but 'why' you feel the way you do. However, ideas coming from Metaphoric Thinking need to be treated with caution. Their usefulness and relevance must be tested by Critical Thinking about their practicality.

METAPHORS AS AIDS TO MEMORY AND RECOLLECTION

Because metaphors can generate physical and visual images that have emotional associations, they are easy to recall. Information is more easily connected to images that are already familiar, like birds, animals or sports players (Buzan, 1993). This information can be filed into an existing schema (Gordon and Poze, 1980). The new information can be 'parked' – as in a 'Microsoft window' – while people relate to it, make connections with it, or explore its implications. Associated thought paths can be followed for as long as they seem profitable. Meanwhile we are not afraid of losing new information because it is 'parked' in the working space created by our metaphor. When a metaphor is memorable, the information, which we associated with it, will be easy to retrieve. Metaphors work like icons on a computer screen. By clicking on your metaphorical 'icon', you can recover not only the associated information and feelings, but also the starting points for all the mental pathways you have explored already. If a particular pathway turns into a 'dead end', you can easily retrace your steps and go back to your original metaphor and from there set off again to explore a new path.

USING METAPHORS TO INTEGRATE HIGHER ORDER APPLIED THINKING

The metaphor not only helps you to remember and recall things, it enables you to integrate higher order Applied Thinking skills, like critical, creative and reflective thinking. The metaphor creates links in the neural pathways that make it easier to 'see the big picture' and to retrieve the new ideas by following the links around your internal neural net. This is particularly useful to those of you, male or female, who have a typically male brain structure, in which different parts of your brain will be up to 30 per cent less well interconnected than in a typically female brain. Treffinger (1986) defined Creative Thinking as 'the making and expressing of meaningful connections', and Cornelius and Casler (1991) described imagination as 'forming mental images of what is not actually present and combining them with previously unrelated ideas'. This suggests that using metaphors will also help you to develop your creativity and imagination.

Transferable skills

Because Metaphoric Thinking involves finding important commonalties between situations that on the surface appear quite different, it enables you to practise 'transferring' knowledge and connections from one situation to another. In making the transfer, what is required is a 'mental leap', like a spark that 'jumps across a gap' (Holyoak and Thagard, 1995). Good metaphors 'spark off' good ideas that can leap across 'mental gaps' in your thinking. Koestler considered this sparking to be central to humour and Creative Thinking. The ability to link it appropriately to a new context is sometimes called transferable learning and is highly valued in turbulent situations that require you to adapt rapidly to new situations or to a new world order.

Mental 'maps'

For Buzan (1993), the metaphor of the 'map' has been central to his idea of how the mind works. His books on Recollective Thinking skills are organized around the metaphor of 'mapping'. Mental maps display the mental links between ideas, thereby helping you to make patterns and to organize knowledge. They help you to recollect and visualize. If shared with others, they can help you to think aloud in a thinking conversation or dialogue. According to Shore and Kanevsky (1993), using maps as metaphors enhances the webbing of concepts and promotes high level thinking.

Synectics

According to Perkins (1988), synectics is another subset of Metaphoric Thinking. In synectics, people are encouraged to use objects (for example, condiments or chairs) to represent what they think is happening, or might happen, in a situation about which they wish to think. As their ideas progress and develop, they are encouraged to change the arrangement and juxtaposition of the objects. Computers can be used to simulate the synectic processes. The computers create 'virtual objects' that can then be moved around on the screen. War gaming and scenario forecasting are examples. 'Helicopter Thinking' metaphors can be used to overview the situation, or the relative fruitfulness of different thinking strategies. This synergy between the use of objects and the use of metaphors can be reproduced without using physical objects. It is possible to use words to create mental images of objects and then manipulate these mental images, either in our heads or on paper (Cheng, 1993).

PUT ON YOUR THINKING CAP

A good example of Metaphoric Thinking is the way de Bono (2000) used six different coloured Thinking caps to unscramble the Thinking process. Using the 'Thinking caps' metaphor, you can use six different ways of thinking, separately and deliberately, one at a time. The essence of the different coloured 'Thinking caps' is:

▶ *White Cap Thinking* – pure white, virgin white, uncontaminated. Just give me the facts and crunch the numbers, logically and dispassionately.
▶ *Red Cap Thinking* – seeing red: emotions and feelings, hunch and intuition. Paying attention to emotions is important and legitimate.
▶ *Black Cap Thinking* – playing the devil's advocate, looking on the black side. It will never work. Wear your black executioner's hat and try to kill the idea. Black Hat Thinking gives you permission to forgo the benefits of positive thinking.
▶ *Yellow Cap Thinking* – yellow sunshine, brightness, optimism. Yellow submarine – 'our friends are all on board'. This thinking

is characteristic of those with a 'sunny' disposition and a propensity for constructive thinking.

▶ *Green Cap Thinking* – fertile green fields with green shoots springing from the seeds of ideas. This thinking symbolizes new growth and creativity.

▶ *Blue Cap Thinking* – blue eyes, cool, unflustered and controlling. This is thinking calmly about what kind of thinking is needed next.

If you think you need to improve your ability to think metaphorically – using analogies or models – try these activities:

▶ Write down the name of an animal that resembles an organization with which you are familiar. Write down, as quickly as possible, as many words as you can that describe the animal. Think about why you chose that animal. Now repeat the exercise, using an animal that you wish the organization was more like. Finally, think of five changes – three essential and two desirable – that you would like to see in the organization. Small practical changes often have the most immediate impact.

▶ Take a walk and collect objects that represent the way you think others perceive you. Try to work out why you chose the objects that you did.

▶ What colour do you think represents you? What colour would you prefer to be? Does this indicate directions for development?

▶ When explaining something, try to make comparisons with things like sports, DIY, hobbies, politics or child rearing. Remind people of metaphors you have used before. You can use clip-art, or a postcard to remind people of your metaphor.

▶ Try de Bono's metaphor of the Thinking cap. Start by putting on a white cap. This means that until a different coloured cap is chosen, you're trying to think only about what you factually know to be true first hand. Disregard hearsay or speculation. What do you know? Do not consider opinions or feelings, just facts and figures. Jot them down. They can be supplemented later. Try your red cap next. Get any strong feelings off your chest. Keep repeating how you feel until you get calmer. Label the feelings. Feelings are single words – not sentences or speeches. Now it's time to don your green cap. What opportunities are there? What is fascinating, intriguing, or curious? Is there a dilemma or a paradox? What genuine questions occur? What possibilities are there here for growth, exploitation or development? Create a 'green' ideas sheet next to your 'white' sheet. Now don your black cap. Listen carefully to all your fears about things that have gone wrong already and could yet go wrong again. Create a 'black' list and put it alongside the 'white' sheet and the 'green' sheet. Before you get overwhelmed and demotivated by the 'black' list, put on your yellow Thinking cap. What is the best thing that could happen? If you had three wishes about this situation, what would they be? If you had a magic wand what would you want to happen? What vision of the future would inspire you or excite you? Make a 'yellow' list before you put your black cap back on again. What's wrong with these ideals? What constraints are we overlooking? Green cap again – what opportunities might there be among these problems on the 'black' list? Where are the silver linings? Yellow cap again, what ideas still remain possible? What about a purple cap now? Purple is traditionally a religious colour – the cardinal's hat, or the robe of a Trappist monk. Whether or not we can make these green and yellow ideas work, are they 'in right ordering'. Are they moral, ethical or truly 'good'? Would we want to tell our children, or our grandparents, that we were doing things like this? Back to yellow – what could you support that seems a feasible improvement? What action is required? White cap on – let's write up the action plan. Who needs to do what by when, and how will we know when they've done it? This Metaphoric Thinking can be done alone or with a 'Thinking' Companion. Having a Thinking Companion allows you both to think aloud.

2.3.3 Strategic Thinking

This material on strategic Thinking and the following case study exercise are based on *Strategic Thinking* (Wootton and Horne, 2010c). *Strategic Thinking* takes you step-by-step through the questions to ask in order to formulate strategies and write clear and concise strategic plans. Based on three core actions – creating knowledge, innovating ideas and implementing change – strategic Thinking consists of hundreds of examples and advice on:

▶ How to gain a deeper understanding of your market.
▶ How to develop a strategic vision.
▶ How to think critically about proposals.

- How to survive and thrive in a recession.
- How to implement and manage strategic changes.

With a section covering key aspects of leadership and neuroscience, and prompt sheets, action plans and useful summaries, this is an all-in-one strategy manual for marketers, leaders, managers and business students.

Trust and truth – Is s(he) lying to you?
It is clear from brain scans that the brain of a liar has to work much harder in more areas than someone recovering memories of truth. Still, normally, you won't be able to tell. Under test conditions, most people spot only half of false statements made to them – barely better than random chance. You can improve on this by giving the busy brain of a liar even more to do. Their brain will often crack under the extra work load. Try any of the following:

- Ask the suspected liar to draw the events, places or items they have been describing.
- Ask for sustained eye-contact – this is hard work and liars look away more often than truth tellers.
- Ask them to retell their story from the end, backwards.
- Few people's brains can sustain this work rate and liars will start to think and talk very slowly, or just confess.

Case study: Marketing leadership and management action in turbulent times

This is a practical case study of the strategic action that you would need to take as a marketer or as a manager during turbulent times.

Introduction: Leadership and action in turbulent times

When faced with immediate or looming difficulties, many managers become paralysed by stress and anxiety, or depressed by head-in-the-sand fear and denial. They do not realize the effect this has on their brain chemistry. They deprive their organization of strategic Thinking at a time when the organization needs it most.

In tough times, lack of good strategic Thinking is often fatal – as it was for retailer Woolworths in the UK in 2008. In tough times, employees look to their managers for clear answers to the questions on their minds, and for clear directions in which to expend their efforts. During the Great Depression of the 1930s, Roosevelt warned managers about 'unreasoning fear … which paralyses the efforts needed to convert retreat into advance'. If you don't reason as a strategic thinker, your fears will remain 'unreasoning', and your organization will be unable to 'convert retreat into advance'. To be reassuring to shareholders, as well as employees, even as you spell out realistically the difficulties you have analysed, you must paint a positive picture of the future beyond the present crisis. You must paint very specific stepping stones and point out the pathways. This is because an important part of maintaining morale in difficult times is to communicate face to face. You will need to get out of your office and walk your patch. This will have the added benefit of enabling you to cross-check frontline intelligence to feed your strategic Thinking process. It will enable you to listen specifically to customers, partners, distributors and suppliers. An important response to difficult trading conditions, or a shortage of credit or cash, is to trim the operation. It is essential that decisions about which products to phase out, which customers to let go, and which research and development to suspend, are based on market-led strategies.

MANAGING TURBULENT TIMES – THE CASE STUDY QUESTIONS

Fill in your best responses to the 14 questions below. Then look ahead at 'Thinking aloud about strategy in turbulent times' and write any additional notes that you find useful.

....

Case Study Question 1
To whom will people in an organization look in turbulent times? Why is this? Why is it important that strategies are market led?

Case Study Question 2
Who is best placed to implement a survival strategy in turbulent times? Why?

Case Study Question 3
Who is best placed to try to forecast the future in turbulent times? Why?

....

Case Study Question 4
If chaos continues, what are some of the threatening possibilities ahead for the world's economies and markets? Who is best placed to see through the mist and why?

Case Study Question 5
What is going to be the most critical thing to keep your eye on in a crisis? Why?

Case Study Question 6
How can you raise cash in a crisis? Who should be in charge of managing the cash in the short term? Why?

Case Study Question 7
Thinking about your need to know – your need to create usable knowledge out of the inevitable confusion caused by turbulent times – where should you look for good intelligence? How should you set about gathering your intelligence?

Case Study Question 8
In turbulent times, what might you need to do about your suppliers and your supply lines? What information will you seek from your suppliers?

Case Study Question 9
In turbulent times, you may need to 'downsize in a downturn'. How will you decide who stays and who goes? What will be important about the way you take these decisions?

Case Study Question 10
What will you do about recruiting in a recession? Why?

Case Study Question 11
What about sales staff when times are tight? How will you think about what they have to say? Why?

Case Study Question 12
What about the training budget in tight times? What will you do about training? What methods will you favour? Think particularly about sales training – how might the focus on training for sales staff need to change? Why?

Case Study Question 13
What about product pricing in a pinch? Prices up or prices down? Why?

Case Study Question 14
What about research during a recession? What about development during a downturn? Will you increase or decrease your spending on research and development? Who should decide? Why?

Now turn to 'Thinking about strategy in turbulent times' and revisit your answers to each of the above questions then write in any additional notes you find useful. Finally, review all your answers and draft a crisis communiqué to employees in an organization in turbulent times.

THINKING ABOUT STRATEGY IN TURBULENT TIMES

Thinking about case study questions 1 and 2: Marketing and management in turbulent times
At times of organizational crisis, people look to their leaders and their managers for strategies that will enable them to survive and

thrive. These strategies must be market led. Market-led strategies must be informed by intelligence gathered from those who are closest to customers, clients, competitors and suppliers.

It is the marketing team that must specify what needs to be done; it is for executive managers to decide how best to do it. The marketing team must specify what to do because they are closest to what is changing in the world of customers, clients, competitors and suppliers. Executive managers must then decide when and with what resources the marketing strategy is best implemented. Executive managers have their hands on the operational levers, people, money and resources. When times are tight, the CEO must personally mind the money and personally manage the implementation of the market-led strategy. In turbulent times, market-led strategists must not fear what they see coming, for this will impair the quality of their strategic Thinking. Rather, they must see it coming before the competition does, and urge the CEO to move faster.

There are always opportunities in chaos. The trick is to spot which opportunities are in a strategic direction that will take advantage of what you think will happen after the crisis recedes. Luck favours the prepared mind and the best preparation in turbulent times is Strategic Thinking.

Thinking about case study question 3: Foretelling the future in uncertain times

No one can know the future, even in normal times. Because the work of marketers is always about the future, marketers are more used to having to guess. Because the focus of marketers is outward – on the outside changing world – the guesswork of marketers is likely to be better informed than the guesswork of managers whose focus is internal.

Thinking metaphorically, a marketer is like the cox in a rowing boat. The CEO is the leading oar. The leading oar knows the limitations of his or her crew, can set a sustainable pace and be seen to be leading by example. But the marketing cox is the only member of the crew who can see where the boat is heading, even though he or she must peer through the mist and the spray. Only the marketing cox can read the surface ripples and guess from the line of the riverbank what might lie around the bend. The marketing cox can position the boat so as to avoid obvious rocks and the worst of the white water. The marketing cox can make a quick detour to collect low-hanging fruit from the bushes on the riverbank, taking care not to get stranded on the mud by a rapidly turning tide.

Thinking about case study question 4: Competing in chaos
Life in a competitive market may well be 'what happens while you're making other plans' (John Lennon). But that is no reason why what you do in an organizational crisis should not be informed by what you think might happen tomorrow. As a marketer, you do not need to call the future perfectly. Even in calmer times you were never able to do that. You need to get more calls right than your competitors. In turbulent times, that is not as difficult as it sounds, because in turbulent times your competitors are likely to make mistakes. In Formula One, the main opportunities you get to overtake are when there is a crash or a sudden storm. Thinking by analogy, there will always be crashes – in credit, in economies, in times of war. In the shorter term, the US Dollar and the UK Pound will likely crash against the currencies of China, India and the Middle East, and maybe later against the currencies of Russia and Brazil. International money markets may become nervous about lending to Greece, Spain, Portugal, France, the UK and even the US. This will herald problems for the Euro, the Pound and the Dollar. Inflation may loom and recession will threaten to return. This will bring opportunities to export, but threats to supply. Commodity prices, energy prices and prices of metals will rise. Weather changes will cause shortages in sugar and rice. Industries allied to aid will prosper. Amid this encircling gloom, only the strategic light of a marketer can call the best way forward.

Thinking about case study questions 5 and 6: Minding the money
The most critical metric in business is cash.

Whether times are turbulent or not, you need technology that gives you your cash position in real time. Cash comes from reducing stocks and debtors and selling assets. In a credit crunch, all three should be monitored daily by the CEO. (The CEO needs to delegate Strategic Thinking to the marketing team while he or she manages the money.) Short-term cash needs to be prioritized over margins. Forecast your worst-case scenario. Strategic leaders should always be conservative when forecasting the cash flow. Marketers need to lower cash breakeven points by pruning sales growth in cash-hungry product lines or costly distribution channels. The quickest and most cash efficient way to prune cash-hungry products is by increasing their prices. Cash growth is more important than sales growth. Cash will enable you later to buy up the order books or brands of less cautious competitors. For the CEO, cutting back creates opportunities to de-layer administration and to produce leaner, flatter structures that move more people into direct face-to-face or voice-to-voice contact with customers. Many of your customers will prefer this to the screen-to-screen contact offered by your competitors. You will emerge stronger than your competitors. You will be more flexible and quicker to respond to the re-emerging needs and wants of the markets to which you have stayed close. You will be in a better position than your competitors. Not perfect, but better – and that is what counts.

Thinking about case study question 7: Creating knowledge in confusing times

This requires deep immersion in the broadest possible range of information that is relevant to your customers and relevant to the drivers of change in your customer's country and culture. The Applied Thinking Approach will turn this information into usable strategic knowledge, on which profitable action can be based today, and on which profitable change can be based tomorrow. It matters crucially that you use a wide variety of triangulated sources of information to feed your Strategic Thinking. Do not spend all day, every day, in your office. Be seen to be interested in everything that might affect your customers or your competitors. Listen to your sales staff. Discount their optimism (or their pessimism) and think what the things they say might mean. What might this information mean for the business today, and in the future?

Thinking about case study question 8: Watching the bottom line and the supply line

Strategic leaders need to think about the bottom line today. They need to do so in the light of the product line and the supply line of tomorrow. Listen to your suppliers – not only to secure good service levels for your customers, but to gain intelligence about cash, liquidity and competitive activity. Returning to our metaphor of boats in stormy waters, in order to make 'headway' against unfavourable 'head' winds, you may need to tack. (Tacking is what sailors do to still make progress when the prevailing wind is not in their favour.) You may need to ship oars, or tread water, while you lighten your load. Volatility may shorten the CEO's strategic focus, but marketers must not lose sight of which way is 'upstream'. Do not trust numbers alone – dig into them to discern their meaning. Use Verbal, Empathetic and Visual Thinking, besides

Numerical Thinking. Your constant enquiry, interest and questioning will convey to your people that urgency is required to 'head' off the crisis.

Developing vision
As a strategic leader – whether in the backseat or the driver's seat – it is of course your job to look ahead. But that is no reason to ignore what you can see in your wing mirrors or your rear-view mirror. Even in good times, the horizon is usually hazy and seeing beyond it is impossible. This is what makes radar and GPS invaluable! Pursuing our 'driving' metaphor, even when driving conditions are difficult, you should not abandon your forward focus. Your forward focus helps you to decide which way to swerve to avoid obstacles on the road ahead.

Thinking about case study question 9: Downsizing in a downturn
A strategic leader's view of the future must inform today's decisions about who stays and who goes. It is important to keep people who enjoy change. There may be more than you think. According to our research (Horne and Doherty, 2003) about one in four people enjoys change. It should be a marketers' view of the future, rather than the possibility of local grants, that should determine which factory or office the CEO decides to keep open and which to close or to mothball. Any possibility to sell factories or offices for cash must be considered, even if you are offered a price well below the figure in the balance sheet. No point in going bankrupt with a strong balance sheet. (In any case, you cannot borrow against even a strong balance sheet when no one is lending!)

Taking difficult decisions in difficult times
Taking decisions in difficult times helps to rally the morale of the people. Leave the decision as late as you reasonably can – then decide, don't dither. They will despair if you dither. Honesty, openness and transparency – sharing the thinking behind your decisions – will build your credibility and their confidence. That is why it is important to think strategically. You cannot be open and honest when answering questions to which you have not given prior thought. Time on the front line helps you to keep abreast of your people's concerns, and to anticipate the questions they are likely to ask. Answer as straightforwardly as you can – as clearly and concisely as you can. If you don't know the answer, say so immediately. Do not conceal impending storms for fear of spreading alarm. There are straws in every wind. Fears of the unknown meaning of straws in the wind will be much worse than their fears once they know the worst. In the meantime, news of what threatens will create much needed urgency to implement changes.

Thinking about case study question 10: Recruiting in a recession
When assessing your staff and top team, invest in the highest
quality marketing staff. It is the judgement of marketing staff that
must determine your market-led strategic direction. Advertise for
top marketing people, despite any trading difficulties. In times
of turbulence, all manner of unexpected talent will respond to
recruitment publicity. Such publicity will be good for internal morale
and for your industry standing. Some applicants will be all too ready
to give you information on competitive activity. You need the best
marketers because it is marketers who need to tell the managers what
to do and where to do it. The Strategic Thinking of marketers will be
customer-led and market-led, and that is what the organization needs
most, before its managers can quickly work out how and where to
implement the strategic changes required. In difficult times, marketers
need to determine implementation milestones that are close together,
and managers need to monitor progress against them every day.

Thinking about case study question 11: Selling when times are tight
Although we have said that sales people are vital sources of frontline
intelligence to feed into strategic Thinking, the significance of sales
intelligence must be assessed by the marketing team. This is in part
because sales people are frequently over-optimistic and sometimes
overly pessimistic, and in part because it is marketers who must take
the lead in explaining the strategic intent that needs to inform every
decision taken by managers.

Threats of economic downshift or business recession are particularly
disconcerting to sales people. Sales people are hunters who tend to
operate best in a world where targets (and rewards) always increase:
all the more reason in recessionary times for their sales intelligence
to be carefully assessed by their marketing colleagues. In the last ten
years, most sales people have managed to increase sales revenue (and
their own commissions) by skilful offers of volume discounts, and
by persuading customers to accept lower cost, imported substitutes.
In times of tighter credit, some high volumes of low-margin business
may need to be pruned as part of a strategic move to lower the
organization's cash breakeven point. Giving up customers and sales,
especially high-volume sales, does not come naturally to sales staff.
Besides providing strong strategic leadership to managers, senior
marketers will need to provide strong operational leadership to
the sales and marketing team. The number of sales staff may need

to be reduced and this will affect morale. Structures, staffing and key performance indicators will need to be realigned as part of the implementation of the strategic changes required by the market-led strategy.

Thinking about case study question 12: Training in tight times
Improved morale, sharper focus and increased performance should repay the cost of training. Avoid expensive conferences. Favour one-to-one coaching, mentoring and frequent review. During times of economic difficulty, your customers will also have problems. Retrain your people to listen to the customers' problems and to help find solutions to them, rather than dwelling on their own. Empathetic, reflective and creative Thinking and a good memory will be highly valued.

Train sales people and frontline staff to act as intelligence agents. They can be the human ears and eyes of the organization. In a credit crunch, train them to make hard-headed assessments of the survival prospects of their key accounts. Which will survive? Which will thrive? In which customers should your market-led strategy invest? Who will pay their bills? Who will pay them on time? If strategic divestment of some customers is required, do not leave them in the lurch. Work with them. Help them to re-source. A manager in a divested company may turn up later in one of your key accounts; it does not pay to make enemies. Train sales and support staff to be business consultants. Can they find ways to improve the prosperity of their customers? Improve the customers' business and share in their prosperity. Shift the focus away from helping to reduce your customers' costs through lower prices and higher discounts. Focus instead on increasing your customers' earnings.

Thinking about case study question 13: Product pricing in a pinch
In an economic downturn, raw material costs, commodity costs and even some energy costs may dip in the short term. Your customers may expect your prices to track any fall in your input costs. Beware. Volume decline may have left you with increased overhead costs per unit. You may also have a declining cash flow from which to meet your current liabilities and with which to service your pre-existing debt. You may actually need to increase prices. If you do, target first those areas of business that tie up most of your cash for longest. Marketers can contribute to lower cash breakeven points by cutting,

or deferring, spending on promotion. For example, they may contract out to agencies that are so desperate for work that cash-friendly deals can be done. Some savings can be reinvested in customers, products or markets that are likely to recover soonest.

Thinking about case study question 14: Researching in recession – developing in a downturn

Any decisions about the research and development (R&D) budget must be strategic and that strategy must be market led. Assign some of your most entrepreneurial marketers to leadership roles in the R&D department. As present crises become past problems, research and development may hold the key to reinventing the future. That is why R&D must be directed by strategic leaders. That is not to say that R&D expenditure should be immune from the rigours of cash management and liquidity control. On the contrary, in good times, R&D departments tend to spawn pet projects and cosy corners full of blue sky thinkers. In contracting economies, these cannot be afforded. Not all the savings should be returned to the treasury. Some should be used to hasten the development of those projects that are most likely to yield cash.

In tighter times, focus your R&D on making the same things simpler, smaller or cheaper. Consumers will be more interested in inexpensive functionality than in paying for product features that they rarely use or may not even understand. Put a high value on obtaining strategic intelligence about the R&D projects that your competitors are working on. Monitor their trade recruitment and target your own recruitment at their specialist staff. You will be surprised how much job applicants will tell you at a recruitment interview. Sometimes the expertise of just one R&D recruit can shorten your time-to-market by several years, thereby saving you cash and advancing your cash flow. Remember you don't need to be fast-to-market, just faster than the competition. In troubled times, your competitors may handicap their R&D teams by making arbitrary across-the-board cuts in research and 'risk' capital. If your competitors are handicapped, it should not be too difficult to overtake them.

Summary

In Part 1, you learned about the way your brain works when you are thinking well, and how you can increase the cognitive capacity of your brain and engender the chemical conditions in your brain that favour your brain's ability to think well. You learned about specific exercises you can do to enhance particular parts of your brain and the connections between them, and also about the role of Thought Experiments and real world Dilemma training. In Part 2, you have learned about the basic, higher order and advanced components of Applied Thinking. You have looked at the Applied Thinking skills that you can develop to exploit the increased cognitive capacities of your brain. You have examined some of the world's most advanced models of the way basic, higher order and advanced thinking skills can be combined to enhance Applied Thinking. You have looked in detail at development of Numeracy and Mathematical Thinking; Creativity and Creative Thinking and at advanced techniques such as Metaphoric and Systemic Thinking. Finally, you have applied your Applied Thinking skills to the real world problem of taking difficult decisions in difficult times.

Part 3 will look at how you can give a further boost to the performance of your brain using a ten-day programme and how you can use a four-step approach (4S©) to developing your Creative Intelligence.

Part 3

Developing creative high intelligence and Advanced Applied Thinking

3.1

The neuroscience: From genius to Advanced Applied Thinking

In this section you will:
- *learn about high IQ and the neuroscience of creative intelligence*
- *learn how to boost your brain*
- *match your mind against Mensa.*

3.1.1 High IQ and the neuroscience of creative intelligence

WHAT IS GENIUS?

It is common for discussions of genius to quickly cite the same examples: Goethe, Shakespeare, Einstein, Mozart, Donatello, Rodin, Beethoven, Michelangelo and Leonardo da Vinci. People with brains like these are not the focus of this book. Instead, in Part 2, we focused on things that you can do – steps you can take. For example, section 2.2 showed you the steps that you can take to improve your ability to think creatively. All Applied Thinking leads to actions – in this case creative actions, i.e. the kinds of actions which, seen by others, lead others to say 'You are creative'!

This observed 'creative intelligence' is the result of explicit Applied Thinking and it does not depend on your having a creative 'intuition' that relies on unconscious processes.

GENIUS AND INTUITION

It is easy to be seduced by intuitive common sense but plausibility does not always equal truth. When time pressure means you have to rely on intuition, common sense and street wisdom, remember that luck favours the prepared mind. Chabris (2011) suggests that you prepare your mind against six common-sense delusions:

WHAT IS HIGH INTELLIGENCE?

The term IQ is much abused. Originally devised more than 100 years ago by Alfred Binet, IQ is a quotient that is held to be a measure of relative intelligence, i.e. mental age ÷ chronological age. If your mental score is average for your chronological age, your IQ will be 100. The usefulness of IQ scores alone is contestable. Intelligence is much more than IQ. There are many different forms of intelligence (Gardner, 1999). Advanced Applied Thinking prioritises Creative Intelligence.

Long-term follow-up studies of several hundred children whose IQs were rated at genius level about 50 years ago have indicated that classic IQ measures of verbal, numerical and spatial intelligence and general knowledge (memory) have proved to be good indicators of performance in education. However, high IQ children have also turned out to be healthier and physically fitter. This complicates the correlations, because physical fitness is a known correlate to mental fitness (sections 1.2 and 1.3). Unfortunately, the high average performances of the high IQ children conceal some tragic examples of underperformance. One problem is that the IQ measures used did not include creative intelligence, which is now at a premium in job markets around the world. Scores obtained on traditional IQ tests alone should be viewed with some caution – restraint if they are very high, scepticism if they are very low. The tests and models used in this book are related to creative intelligence and are more closely allied to what you need at home, at work and at play. They relate to the thinking skills you need to live your life as well as the thinking skills you need to earn a living.

GENIUS AND PERSONALITY

This relationship has been explored by Josephine Fulton (2006) with the help of Robert Allen, former head of Mensa Psychometrics. Geniuses are obsessive. William James (1942–1910), a pioneering American psychologist and philosopher, described geniuses as often missing appointments, leaving letters unopened, or at least unanswered, and often neglectful of family and domestic duties. They are often in hock to their genius – quite unable to turn away from their current thoughts. They are often terrified that they may lose track of the way their thoughts are running. They know that ideas are fragile and that, if derailed, they may be lost for ever. There are no known 9 to 5 geniuses. Although some end up rich and famous, many more end their lives unknown, or in unhappy penury. Mozart, for example, was buried notorious, in a pauper's grave. Genius is not a cute career choice. Applied Thinking is a better lifestyle choice. Applied Thinking in action can seem like intuition or just a lucky guess. But, as we have learned in Part 2, you can make your own luck. Lucky intuition favours the knowledgeable prepared mind.

Geniuses have a capacity for delayed gratification and enough self-belief to know that a solution, an invention, or book, will emerge from their thinking. Genius is a variant of patience. It is more than mere flair. Geniuses are obsessed with endeavour for its own sake. They are constantly pushing boundaries. They are hard to live with. Even when Beethoven was going deaf, he wasn't deterred from writing music. Even though he could have retired to fame and to a good income, he sawed the legs off his piano so that he could use the floor as a sounding board. He was in it for the music, not the material gain. When geniuses focus intently on their subject, they can feel remote from the feelings and concerns of normal people – like paying bills, or opening brown envelopes, or doing housework. The head of a genius is often full of obsessive, sometimes dangerous thoughts. A genius quite often thinks the unthinkable.

GENIUS AND THE UNTHINKABLE

Thought experiment
What is your most recent dangerous thought?

What do you believe, even if you don't know how to prove you are right?

If you need inspiration, here are some examples.

> *Thinking the unthinkable: examples of dangerous thoughts*
> **Are you outraged that, having no proof, it is possible to think:**
>
> ▶ that men and women are basically the same
> ▶ that events in the Bible are fictitious
> ▶ that the environment got better during the last century
> ▶ that our planet's climate is not changing
> ▶ that victims of rape or sexual abuse do not suffer lifelong damage
> ▶ that native Americans despoiled their country
> ▶ that the tendency of soldiers to rape is innate
> ▶ that terrorists are generally educated, mentally healthy and morally driven
> ▶ that Jews on average are more intelligent than Gentiles
> ▶ that the incidence of rape would decrease if prostitution was legalized
> ▶ that heroin and cocaine should be legalized
> ▶ that homosexuality is a mental illness
> ▶ that parents should be able to kill their defective children
> ▶ that religions have been responsible for more deaths than Nazism
> ▶ that the torturing of suspects is right under the right circumstances
> ▶ that unwanted babies should be auctioned to the highest bidder
> ▶ that there should be a legal trade in transplantable organs
> ▶ that average intelligence in western countries is falling because we allow dull people to breed more children than smart people.
>
> *What dangerous thoughts have you had recently?*

GENIUS AND VISION

Another attribute of genius is vision – the capacity to see things not apparent to others. But just seeing things can drive you mad. Applied Thinkers look proactively, and are good at seeing what they seek. Applied Thinkers explicitly seek out things that will give them a novel solution, a distinctive decision, an innovatory plan. Applied Thinkers deliberately seek comparative advantage.

While a genius may be content to have an entirely new idea, Applied Thinkers are much more demanding. Applied Thinkers will want to ask 'Useful to whom?' and 'By what criteria?'. Visionary ideas are relatively cheap. Many people were relatively quick to see the leaps from propellers to jet engines to space travel. Science fiction, for example, is commonly ahead of science fact. It took Applied Thinking to work out how to get a man on the moon.

Leonardo da Vinci was a genius. He sketched an aeroplane and a submarine at a time when nearly no one could have seen or imagined such a thing. Yet Leonardo's sketches remained just that – sketches. Donatello, on the other hand, was a visionary genius and an Applied Thinker. Donatello looked at a huge block of stone and 'saw' inside it a beautiful David. Donatello needed a lot of patience, and a lot of skill, borne of a lot of practice, to produce his David masterpiece. Working with a chisel and a hammer is hard work – Applied Thinking and Creative Intelligence owe as much to perspiration as inspiration.

GENIUS AND INSPIRATION

To inspire is to breathe in. There is some evidence that how you breathe in and out affects the EEG trace of your brain (EEG traces show how the electrical activity in your brain rises and falls over time). Typically an EEG trace would show a wave-like pattern. Changing your breathing can increase the length of these waves – increasing the chance that you will have a big brainwave! As we saw in section 2.3, even if you are not a born genius, as an Applied Thinker you can learn to think creatively. Applied Thinkers learn to immerse themselves in information in order to incubate ideas and inspiration.

GENIUS AND GENDER – COULD A WOMAN EVER BE A GENIUS?

Thought experiment

First: Imagine that you have asked a large enough sample of randomly selected representatives of as wide a variety of professional backgrounds as you can, to name up to ten geniuses.

Second: Look to see how many women are on their lists.

Third: You will probably find there aren't any – so why do you think that is so?

According to Josephine Fulton, even though educated politically correct female respondents sometimes mention Marie Curie, even the most embarrassed women struggle after that. Why is this? The areas where genius has traditionally been found include philosophy, science, literature, art and music. Until relatively recently, it could be argued that women have been actively discouraged from working in many of these areas. This argument seems insufficient to account for the dearth of female genius. Maria Callas (opera) and Margot Fonteyn (ballet) are undoubtedly top talent, but not ranked as genius. Unless the public believe you are a genius, you aren't a recognized genius. The public (of whom 50 per cent are women) seem to prefer males for their attributed title 'genius'. A genius will often play with ideas for their own sake. A genius will often appear to be talking about ideas for the sake of talking. Many women cannot understand this. Many women do not wish to join in at a purely theoretical or hypothetical level. Women are generally more practical. Such women could make better Applied Thinkers than these apparently narcissistic, largely male obsessives. Men have more idle time for idle thoughts, and idle thoughts, like idle fingers, make more mischief.

GENIUS AND EVIL

In your thought experiment on thinking the unthinkable you explored the idea that thoughts can be dangerous. Can genius be evil? Was Hitler an evil genius? Certainly he was obsessed. Certainly he had a vision – he set it out in detail in a book called *Mein Kampf*. Hitler has many characteristics of a genius – obsessive and persistent – perspiration as well as inspiration. He survived ridicule and imprisonment for his ideas. His path to power was long and hard, demanding great fortitude. The characteristics of both evil and genius are there. If there is such a thing as an evil genius, then Adolf Hitler was one and Joseph Stalin was another. Applied Thinkers thus need to build in checks.

▶ 'Is the proposed change a change for the better?'
▶ 'Better for whom?'
▶ 'How is to be judged?'

While geniuses are driven to do what they must, Applied Thinkers do what they can. But Applied Thinkers only do what they can when they think it is right to do so.

GENIUS AND CREATIVE HIGH INTELLIGENCE

The role of thinking skills

When you use the thinking skills set out in sections 2.1, 2.2 and 2.3, in the particular combinations and sequences illustrated in Figure 2.1, this produces Advanced Applied Thinking. This will enable you to solve problems, take decisions and make plans when others cannot. When you favour the use of thinking skills that combine to produce creative thinking (Figure 1.9), the solutions you produce are more likely to be original, the decisions you take are less likely to be predictable, and the plans you make are more likely to be innovative. Others are now more likely to say that you are not only intelligent, but creative as well. If, in addition, you use physical and mental exercises similar to those in this book and if you make some of the lifestyle choices advised in *Train Your Brain* (Wootton and Horne, 2010a) and *Keep Your Brain Sharp* (Wootton and Horne, 2010b), your intelligence will be increased, thus bringing into view the possibility of developing creative high intelligence. You will use Critical Thinking (Figure 2.1) to evaluate your creative options. You will use a number of criteria, including:

▶ How original, novel or distinctive are these ideas compared to those of other people? Do they confer any comparative advantage and to whom?
▶ How useful is this outcome? To whom is it useful and how is useful to be judged?
▶ What are the risks of adverse unintended consequences – how serious are these and how probable?

WHAT IS THE NEURAL BASIS OF CREATIVITY?

To comprehend the limitlessness of the number of creative connections that the brain can make and myelinate, it is necessary to take a close look at the neurons described in section 1.1. You saw there that conscious thinking in the cerebral cortex is supported by between 22 and 100 billion neurons, each with an axon, each having dendrites that wave across synaptic gaps at the dendrites of neighbouring neurons.

Creative thinking involves sub-cortical areas of the brain that have even more neurons than the cerebral cortex, e.g. a further trillion in the tiny cerebellum alone. This brings the total number of neurons that can creatively connect to each other to around a trillion.

A closer look at the dendrites on each neuron reveals that they each have between 1000 and 10,000 spines, each of which can create synaptic connections with between 1000 and 10,000 spines on the dendrite of a neighbouring neuron. The number of possible permutations of creative connections is now around a quadrillion. Important for creative thinkers is the discovery that these connections are active, 24/7, even when you are asleep. Fuelling this constant flux of connectivity consumes about 25 per cent of your food even on tick-over. Raising the rate of your mental work lowers your weight! The possibility of creating a change in your mind is always with you, even in your sleep. How many times have you changed your mind about something, having decided that you will 'sleep on it'?

CRADLING CREATIVITY

Creative people often come from unpropitious homes. So what can nurture their talent? Nancy Andreasen (2006) discovered that 'having intellectual freedoms, novel experiences and a sense of being different' were all helpful. Also helpful, she found, was contact with a critical mass of other open-minded people, and a feeling that any competition for attention, recognition or reward is fair. Patronage and general economic prosperity also help. Specific advice on how to nurture your own creativity can be found in section 3.2 and in *Train Your Brain* (Wootton and Horne, 2010a) Chapter 9.

ON BEING CREATIVE

Astronomer Carl Sagan was very sombre about the prospects for a society that would be dependent on science and technology, but in which few had any understanding of science and technology. Neuroscience and scanning technology have shown you how malleable and vulnerable your brain can be. You need to use that knowledge to protect your brain, and your individuality, from the further harmful effects that science and technology can have. Your best hope lies in developing creative intelligence. As a minimum, developing your Creative Intelligence will optimize your economic prospects, because your Creative Thinking and creative intelligence can confer competitive advantage on your employer. This will enhance your prospects of employment. But it will do much more than that. Nothing will increase your self-starting energy, your self-esteem and your sense of individuality more than producing creative ideas that are uniquely yours.

BOOSTING YOUR CREATIVE INTELLIGENCE

Do not confuse or conflate prodigious born talent with Creative Thinking. You cannot choose to be born with prodigious talent but you can choose to develop your Creative Thinking by working on the components of Creative Thinking modelled for you in Figure 2.4 in section 2.2 and by following the 10-day plan set out here.

3.1.2 Boosting your brain: a 10-day plan

Your preparative shopping:

▶ Protein: eggs, tofu, low-fat pouring yogurt, varied beans, nuts, seeds.
▶ Multi-vitamin and mineral supplements.
▶ Carbohydrates: berries, plums, apples, pears, tomatoes, beetroot, porridge oats, bran, wholemeal pasta, sweet potatoes, oat cakes.
▶ Fats: avocado, olive oil, olives, nuts, hemp oil.
▶ Drinks: coffee (not instant), teas: green, ginseng, ginkgo biloba, redbush.
▶ Spices and herbs: ginger, turmeric, fennel, chilli, garlic, sage, rosemary, basil, mint and coriander (the herbs, where possible, should be fresh and growing in indoor pots).
▶ A new on-offer classical CD.
▶ A meditation or relaxation CD.
▶ A prospectus from your local sports/leisure centre.
▶ Details of days when local markets have fresh, not farmed, fish.
▶ A local community theatre programme.
▶ A hard backed A4 book or page-a-day diary, suitable for use as a journal.

PLANNING YOUR 10-DAY BRAIN BOOST

Design a 10-point daily checklist to keep in your journal:

1 Did I do 30 minutes of exercise that raised my heart rate?
2 Did I take my vitamin and mineral supplements?
3 How many times today did I do ten minutes of meditation/relaxation to my CD?
4 What did I learn, that was surprising to me, today?
5 Did I eat breakfast, e.g. fruit, yoghurt, just one coffee?
6 Did I eat lunch, e.g. protein, salad, vegetables, with green tea/water?
7 Did I snack to avoid hunger, e.g. nuts, fruit, water?
8 Did I drink two litres of water?
9 Did I chat to a friend or neighbour or random person/expert?
10 Did I commit one random act of selfless, unsolicited, gratuitous kindness?

Follow the 10-day brain boost plan

The 10-day brain boost plan (Horne & Wootton, 2011)

Day 1   Decide what you are going to learn this week and make the arrangements (book, course, search).
Complete your checklist and think about what sport you will do on day 4.

Day 2   Cook or prepare all your own food today using the shopping. Ask around if you need a recipe.
Complete your checklist.

Day 3   Make today a music day.
Listen to your new classical CD and an old favourite.
Complete your checklist.

Day 4   Do your sport today (play or learn).
Complete your checklist.

Day 5   Write out a list of ten things you are grateful for today.
Keep referring to the list during the day.
Complete your checklist.

Day 6   This is a sleep day.
Go to bed one hour earlier (no TV or screen in the bedroom).
Complete your checklist.

Day 7 A screen-free day today.
No TV, computer, or mobile phone for 24 hours.
Complete your checklist.

Day 8 A double couple day.
If you are in a committed relationship, think about
how you could make love twice today. (Even if you do
not manage to, thinking about it all day will produce a
helpful regime change (chemical).)
Complete your checklist.

Day 9 Go to the fish market and buy fresh (not farmed) fish to
grill or bake. (Wild salmon has desirably high levels of
omega 3.)
Complete your checklist.

Day 10 Today is laughter day.
Seek out someone with the same sense of humour as you.
Or buy a funny book.
Or watch a funny DVD.
Or go to a community comedy club.
Complete your checklist.

Day 11 Start your next 10-day brain boost plan at Day 1.

Either before or after your brain boost, you might want to measure
your mind against members of Mensa. Here are some problems that
even many Mensa members could not solve.

3.1.3 Match your mind against Mensa

WHAT IS MENSA?

Mensa is an international social club whose members aim to meet at
least monthly for social contact, brain research and the fostering of
human intelligence. Mensa is also a Latin word for 'table' or 'month'
or 'mind'. The only qualification for membership is a high IQ.
Most puzzles you see in newspapers could easily be solved by most
members of Mensa. For Advanced Applied Thinkers, only puzzles
that could not easily be done by all Mensa members have been
included in this 'Match your Mind' challenge.

In Part 2 you read how you can raise your thinking skills to advanced
levels by combining basic and higher order thinking skills as shown

in the Advanced Applied Thinking Model, Figure 1.1, Section 1.1.1. In section 2.2 you also saw how you can make solutions, decisions and plans more creative. Here in Part 3, you are looking at how to make your solutions, decisions and plans not only more creative, but more intelligent. You are learning how you can develop creative intelligence. To assess how creatively intelligent you are already, try your hand (or better, your head!), at the following problems, posers and puzzles.

Problems, Posers, Puzzles
What constitutes a Problem, Poser or Puzzle? Typically, two things:

1   The information is not all relevant, not all accurate, not all complete, not all reliable and often not all there. (Mensa members are expected to have remembered information about the world and to bring it to 'the table'.)
2   There is more than one option and there is some uncertainty, or lack of clarity, about those options.

The problem usually includes the need not only to generate more options, but then to reduce the number of options by developing some criteria for selection, and then selecting the best option.

In this process there is a lot of scope for judgement and for the balancing of probabilities. (If the 'problem' is simply a chain of decisions, where there is only one logical choice at each decision point, you may as well give it to a computer.) Mensa minds are only needed when there are options at each stage and a balanced creative choice is called for. Do not be surprised, therefore, if you come up with a solution not found by past Mensa members.

After Victor Serebriakoff, former Chairman of Mensa.

THE 'MATCH YOUR MIND' AGAINST MENSA CHALLENGE

The percentage of Mensa members who could *not* solve each problem is shown, in brackets. Answers are in Appendix 1 at the back of the book.

Ten mental matches
Mental match 1: (75%)

At rush hour, my surname is seen by thousands who say I'm to blame. Who am I?

Mental match 2: (75%)

If to be full of care is to be careful, what word, containing the same letter three times consecutively can sometimes describe a dryer?

Mental match 3: (75%)

What does column A have, that column B does not?

A	B
Soccer	Tennis
Hockey	Baseball
Lacrosse	Golf

Mental match 4: (90%)

What is the difference between the words in column A and column B?

A	B
More	Pledge
Mail	Party
Pairs	Plan
Louse	Exit

Mental match 5: (80%)

What is different about the words in column A compared to column B?

A	B
Grove	North
Date	Pile
Age	Dairy
Or	Item

Mental match 6: (90%)

What is different about the words in column A compared to column B?

A	B
Page	Fang
Graft	Brought
Zing	Bag
Grouch	Gift
Gone	Gnome

Mental match 7: (95%)

What is the next letter?

P N B R ?

Mental match 8: (75%)

You may add any two letters to the following to make a word

A A C C U

Mental match 9: (90%)

It's a burning issue when boxers turn and sound like part of the job.

Mental match 10: (90%)

Which chemicals compounds contain Se, Mo, Fl and H?

If you got even two of these correct, your intelligence is likely to be in the top 2 per cent of the population, and you might want to consider joining MENSA! (www.mensa.org)

Ten cunning conundrums
The percentage of Mensa Members likely to get the answer wrong is shown in brackets. Answers are given in Appendix 1 at the back of the book.

Cunning conundrum 1: (15%)

A GM modified leylandii tree was found to double its height every 24 hours. You measured its height on a Tuesday. It was 20 metres high. On what day would it have been 2.5 metres high?

Cunning conundrum 2: (45%)

A slug is climbing out of a 20-metre wet sided well. During the night it climbs upward 3 metres. During the day, the slug sleeps and slithers 2 metres down again. How many days will it take the slug to get out?

Cunning conundrum 3: (16%)

O T T F F S S E N ?

Cunning conundrum 4: (15%)

You have two items – an expensive one and a cheap one. The expensive one cost you £100 more than the cheap one. Together they cost you £110. How much did the cheap one cost?

Cunning conundrum 5: (30%)

Two trains are travelling towards each other at 100 mph on separate tracks and a fly is flying back and forth between them at 60 mph. How far will the fly have flown at the time the fronts of the trains pass each other in 45 minutes' time?

Cunning conundrum 6: (50%)

You are driving alone on a dark night. You are driving to Arnside. You pass a sign that reads, 'Welcome to Lancaster' and shortly afterwards a sign, 'Thank you for driving carefully through Lancaster'. You come to a five-way crossroad to find that the signpost has been blown over. One of the signs says 'Arnside'. How do you alone find out which road to take?

Cunning conundrum 7: (5%)

A new Virgin pendolino train travels from Lancaster to Manchester in an hour and a quarter, yet can only manage the return journey in 75 minutes. What might account for the difference? What explanations could you brainstorm?

Cunning conundrum 8: (15%)

What word becomes smaller by adding additional letters?

Cunning conundrum 9: (30%)

Under international aviation law, if a plane were to go down exactly in the middle of the Pacific Ocean, where must the survivors have to be buried?

Cunning conundrum 10: (30%)

A BMW M5 is approaching the Mont Blanc Tunnel. It is running on its reserve diesel fuel tank. It is travelling at 100 mph. There is a lower speed limit in the tunnel of 30 mph and an upper limit of 70 mph. How far into the tunnel does the M5 manage to go?

If you worked out more than four of these classic conundrums, you should think about joining MENSA (www.Mensa.org).

Mensa members' top 10 tips for increasing your IQ

Drawing on their personal experience of increasing their own IQ, 327 MENSA members advise:

1 Read, on as wide a range of new topics as possible. Read to children. Join a book club.
2 Stay in touch with news and current affairs – newspapers and magazines are better than a searchable internet source, because you are more likely to read something unfamiliar. Discuss events with friends.
3 Learn a major new thing every year. Enrol in a new weekly class every year, especially classes involving your hands or music.

4 Play word games and do brain training puzzles with other people.
5 Exercise with others and eat healthy food together: avoid alcohol, caffeine, nicotine and unsaturated fats.
6 Play strategy games like Chess, Go, Hex and Diplomacy.
7 Limit your own TV viewing. No TV for kids. No screens in bedrooms.
8 Go to cultural activities (dance, music, opera, theatre, galleries).
9 Travel with others to as many different places as possible. Learn the new language before you go.
10 Share physical outdoor all-weather activities like walking, climbing, sailing, martial arts.

....

20 analytic analogies

Like doing conundrums, analysing analogies is a way to practise components of metaphorical thinking. Section 2.3 demonstrated that metaphoric thinking is one of the most advanced thinking skills and one with a high success rate in making creative advances in scientific theory and technological innovation, often conferring great value in twenty-first-century economies.

The percentage of Mensa members likely to give up or get it wrong is shown in brackets.

Analytic analogy 1: (70%) Potatoes are to peanuts as apples are to …?

Analytic analogy 2: (15%) Spain is to Argentina as Portugal is to …?

Analytic analogy 3: (15%) Celsius is to 0° as Fahrenheit is to …?

Analytic analogy 4: (33%) Loops is to spool as straw is to …?

Analytic analogy 5: (20%) 2 is to 8 as 5 is to …?

Analytic analogy 6: (20%) A is to E as B is to …?

Analytic analogy 7: (20%) Black Beauty is to horse as Lassie is to …?

Analytic analogy 8: (5%) Palette is to artist, as kiln is to …?

Analytic analogy 9: (20%) Ceylon is to Sri Lanka, as Constantinople is to …?

Analytic analogy 10: (10%) Star is to constellation as constellations is to …?

Analytic analogy 11: (86%) Onions are to leeks as crocuses are to …?

Analytic analogy 12: (30%) Reagan is to Carter as Truman is to …?

Analytic analogy 13: (33%) Tail is to comet as Broca is to …?

Analytic analogy 14: (96%) Roquefort is to France as Liederkranz is to …?

Analytic analogy 15: (12%) Drawer is to reward as Anna is to …?

Analytic analogy 16: (36%) Florentine is to spinach as Parmentier is to …?

Analytic analogy 17: (60%) Wolves are to pack as whales are to …?

Analytic analogy 18: (8%) Horn is to South America as Good Hope is to …?

Analytic analogy 19: (32%) Conforming is to orthodox as non-conforming is to …?

Analytic analogy 20: (8%) Profitable is to remunerative as fallacious is to …?

If you analysed nine or more of the analogies correctly, you might want to consider joining Mensa (www.Mensa.org).

You have attempted examples of some of the world's hardest tests of the components of creative intelligence, matching your wits against members of Mensa, whose IQ has to be at least in the top 2 per cent in the world, just to get in. If you enjoy these and would like more practice, refer to the recommended reading in Appendix 3, or do the puzzles in the Mensa club magazine. Better still, since the 'game' might be your best coach, involve yourself in paid or voluntary work that requires you to solve problems creatively.

3.2

....

Developing creative intelligence: The 4S© Way

In this section you will:
- *do some Thought Experiments involving AAT*
- *find out what steps to take to get things done*
- *learn how to boost your Creative Intelligence the 4S© way.*

3.2.1 Applied Thinking

'Applied Thinking not only helps you to see through things, it also helps you see things through.'

Terry Horne 1997

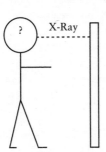 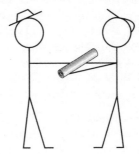

Figure 3.1

Thought experiment 1
Imagine an ice cube tray in which each frozen ice cube is a separate department at work, or a separate person to whom you needed to relate (at work, in your family or in a team).

If you can get the ice cubes out and into a glass, you could develop some inter-personal or inter-disciplinary thinking. As you put more energy or warmth or work into mixing the cubes in the glass, they will slowly melt. What you might get is collective group intelligence and some very Advanced Applied Thinking (Figure 3.2).

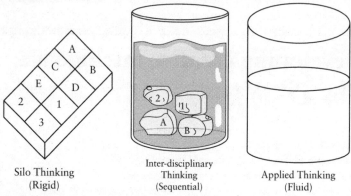

| Silo Thinking (Rigid) | Inter-disciplinary Thinking (Sequential) | Applied Thinking (Fluid) |

Figure 3.2

Thought experiment 2
Imagine your department, or your discipline, or your partner, or your child, as a biological cell:

▶ Think about the boundaries – rigid, fluid, or atrophied?
▶ Think about nutrients and resources.
▶ Think about inputs and demands and influences.
▶ Think about outputs and waste disposal.
▶ Think about the feedback and control mechanisms.
▶ Think about environments – favourable and fatal.
▶ Think about the wider systems to which your cell belongs.
▶ Think about processes your cell uses to transform inputs to outputs.

Thought experiment 3
Think about yourself as a Russian Doll (Figure 3.3). What different contexts do you inhabit? In what order are they nested?

Figure 3.3

Thought experiment 4

Imagine the components of Applied Thinking as different colours of light flowing into a prism and combining into a bright white light that you can shine to help to illuminate problems. Notice how different people and different problems, in different contexts, absorb different components of your thinking spectrum. This leaves them looking a different colour to you, and you looking a different colour to them.

Professor Edward de Bono made use of the colour metaphor with his thinking hats (section 2.3).

3.2.2 Applied Thinking: The steps to take to get things done

One of Professor Edward de Bono's great contributions to life was to get people interested in thinking as something they could do consciously and deliberately and with some hope of improving the way they did it. He has become rightly famous for his work on helping people to think 'laterally'. De Bono made his ideas more accessible when he wrote 'Thinking Hats' – a practical metaphor that can help you to remember what to do, particularly when trying to produce or write a plan. Applied Thinkers add concern about the steps that you need to take to implement the plans you thought to make. Steps need feet and feet need shoes, hence the metaphor – the different shoes that you might need to wear, in order to take the steps you might need to take, in order to implement the plans you have thought to make. Applied Thinkers can make use of de Bono's 'six different shoes for six different steps' metaphor.

> *Taking steps to get things done*
> **1 Grey slip-on shoes**
> Grey is for murky, misty, unclear. Your slip-on shoes need to be quiet and unobtrusive, as you check out the situation. Try to be as neutral and open-minded as possible.
>
> **2 Yellow wellington boots**
> It has become clear that you have an unstable, unpredictable, dangerous or emergency situation on your hands. There is risk of loss and risk of panic. Put on your yellow wellies – yellow is a common colour for emergency services. Act first to reduce danger and to get your people out of the firing line. Put someone, if not yourself, clearly

in charge of co-ordinating a rescue mission. Make sure everyone knows who this person is and how to communicate with each other. Check everyone knows what they are doing and enough about what everybody else is doing. Get someone looking for expert advice as your emergency will more often than not have happened to someone else before. Second-hand experience can be beneficial.

3 Red soft slippers

Always have some soft slippers handy. Red is for emotion. Always be prepared to slip on your slippers and listen with sympathy and compassion. Think empathically. Offer practical help, care about all people. There is no hierarchy among the distressed. Aim first for understanding, then for action.

4 Blue riding boots

Assume command. Riding on horseback signifies your greater ability to see and be seen as in control, and taking charge. Maybe you are just doing what you're paid to do – taking responsibility for decision making, with some exposure and some risk. In blue riding boots, you are in role – discharge it fully but within its constraints. In no role can anyone make you do what you believe to be wrong, illegal or immoral. Blue is for cool dispassion and keeping a cool head, when all around you may be losing theirs. But you are not to be hard hearted – you have your soft slippers in your saddle bag!

5 Black formal shoes

Things are calm enough to hand back to formal systems and procedures – the administration, the bureaucracy. Black is for putting it down in black and white. Write things down so that the system can continue to take decisions in your absence.

6 Brown brogue shoes

Feet on the ground, walking the job, working out who needs to do what, when and where, and how you will know it's been done? Brogues are sensible, down to earth all-purpose shoes, for walking or talking. Brown is for soil. You are grounded in the work of your people, your customers and your family. The brown brogue style is pragmatic, political and practical. Getting done what can be done – the art of the possible. Show flexibility; change your mind if you must, but not your priorities or your destination. As you walk about, remind people who they are, where they are going and why. Encourage personal initiatives, but follow up and keep control.

> Do what works and get it done. Do the obvious and familiar unless surprise and change have overwhelming merit. If it's not broken don't mend it. Change out of your brown brogues only when you have to, but often enough to check that your other shoes still fit! Now that you have more advanced brain work to do and more advanced thinking skills with which to do it you may want to develop your Applied Intelligence. Here's a four-step way to boost your brain power and your creative intelligence.

3.2.3 Boost your brain power and your Creative Intelligence the 4S© way

4S© STEP 1 PRIME YOUR BODY AND YOUR BRAIN

Your brain can change in response to the way you exercise and the way you breathe. It can change in response to what you eat, drink and smoke. It is changed by what you do and what you don't do. Your brain, it appears, can change its structure in response to your lifestyle. Your brain is able to adapt in this way because, according to Colin Blakemore, Chief Executive Officer of the UK Medical Research Council, your brain is not only a chemical factory, it is an extremely busy chemical factory. Your brain needs energy for more than 1 million chemical reactions every second! Your brain can be changed by what you do with it. Neuroscience now helps to design exercises for you to do and problems for you to solve.

Your brain is not only changed by what you do with it, it is also changed by what you do to it. Here we will look at the effects of diet, exercise, sleep, drugs, sex and dark chocolate on your brain.

Food for thought
1 Under normal circumstances, the brain uses mainly glucose for energy. With the aid of oxygen, B vitamins and minerals, the glucose is oxidized to produce water, carbon dioxide and energy – enough to fuel a million chemical reactions a second!
2 Neurons, and the sheaths surrounding their axons, need to be kept in good condition and phosphatidyl choline is essential for that maintenance. But for phosphatidyl choline to work it needs certain B vitamins.

3 Folic acid and selenium have been found to boost cognitive functioning. Folic acid is found in dark leafy green vegetables. Selenium is a mineral found in seafood, wholegrain breads, nuts and meat.

4 Boron, iron, magnesium, selenium and zinc aid mental activity. Boron is found in broccoli, pears, peaches, grapes, nuts and dried beans. Zinc can be found in fish, beans and whole grains. Vitamin C can be found in citrus fruits and salads (it enhances the absorption of iron and iron helps to form ferroxyhaemoglobin, which is used to carry oxygen in your blood, to your brain). Magnesium is found in dark chocolate.

5 In humans, neurotransmitters like dopamine and norepinephrine are essential for mental alertness and acuity, and for high speed calculation, evaluation and critical thinking. Eating protein increases the supply of neurotransmitters. The implication is that you should eat more protein if you wish to be mentally alert and quick thinking. (Some of the lowest rates of dyslexia in the world are found in Japan, which has the highest per capita consumption of fish.)

6 Eating blueberries, strawberries and spinach can reverse some deteriorations in thinking ability. (Dark chocolate has ten times the level of the flavonols that are responsible for this beneficial effect – try four small squares a day (Wootton and Horne, 2010a).)

Dieting, snacking and grazing

The British Association for the Advancement of Science reports that whether or not people who diet frequently lose weight, they certainly lose mental performance. Thinking consumes energy and needs fuel. Where possible, try to have evenly spaced snacks rather than a few large meals. Large meals are often preceded by reduced ability to concentrate and followed by periods of drowsiness. However, do not snack on sweets, biscuits or refined, fatty or salty carbohydrates. Snack on proteins such as yoghurts, cheese, nuts or seeds.

Sweets

People who become anxious frequently crave the tranquilizing effect of serotonin. Serotonin is formed from the tryptophan released into their blood when they eat carbohydrates. Perhaps that is why people who are over-anxious often crave sweet things. Sweet things are usually sweet because they contain refined sugar. For the anxious person, this has the advantage that refined sugar is very rapidly absorbed by the body, so the calming effect is almost immediate. A serious downside, however, is that you can get an over-production of insulin. Excess insulin provokes hunger-like pains and makes mental concentration very difficult. It also produces craving for more sweet food and so the cycle gets worse. Body weight as well as mental functioning can then suffer.

A mindful meal – a mindful mouthful

▶ Switch off the TV, radio, DVD, iPod, computer. Put aside the newspaper, magazine or book. Give attention to your eating.
▶ Don't just eat – dine. Arrange your food attractively on your plate – do not make unappetizing, messy piles. Notice the colours, the textures and the smell of your food before you start. Pause and drink your glass of water.
▶ Appreciate the tastes and textures and try to detect the different ingredients in the food as you chew it in your mouth. Discuss the tastes with your dining partner, if you have one.
▶ Rest your cutlery on your plate while you chew each mouthful – 12 times.
▶ Make each mouthful a choice, not a habit driven reflex to refill your mouth.
▶ Give your brain time to tell you when it has had enough.
▶ With rich cooked food, it is easy to eat more than your brain knows you need, before your stomach signals 'full'.

Detoxify your brain
1 Detoxifying drinks
Try carrot juice, beetroot juice or celery juice, or try blending 4 tbsp pure olive oil (or almond oil), with 8 tbsp fresh lemon juice, adding 6 cloves of garlic and fresh ginger to taste. (But not if you have gall stones!)

2 Detoxifying foods
These include kedgeree, muesli (wheat free), fish (not fried), vegetable curry with wholemeal rice, baked potatoes, houmous, thin vegetable soups and omelettes or try making Kichadi:

Take one cup of basmati rice plus a half cup of mung beans (washed) and heat them in olive oil. Add half tsp of fennel, coriander, cumin, ginger and turmeric. Stir and add the drained rice and beans. Cover in water and boil. Simmer for 1 hour. Add root vegetables after 20 minutes. Add leafy vegetables for the last five minutes. Add fresh coriander and/or basil and/or mint and/or sage before serving.

From *Think Yourself Thin* (Horne and Wootton, in planning)

The positive effect of relaxation on thinking
Gelb (2003) reports that the tested cognition and memory of people taught how to relax is 25 per cent higher than in a control group. He found similar gains when posture was improved prior to thinking tasks. According to Bagerly, Gelb massage and yoga can increase

relaxation and slow the frequency of the electrical brainwaves in your head (you literally get bigger brainwaves!). Excessive stress and anxiety impair thinking. Relaxation lowers the cortisol associated with both.

The effect of aerobic exercise

Dienstbier (1989) reports that aerobic exercise enhances thinking performance. Brain activity is fuelled by oxygen. Aerobic exercise increases the supply of oxygen to the brain. Herman-Toffler (1998) divided people into three groups: group one was given vigorous aerobic exercise; group two was given moderate anaerobic exercise; and group three was given a placebo activity not involving exercise at all. The two exercise groups consistently showed significantly higher scores on reasoning and thinking tests than the non-exercisers. The exercise regimes were rotated around the groups and the most enhanced reasoning and thinking scores continued to be achieved in the group that was exercising aerobically. However, exercise to the point of exhaustion induces sleepiness, which impairs thinking. Only do hard exercises later in the day if you need help to get to sleep.

The effect of sleep on thinking

Horne (2010b) has found that impaired sleep reduces performance on many mental tasks.

According to Coren (1996) scores on intelligence tests decline cumulatively on each successive day that you sleep less than you normally sleep. The daily decline is approximately one IQ point for the first hour of sleep loss, two for the next, and four for the next. After five successive days of sleeping less than you need, your IQ can be lowered by up to 15 points. This means that a person of normal intelligence could have an effective IQ of only 85, the level at which you would need special education in order to learn. Even a very bright person (IQ of 120 plus) can be reduced to robotic, autopilot thinking by shortage or disturbance of sleep. Alcohol can induce sleep but it impairs the quality of the sleep.

The effect of alcohol on thinking

Alcohol depletes vitamin B1, which is essential for the thinking process. Heavy drinkers risk a brain disorder called Wernicke-Korsakoff syndrome, a progressive memory deficit. Sufferers normally recover their ability to speak and walk, but do not recover their ability to think. The condition seems to be irreversible. There is some evidence that 1, maximum 2, units of alcohol, preferably red wine, champagne or malt whisky, may confer enough health benefits to justify the loss of mental performance as long as you drink extra water to counter the diuretic effect of the alcohol. Your call!

The diuretic effect of tea, coffee, coca-cola and caffeine

Caffeine is found in tea, coffee and cola drinks and in some food products. Caffeine can quicken your reaction time and prolong your vigilance during demanding tasks. However, there is a need to keep doubling your intake of caffeine to have the same effect and eventually a plateau is reached. The caffeine also acts as a diuretic; you keep urinating, causing dehydration. This produces lethargy and reduces your cognitive performance. Nutritionists recommend that you drink 8 to 15 glasses of water a day, depending on your body size, the weather and your activity level. Water is preferable to tea, coffee, soft drinks or fruit juices. If you must have caffeine at all, one cup of real black (not instant) coffee, when you most need it, will also provide some antioxidant protection for your brain.

The effect of smoking on thinking

Smokers self-report increased mental alertness and improved performance on a host of cognitive tasks after one cigarette. However, this positive effect is soon countered by an adverse effect on the oxygen-carrying capacity of the blood. Smoking ties up the haemoglobin that carries the oxygen in the blood. Damage to lungs limits the body's ability to absorb the oxygen needed to support mental activity.

The effect of drugs on thinking

Cannabis Regular users progressively reduced their baseline of brain activity compared to a matched control group, with lower proactive energy levels, lower completion rates on personal goals and plans, lower reported pleasure in anything, and reduced interest in using their bodies or their brains (Mathew, 1997).

Ecstasy Users of ecstasy are left with seriously depleted levels of serotonin. This makes it difficult to concentrate, to complete mental tasks or to sleep. This will, in turn, impair the ability to think (Kish, 2000).

Cocaine When an endorphin molecule in your body jumps a synaptic gap and finds a receptor site, you experience pleasure. Normally the endorphin will then detach. A cocaine molecule will lock the endorphin onto the receptor site so that you will continue to experience the pleasure. Once the cocaine has been metabolized, you will be short of endorphins and you will crave a repeat experience. You are hooked.

The more cocaine you use the more the blood vessels in your brain will become constricted. This constriction will impair your ability to think and will eventually damage your brain and may kill you.

Dark chocolate boosts the brain

Dark chocolate boosts your brain while protecting you from heart disease and cancer. Eating approximately 20–150 g (maximum of four small squares) a day of dark chocolate can improve your learning and your memory. Improved blood flows carry more oxygen to the brain, enabling you to think quicker for longer. Your blood vessels relax, reducing blood pressure, brain damage and risk of heart disease.

Dark chocolate contains PEA (phenylethylamine). PEA activates the neurotransmitters in your brain that control mental attention, concentration and alertness. Your levels of PEA go up naturally, without chocolate, when you are gripped by a great movie or are enjoying a good book, or are wholly engrossed in a football match, a work project or a computer game. Elevated levels of PEA can cause you to lose track of time. This is why time seems to fly when you are enjoying yourself.

You need the magnesium in dark chocolate to decrease the coagulation of your blood. This will help your heart to deliver more oxygen to your brain. This will not only raise the thinking speed and thinking power of your brain, it will also protect your brain from the damage caused by high blood pressure. One of the easiest ways to add magnesium to your diet is to eat dark chocolate.

Dark chocolate contains monoamine oxidase inhibitors (MAOIs). These allow the levels of serotonin and dopamine in your brain to remain higher for longer, alleviating depression and producing feelings of well-being.

Free radicals attack and oxidize the DNA in your brain, creating growth points for tumours, as well as the onset of premature ageing. Cheng Lee at Cornell University, USA showed that dark chocolate is rich in antioxidants, called flavonols. Flavonols mop up the free radicals before they can oxidize your brain. Dark chocolate is twice as rich in antioxidant flavonols as red wine, and three times richer than green tea. The flavonols in dark chocolate also make your blood platelets less likely to stick together and thus less likely to cause brain damage through a stroke. Lee found that a normal cup of drinking chocolate, based on dark chocolate, contained about 600 mg of the flavonoid epicatechin.

Eating dark chocolate substantially increases your mental speed and energy because it contains the brain stimulant theobromine. (Dark chocolate is virtually free of caffeine, which can also give your brain a temporary boost, but caffeine has fatiguing short-term side-effects and more dangerous long-term side-effects.) Dark chocolate contains about 21 per cent theobromine (up to 450 mg per oz). Theobromine works as a brain stimulant by relaxing muscles helping to dilate veins and arteries thus allowing blood to flow more easily to the brain. The effect of theobromine is gentler and more sustained than that of caffeine. It lasts four times longer and is kinder to your heart. Theobromine has actually been prescribed for heart patients to help lower blood pressure. Caffeine, on the other hand, is life-threatening to many heart patients, because it raises blood pressure and thus potentially damages the brain. Death is bad for your brain.

Dark chocolate contains PEA (phenylethylamine). PEA activates the neurotransmitters in your brain that control mental attention, concentration and alertness. Your levels of PEA go up naturally, without chocolate, when you are gripped by a great movie or are enjoying a good book, or are wholly engrossed in a football match, a work project or a computer game. Elevated levels of PEA can cause you to lose track of time. This is why time seems to fly when you are enjoying yourself. PEA is present in higher levels in 'blissful' people (Wootton and Horne, 2010b). It is also found in dark chocolate. Good quality dark chocolate can contain up to 2.2 per cent PEA.

ANANDAMIDE IN DARK CHOCOLATE – THE BRAIN'S BLISS CHEMICAL
Dark chocolate contains anandamide. Anandamide is released in your brain when you feel good. It acts on your brain the same way as the THC (tetrahydrocannabinol) in cannabis does. Because anandamide does not act on the whole of your brain, the way cannabis does, you can feel good without losing your mind. You do not feel 'out of it', like you would on cannabis. Anandamide is a natural brain chemical with no known harmful side-effects. In fact, BLISS is strongly correlated with good health and the anandamide in dark chocolate is the brain's own BLISS chemical.

THE SECRET OF ETERNAL YOUTH?
The monoamine oxidase inhibitors in dark chocolate work by allowing increased levels of anandamine and dopamine to circulate in the brain. High levels of anandamine and dopamine distinguish the brains of children from the brains of most adults because, in general,

as you get older, the levels of anandamine and dopamine decrease. This decrease is associated with a decrease in physical and mental spontaneity and joy. You are as young as you act and think and feel, and the monoamine oxidase inhibitors in dark chocolate can help to keep these neurotransmitter levels nearer to the levels of your youth (Cousens, 2001).

Dark chocolate produces endorphins that induce the loving feelings that often lead to sex. The same endorphins also facilitate the euphoria of the 'afterglow'.

The effect of sex on your brain
The effect of sex on your thinking depends on whether or not your pre-sex stress levels are excessive, whether or not you have an orgasm, and what type of thinking you are concerned about. Five of the seven steps to sexual satisfaction release chemicals in your brain that each help your brain to think.

The seven steps in the sex life of your chemical brain are:

Step 1 Both you and your partner each need to have sufficient testosterone in your brain. Low testosterone is the most common cause of low libido. Stresses, fatigue, disturbed sleep, hormone imbalance due to pregnancy, hysterectomy or menopause are common causes of inadequate levels of testosterone.

Step 2 Given you have sufficient testosterone, then desire can generate a rising level of oestrogen, triggering the release of pheromones under your armpits. These may create a reciprocal sexual desire in your partner (the jury is still out on this).

Step 3 Sexual desires release dopamine. Dopamine helps you to think visually. Dopamine will help you to visualize, imagine and fantasize about the different possible places and ways in which you might have sex with your partner. This will further raise your level of desire and the level of nitric oxide in your bloodstream.

Step 4 Nitric oxide increases your rate of blood flow. Besides helping to dilate the labial lips of your vaginal area, or to engorge the tumescence of your penis, the increased rate of supply of oxygen to your brain will enable you to process information faster and to assess problems more quickly. Increased oxidation will leave your head clearer for calculation, decision and action. Nitric oxide readies you for action!

Step 5 If the action is sexual, your oxytocin levels will rise, causing pelvic contractions and raising the possibility of female orgasm. Oxytocin heightens a sense of being wanted, safe and secure. It is a 'trust hormone'. It increases preparedness to think of novel or riskier solutions. It aids creative thinking.

Step 6 The pleasure of sexual activity, especially following orgasm, raises the levels of serotonin in the brain. Serotonin calms agitation, stress and anxiety. Cortisol levels associated with stress are moderated, making calm, logical decision making and calculation easier. High levels of serotonin favour creative thinking.

Step 7 With stress relieved, head cleared and visual and creative thinking empowered, there is an 'afterglow' of satisfaction associated with a rise in the level of PEA. PEA produces feelings of well-being and a tendency to smile involuntarily! PEA is the brain chemical associated with romance and falling in love. It is also produced by eating dark chocolate. (Sometimes life is less complicated if you just eat the dark chocolate!)

If a lucky night, prime your body to keep it tuned during the day. Try one or more of the following:

Top 10 brain tuners	
Tuner 1	Cross and uncross your arms the opposite way to normal (notice how strange it feels).
Tuner 2	Lock and interlock your fingers the opposite way to normal (see how relieved you are to stop doing it).
Tuner 3	Write or type for a while with your non-dominant hand.
Tuner 4	Wink at yourself – or preferably someone else – with your non-dominant eye (the reaction will be enough!).
Tuner 5	Roll your tongue from the side. Both sides.
Tuner 6	Draw with both hands simultaneously.
Tuner 7	Write in a mirror.
Tuner 8	Reach behind your back with your left hand to touch your right foot. Now behind your left foot with your right hand. Repeat as a refresher.
Tuner 9	Ten times … raise your left knee to touch your right hand, then your right knee to touch your left hand.
Tuner 10	Practise juggling.

4S© STEP 2 ASK YOURSELF QUESTIONS ABOUT EVERYTHING?

Thought experiment

Your top ten most important questions – your starters for ten

Can you list your top ten most important questions?

Try subtracting from and adding to the following list of starters for ten.

STARTERS FOR TEN

- ▶ Who allows me to be my natural self?
- ▶ During what activities do I feel my natural self?
- ▶ What is my greatest talent?
- ▶ How can I best serve others?
- ▶ What is my heart's deepest desire?
- ▶ What are my greatest attributes?
- ▶ How am I perceived by my closest friend?
- ▶ What legacy would I most like to leave?
- ▶ How could I get paid for doing what I love?
- ▶ What could I stop (or start) doing today that would most improve my experience of life?

HOW TO USE YOUR TOP TEN QUESTIONS

1 Try holding one of your top ten questions in your mind for ten minutes before sleeping. Keep a pad by your bed to record your waking thoughts. You can incubate insight, overnight.

2 Try writing your responses to one of your questions, without revision or correction. Write for ten minutes without stopping. After ten minutes go back and highlight what jumps out at you. A possible starting line for a poem, or a song or, a note to a friend? Or maybe another good question?

3 If you have a problem asking (or answering), any of your top ten questions ask yourself …:
   a **When** did this problem start?
   b **Who** cares about this?
   c **What** different perspectives can I take?
   d **Where** else has this happened?
   e **Why** is it important?
   f **How** will I know when this problem is solved

4 What if …? Use visual, imaginative, empathic and predictive thinking to set up a mental laboratory where you can test run speculative ideas without outer world risks and costs. What if we

ignored this problem? What if this solution failed? What if we succeeded, what would look different in the world? How would others feel? The whole of the Silicon Valley originated from the question 'What if we made chips smaller?' Try:

What if I enlarged it; made it heavier or made it lighter; changed its shape, colour, direction; tightened it; loosened it; added an X; or took a Y; stayed open 24 hours; offered guarantees; changed its name; made it easy to order, to use; made it recyclable, stronger, softer; harder; portable; twice the price?; What if we paid customers up front, to lease it long term?

4S© STEP 3 TEST, PRACTISE AND AFFIRM

Having used questions and your Applied Thinking skills to turn information into useable knowledge in the inner world of thinking, you must next test your ideas in practice, in the outer world of action.

Test 1: Experience (*after Michael Gelb*)

▶ Spend 20–30 minutes brainstorming a list of some of the most influential experiences of your life.
▶ Against each, write in one sentence what you gained or learned from each experience.
▶ Review your list – what was the single most influential experience?
▶ How has this experience coloured your view of the world?
▶ Can you now rethink some of the conclusions or ideas you formed at the time of that experience?

Michael Gelb suggests that at this stage you 'marinate'.

Test 2: Beliefs (*after Michael Gelb*)
Choose three areas out of:

▶ Human nature, ethics, politics, ethnicity, scientific theories, sexuality, religion, medicine, the meaning of life, art, marriage, money, parenting.
▶ In each of the three areas you have chosen, write down three ideas or beliefs that you hold.
▶ For each belief you hold, ask:
  ▷ Where did this idea come from?
  ▷ How firmly do I believe it?
  ▷ What would it take for me to change it?

- Consider the role played in your belief formation of:
  - Books, internet, TV, radio, newsprint, magazines.
  - People: family, teachers, physicians, religious people, bosses, friends, colleagues.
  - Your own experience.
- What criteria do you use for assessing the validity of information from these three sources? (See Part 2)

Test 3: Mistakes and adversity

- What was your school experience of mistakes?
- What was your home experience of mistakes?
- What was your biggest mistake?
- What did you learn from these mistakes?
- What mistakes do you often still repeat?
- What is the role in your life of fear of making a mistake?
- Write a stream of conscious style, for 20 minutes, on the subject: What I would do if I had no fear of making mistakes.

As an Advanced Applied Thinker, your greatest enemy or adversity is likely to be the loneliness you will feel at being always ahead of others and ahead of your time. Optimistim, affirmations, awareness and a sense of humour may also help. See also Appendix 3 for writings by Martin Seligman or Michael Gelb.

Pick one affirmation from each of the following groups of affirmations. Notice the strengthening effect on you when you repeat and myelinate the feelings induced when you repeat and myelinate one affirmation from each group

RELATIONSHIPS
- I feel ready and willing to allow another person into my heart.
- I feel curious about how I can change for the better for my partner.
- I feel the difference between me and my father (or my mother).

MONEY
- I feel the difference between what I want and what I need.
- I feel worthy of allowing abundance into my life.
- I acknowledge that abundance is already in my life.

CAREER
- I feel worthy of my contributions to the world.
- I feel connected to my inner strength when others read what I write.
- I feel ready to manifest my inner purpose in the outer world.

4S© STEP 4 SENSING AND MAKING SENSE

As a human being at home, at work, at play, or just around in the world, you sense information and then use thinking skills to help you 'make sense' of what you sense. You use your inner world mental laboratory to test out possible conclusions and actions you are contemplating as a result of the sense you are making of what you sense, before taking the first action steps in the outer world. As you take action steps in your action shoes, you can immediately begin to sense reactions in the outer world, and you will quickly need to make sense of those reactions. The quality of the sense you can make of these reactions depends on how well developed is your capacity for picking up and identifying sensations – sounds and words, sights and signals, touch and feelings. Whether these sensations are sensed directly, or are remembered, or are imagined, a scan of your brain reveals that the same parts of your brain are involved in trying to make sense of sensations, whether you remember them, imagine them or are experiencing them in real time. If you miss or mistake what you need to sense to solve a problem, take a decision or make a plan, then no amount of good thinking can produce a creative solution, or a distinctive decision or an innovative plan. So this 4S© Step 4 is about developing the parts of your brain that deal with sensing and sensation.

Ten sensational exercises

Exercise 1	Sit at a table with your feet squarely on the floor, the same distance apart as your shoulders. Remove any spectacles. Rub your palms for 20 seconds to make sure your hands are warm. Rest your elbows on the table. Cup your palms gently over your closed eyes. Exhale deeply for 3 to 5 minutes. Remove your palms and leave your eyes closed while you count quietly to 40. Slowly open your eyes and look around and notice how bright the colours are. Do this once or twice a day.
Exercise 2	Focus on your fingerprint and then switch your focus quickly onto as distant an object as possible. Alternate your near and far focus for a few minutes, several times each day.
Exercise 3	Edit the list of painters below by replacing some with your own favourites if you have any. Find examples of the work of each of them – call in at bookshops, libraries and galleries as you pass them and look for more details.

Use the internet to find where the original works are kept. Plan to find one a year during a trip or a holiday. If you can view the works with someone, even better. Aim to find and refine your list within three years. Michelangelo / Cezanne / Van Gogh / Renoir / Degas / Vermeer / Pollock / Monet / Picasso.

Aim to arrive as the gallery opens. Get an undisturbed hour in front of your chosen masterpiece.

Exercise 4   Visualization is different from reverie, day dreaming or sexual fantasy, though each might feed your creative thinking. In visualization, you create mental pictures of what things will be like, for example, after a change has been implemented. The visualization should be multi-sensory – the smells and the sounds, the heat and the warmth, as well as what you can see in your mind's eye. Empathize with the thoughts and feelings of significant others as they too gaze up at the implemented scene.

As a warm-up, practise recalling in as much detail as possible one of the happiest or best scenes of your life. Feel the feelings and hear the sounds as well as seeing now what you could see then.

Exercise 5   Find one example you like from each of the following six periods of music. If you are not already familiar with this type of music, keep listening to music from each period until you find one piece you like.
- ▶ Medieval (450–1450) – dominated by voice music. Try monastic chants or music by Hildegard von Bingen.
- ▶ Renaissance (1450–1600) – dominated by music in parts. Try Palestrina.
- ▶ Baroque (1600–1750) – dominated by musical counterpoint. Try Bach and Handel.
- ▶ Classical (1750–1820) – dominated by melody and harmony. Try Mozart, Haydn and Beethoven.
- ▶ Romantic (1820–1910) – dominated by melody/harmony. Try Brahms, Chopin, Verdi and Puccini.
- ▶ Modern music from 1910 – dominated by the blazing new. Try Stravinsky and Shostakovich.

Exercise 6   Edit the following list of musical masterpieces to make room for your own preferences:
- ▶ Bach: Mass in B minor
- ▶ Beethoven: Symphonies
- ▶ Mozart: Requiem

- ▶ Chopin: The Nocturnes
- ▶ Brahms: The German Requiem
- ▶ Mendelssohn: The Violin Concerto, 2nd Movement
- ▶ Beethoven: Piano Concerto
- ▶ Strauss, R.: Four last songs
- ▶ Stravinsky: The Rite of Spring
- ▶ Any opera: e.g. Verdi's Aida and La Traviata; Puccini

Aim to find and hear and refine your list within a year (one a month). Explore fine recordings and seek out live performances. Listen with a friend and talk about the performance afterwards or write some notes.

Exercise 7   Notice how all the great music you have found slowly builds emotional, intellectual or physical tension, and then releases it. Jazz does this continuously. Find recordings of Jazz; King Oliver is a good place to start and then compile and complete your own top ten list of jazz tunes. Move to the music. Dance if you can.

Exercise 8   Create a present for yourself, or another person – a perfume to use in the bath. Test and buy as many good essential oils as you can, and some grape oil as the base oil. Include ylang ylang, neroli and bergamont, plus the brain friendly lavender, sage, rosemary, eucalyptus and peppermint.

Exercise 9   Try some dark chocolate; it is good for your brain and your body. Try to choose plantation-grown beans. Malagasy dark chocolate has around 74 per cent cocoa and is highly sought.

Exercise 10   Cook an Indian, Pakistani or Thai dish for a group of friends. Think of what you are doing at a group level as well as food level. Who are you hoping to blend together as a party or as potential future friends? What are their characteristics and why do you think they will get on? What are the ingredients of your hoped-for chemistry? Now think about your meal – think of trying to balance salty ingredients, sour ingredients and sweet ingredients. What will be the role of yoghurt, cream or coconut? How will you cook it? Give them something to nibble on while they wait for you to finish cooking or for other guests to arrive. Check that the food smells and looks as delicious as it will surely taste!

Summary

The 4S© sensational exercises will encourage you to open your brain to new sensory experiences that will leave you with increased residual sensitivity to new information and sensation. In Section 2.3, Systems Thinking gave you a way of thinking about sensed information that enables you to be systematic and in control of your remembered, imagined and captured information and not overwhelmed by it. You learned not to distort information about problems to make them fit your preconceived ideas about solutions. You learned to tolerate complex, incomplete or ambiguous information. You learned that you can be precise in the way you approach things that are vague.

You have now explored popular ideas about genius and you have found that born genius is very rare and, in fact, unnecessary. By looking at what a genius does, and by analysing how to do it, you can become an Applied Thinker – a streetwise practical genius. The best way to train your brain for Applied Thinking is to take advantage of the three discoveries of neuroscience:

1 Thinking involves many separate areas of the brain that need to be connected by well mylenated neural pathways.
2 That the process of thinking itself improves the brain's residual capacity to think (neuromodulation and neuroplasticity).
3 This means that the brain, and the Applied Thinking that it supports, can benefit from neuroscientifically designed brain training exercises of the kind found in sections 2.1, 2.2 and 2.3, as well as the thinking practice offered in the thought experiments and philosophical dilemmas in 1.2 and 1.3. Neuroscience points to the benefits of both brain exercise and thinking practice.

Section 3.3 ends with some very hard brain exercises and very hard thinking practice indeed. This fiendish workout is suitable only for those who are very serious about Advanced Applied Thinking.

3.3

Workout: A fiendish 4S© workout for Advanced Thinkers only

In this section you will:
- *warm up your brain*
- *do some heavy lateral exercises*
- *meet the world's hardest cryptic crossword!*

3.3.1 Warm-ups

TRIANGULAR WARM-UPS

Answers are in Appendix 1 at the back of the book.

Fiendish workout 1: What is the missing number?

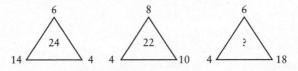

Fiendish workout 2: What is the missing number?

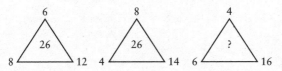

Fiendish workout 3: What is the missing number?

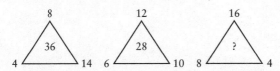

Fiendish workout 4: His father probably knows the answer now.

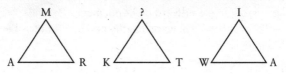

Fiendish workout 5: Initiation

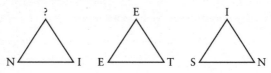

CIRCULAR WARM-UPS

Fiendish workout 6: What is the missing number?

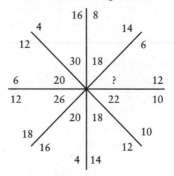

Fiendish workout 7: What is the missing number?

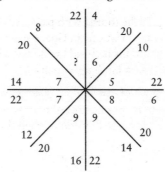

LATERAL WARM-UPS

Coined by psychologist Edward de Bono, mental 'laterals' help you to rapidly solve problems. They are lengthy and near impossible to solve by plodding logic.

Fiendish workout 8: Two brothers were met off a coach by their father. They left the bus station together. None had met either of the others before that moment. How might they have recognized each other? Where will they be going to later?

Fiendish workout 9: You are asleep when the hospital rings to say that Grandma's electric clock stopped at 17:59. What is the problem?

Fiendish workout 10: You are 16 years old. Because of a bad weather warning, you have been let out of school early. This is not much help to you as your parents have not given you a house key. You play ball in the garden and unfortunately you break an original Georgian pane in an original Georgian window. You are scared what your parents will say. Fortunately, they do not blame you, but they do phone the police. Why?

Fiendish workout 11: It was clear to the police officers, who came by minutes later, that the car had gone out of control on the bend at the bottom of the hill and ploughed through a hedge into the ravine 60 metres below them. By torchlight, they could see where the wreckage lay, partially submerged in the river. Suddenly they saw the driver climbing out of the back door of the wrecked car. He dusted his briefcase and began scrambling up the slope towards them. He was not injured. Why?

Fiendish workout 12: If the tourist with pains was from Spain, and the passer-by who had a go was from Goa, when the tourist came back from the hospital to his bed and breakfast, what kind of TV programme was his Jewish landlady watching?

Fiendish workout 13: What can you put in a box without a lid, such that the more of them you put in, the lighter it would become and, if you put in as many as you possibly could, it would probably never be full?

PYRAMID WARM-UPS

Fiendish workout 14: What is the missing letter?

Fiendish workout 15: What's the missing letter?

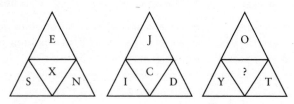

Fiendish workout 16: What is the missing letter?

Fiendish workout 17: What is the missing letter?

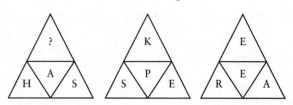

Fiendish workout 18: What's the missing letter? (Clue: Serial Caesareans?)

FOUR SQUARE WARM-UPS

Fiendish workout 19: What is the missing number?

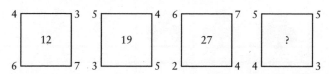

Fiendish workout 20: What is the missing number?

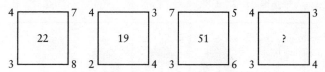

Fiendish workout 21: What is the missing number?

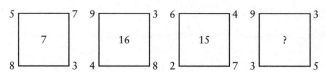

Fiendish workout 22: What is the missing number?

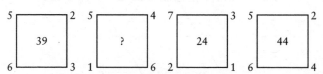

Fiendish workout 23: What is the price of a suit these days, if each collection of suits costs £2100?

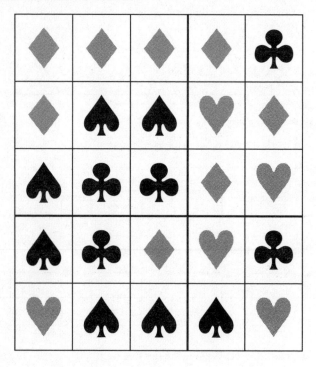

FOUR-STAR WARM-UPS

Fiendish workout 24: Each letter is the initial letter of an anticlockwise set. Find another letter that could belong to the set.

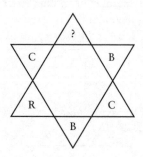

Fiendish workout 25: Each letter is the initial letter of a conceptual set or collection-in-common. Find another letter that could belong to the set. Any letter X is redundant.

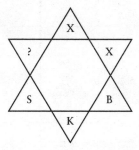

Fiendish workout 26: Each letter is the initial letter of a conceptual set or collection-in-common. Find another letter that could belong to the set. Any letter X is redundant.

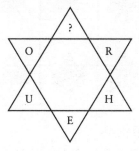

Fiendish workout 27: Each letter is the initial letter of a conceptual set or collection-in-common. Find another letter that could belong to the set. Any letter X is redundant.

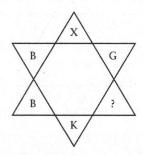

Fiendish workout 28: Each letter is the initial letter of a conceptual set or collection-in-common. Find another letter that could belong to the set. Any letter X is redundant.

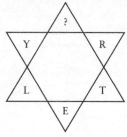

Fiendish workout 29: Each letter is the initial letter of a conceptual set or collection-in-common. Find another letter that could belong to the set. Any letter X is redundant.

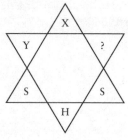

3.3.2 Heavy lateral lifts

Fiendish workout 30: Thinking about coal mines

Two friends emerged from a disused coal mine. One of them had coal dust smudges on his face, the other did not. Only the one with the clean face went off to wash his face. Why was that?

Fiendish workout 31: Thinking about money

Three children each have some coins. Any child has either 25, 10 or 5 cent coins. No child has the same number of coins as another. If each child were to give two coins to each of the other children, then they each would have coins totalling 180 units. How many coins did each child have to start with?

Fiendish workout 32: Finding time to think

When does $8+5=1$?

Fiendish workout 33: Thinking about your will

A wealthy widow willed that she be cremated along with the proceeds of her estate. The family appealed to a judge to annul the will on the grounds that the widow's mind was unsound. He sympathised with the family's situation and found a way to implement the widow's will that still pleased the family. How might the judge have done that?

Fiendish workout 34: Thinking about co-operative fishing

You are the captain of a fishing boat manned equally by two families, making a crew of 30. The ship is in a storm at sea and is in trouble. The ship is taking in water. All the crew agree that half of them should swim for shore to lighten the load, and save the boat from sinking. They ask you for a fair way to decide who goes overboard into the dangerous sea. You say you will line everyone around the edge of the deck and then keep counting round the deck asking every ninth person to jump into the sea. How will you position your family so they get to stay on board?

Fiendish workout 35: Thinking about mailshots

You and nine others advertise your services delivering mailshots. Your first contract payment has just arrived. It is £2,775. You agree to split it between you in proportion to the number of envelopes you each delivered. You will each receive a different amount, but as it happens, the difference between each person's payout and the next higher (or lower) payout is the same. Three of you with the three lowest payouts will together still receive as much as the two highest payouts combined. Yours is the second highest payout. It is £15 less than the person who delivered the most envelopes. How much money will you receive as your share?

Fiendish workout 36: Thinking about nudism

The couple did not sleep in bedclothes. One morning their servant found them both dead. Their bodies were cold and lay very close to each other. The servant could see no evidence of foul play or poison. When the bodies were moved, the bed was found to be cracked. What do you think happened?

Fiendish workout 37: Thinking about the importance of exploration

The couple were intrepid explorers but they had got into trouble. They were feeling very cold so they decided to build a fire using combustible materials from their vehicle. They took some dry papers from their vehicle, but their emergency matches would not work, even though they had been sealed in a plastic container that seemed to be in perfect condition. They tried making sparks from the vehicle's battery. They struck stones together, which made plentiful sparks. They used a lens to focus the sun's rays. This was very hot. Hot enough to burn their fingers and to melt the plastic match box, but it would not make the dry paper even smoulder. The air was not damp or humid. What do you think might be the problem and how could they get the fire started?

Fiendish workout 38: Thinking about Constitutional Law

The King has died. Under the constitution, the Queen will become Head of State until their oldest child is old enough to be crowned King. The King and Queen's oldest children are twins, born by caesarean, at exactly the same moment. How to choose the king? One of the twins is intelligent and kind and loved by everyone. The other is not so bright and is unpopular with the people and the Parliament. Even the Queen admits to not liking him much. Yet the Queen agrees that he should be the child who is to be king. Why might she do that? (There are no marriage issues, treaty issues, or corruption.)

Fiendish workout 39: Thinking about industrial pollution

A chemical plant caught fire at midnight. The fire was producing lethal fumes that were heavier than air. A 60 mph wind was forecast for 3 a.m., blowing directly east to west. The fire brigade estimated that it would take ten hours to quell the fires and the flames. The wind got up as forecast at 3.20 a.m. and blew for 3 hours 20 minutes before suddenly reversing direction and blowing directly west to east. The delay in the wind getting up had allowed the police to concentrate on evacuating the downwind area to the east of the chemical factory fire. No evacuation had occurred to the west of the factory fire. Almost everyone missed in the police sweep died or had very severe residual medical problems. At the subsequent inquiry, it was found that rainfall or closing doors and windows had little or no effect on the lethal effects of the fumes. Surprisingly the inquiry learned there had been very few casualties downwind to the west. Why was that?

Fiendish workout 40: Thinking about racism

Drake and his mates lived in a mixed ethnic community in England. Most years they took a winter break somewhere warmer than the United Kingdom. They liked the idea of a winter break in the sun. Last year they decided to get up a large party to go with them.

Their decision had tragic consequences. The plane crashed killing 300, including Drake's mates. Some of Drake's mates were not killed outright but they were badly injured. The emergency services did not prioritize them to be taken by ambulances to the major incident hospital nearby. Why not? (The subsequent inquiry found no evidence of racism on the part of the emergency services and no evidence of malicious terrorist intent, negligence or toxic virus.

Fiendish workout 41: Major change is hard

Jean's father got a promotion on Friday, and on the following Monday they moved into a new house. The next day, Jean, who was 14 years old, with normal hearing, could not understand anything that happened in school. Why not? (The problem was not the different accent of the teachers or the other pupils. The teachers all spoke English, just like in any other American school.)

Fiendish workout 42: The world running out of oil

To make his point, the Professor fitted a globe with oil and unplugged the hole at the South Pole. He showed his students that the oil would run out in four minutes. To demonstrate the effect of doubling the rate of oil consumption, the Professor refilled the globe with the same oil, and this time, simultaneously unplugged two identical holes, one at the South Pole exactly as before, but this time with an additional hole exactly on the equator. He waited, confident that the oil would run out in half the time. Why was the Professor red faced?

Fiendish workout 43: The right to roam

Four walkers crossed a bridge and climbed a hill to a gate that barred the public right of way. The gate carried a notice warning 'Beware of Bull'. They could see the cattle a long way away in the corner of the field, so they climbed over the gate. Before they could get to the gate on the far side of the field, the walkers were charged by a bull. They did not run. They were not unduly scared despite the fact that the bull that charged them was fully grown and very fit and strong. Nevertheless the walkers made a formal complaint. Why?

Fiendish workout 44: Taking responsibility seriously

Bill had not slept well the night before. He was very tired so he turned off the light and got into bed. His alarm failed to work but he was woken by his radio, on which he heard that 127 people had died during the night and that Bill was responsible. Why?

Fiendish workout 45: Collateral damage

The forest fire had raged 10 kilometres away from the nearest water. Around 36 hours after they managed to put out the fire, they found her body in open ground. She had not been burned or asphyxiated. She was wearing breathing apparatus. She was wearing a protective clothing that showed no signs at all of heat or burning. There was no evidence of foul or sexual play, though both her legs were broken. She had not walked far. How did she come to be there?

Fiendish workout 46: Love of learning

Joan is reluctant to go to school and often arrives a few minutes late, often without having done homework. She avoids taking tests. There are 30 children in her class and 29 are very good students. Yet Joan is rarely reprimanded. Why not?

3.3.3 Sudoku, ladders, propellers – and the world's hardest crossword?

SUDOKU

Sudoku requires several parts of your brain to work together to support numerical, visual, emotional and critical thinking. As patterns emerge, and fragments are remembered, in more than 30 different areas of your cerebral cortex, many neural links are activated. Many of these neural linkages involve your hippocampus, which plays a central role in your memory. When you play Sudoku or Scrabble or do cryptic crosswords, these neural links are run over and over again, thickening the myelin insulation around the axons of your brain cells and thereby improving the speed and the accuracy of your thinking. Emotional thinking is involved in managing your impatience, frustration and disappointment and you feel the need to compete with yourself or with others. Answers are in Appendix 1 at the back of the book.

THE RULES OF SUDOKU

A Sudoku puzzle is usually a 9×9 grid subdivided into nine squares – like noughts and crosses.

The puzzle starts with some given numbers – called clue numbers – already inserted. The object of the game is to fill all the empty boxes such that each row, each column, and each 3×3 large square, contains the numbers 1 to 9 – without repeating any number.

Tips on solving Sudoku puzzles

Use an HB pencil with an eraser in the end, or a ballpoint pen that has more than one colour.

Start by picking the 3×3 grid that has the most number clues already given. Look at the rows and columns going through the square you have picked. Pick a row or column that has several clue numbers already in place. Pick a vacant square in the grid you have chosen to work on.

In pencil, or in green ink, enter in a small font the 'missing' numbers, i.e. missing from the 3×3 square, and the row and the column in which the empty square is sitting. If there is only one such number, you have found your first answer number. Enter the answer number in the vacant grid square, by over-striking your missing numbers in black ink. Write the answer number as big as the clue numbers.

Repeat for all the empty squares in the row, the column and the 3×3 square. By elimination, each time you enter a big black answer number, you can erase or strike out the small missing numbers that you have entered in other places in the row, column or 3×3 square. As soon as you have only one missing number left in a small square – that is an answer number, so over-write it large and black.

Sudoku 1

	8				5		4	1
		3		9				
		4						6
	9	7						
	5		6		1		3	
						4	5	
3						1		
				1		7		
1	6		3				8	

Sudoku 2

6		3		2				
			3	9	8			
	1	9			4		8	
4					9		7	
		7				5		
	9		2					6
	5		4			7	1	
			9	7	2			
				8		4		2

Sudoku 3

5	2	4						
			5			9		7
	8						5	
					5	6	4	3
4				7				1
3	1	2	8					
	6						7	
7		8			2			
						2	3	9

Sudoku 4

		5					7	
	2		8					4
6					3			
	4		9			2		
				1				
		7			5		4	
			2					8
3					6		5	
	9					1		

Sudoku 5

	2		4				3	
					1			
		8		5		9		
		9						6
	3						2	
6						8		
		7		8		5		
			2					
	4				3		1	

Sudoku 6

		2	1			7		
					6			
4				3				8
3							5	
		6				1		
	5							9
				4				3
			2					
		1			7	6		

Sudoku 7

	5						7	
		2				8		
3				1				5
			8		4			
	7						3	
			2		6			
1				5				7
		6				4		
	9						1	

Sudoku 8

	2				6		5	
			3					
		8		1		4		
9					7			
	3						6	
		1						9
		7		8		1		
					2			
	6		5				3	

Sudoku 9

					4			
		3	2			6		
	7			5			9	
9							7	
		6				1		
	5							8
	8			9			5	
		1			6	2		
			4					

The usefulness of Sudoku in training the brain finds support from Susan Greenfield's model of the chemical brain and from David Snowdon's nun study. Oral recitation, repetitive brainwork, and the drafting and redrafting of written work not only gives your brain a memory upgrade, but, at the same time, they expand your brain's general cognitive capacity.

NUMERICAL LADDERS

Now try to some numerical ladders. As with all sensible exercise circuits, each begins with a warm-up, before you strain your brain on the final lift. Answers can be found in Appendix 1.

Numerical ladder 1

EASY	36	+3/4 OF IT	÷9	×5	DOUBLE IT	+14	÷7	×4	-1/4 OF IT	TRIPLE IT
MEDIUM	28	÷7	CUBE IT	+3/8 OF IT	×2	+32	-1/4 OF IT	TRIPLE IT	-3/4 OF IT	+87
HARDER	333	+10	÷49	×16	-3/4 OF IT	-3/7 OF IT	×15	+7/10 OF IT	DOUBLE IT	÷8

Numerical ladder 2

EASY	19	+6	×3	÷5	-11	×9	+1/3 OF IT	HALF OF IT	+60	DOUBLE IT
MEDIUM	16	+82	+36	×2	+1/2 OF IT	÷3	-64	×8	HALF OF IT	-164
HARDER	17	×9	+374	-359	÷6	×8	÷4	+1/4 OF IT	TRIPLE IT	×4

Numerical ladder 3

EASY	48	÷4	-1/4 OF IT	×6	DOUBLE IT	+24	+1/3 OF IT	TRIPLE IT	+20	÷4
MEDIUM	135	-3	÷11	×13	+3/4 OF IT	×2	+2/3 OF IT	+7/10 OF IT	÷7	-138
HARDER	121	DOUBLE IT	-56	-1/3 OF IT	+20	+7/12 OF IT	DOUBLE IT	+3/8 OF IT	+1/3 OF IT	÷4

Numerical ladder 4

EASY	36	÷3	+43	−19	×4	HALF OF IT	TRIPLE IT	−1/4 OF IT	HALF OF IT	÷9
MEDIUM	66	×5	−276	÷9	×14	÷12	÷89	DOUBLE IT	−1/3 OF IT	HALF OF IT
HARDER	96	+13	−65	×3	−1/4 OF IT	÷3	×19	DOUBLE IT	÷3	HALF OF IT

Numerical ladder 5

EASY	22	÷11	×5	DOUBLE IT	+136	÷12	×4	−1/2 OF IT	TRIPLE IT	+22
MEDIUM	84	÷7	DOUBLE IT	+3/8 OF IT	×2	TRIPLE IT	−1/3 OF IT	÷4	+87	÷8
HARDER	476	+10	÷9	×3	DOUBLE IT	÷3	−2/3 OF IT	+5/9 OF IT	DOUBLE IT	−1/2 OF IT

Numerical ladder 6

EASY	22	÷11	×5	DOUBLE IT	+136	÷12	×4	−1/2 OF IT	TRIPLE IT	+22
MEDIUM	84	÷7	DOUBLE IT	+3/8 OF IT	×2	TRIPLE IT	−1/3 OF IT	÷4	+87	÷8
HARDER	476	+10	÷9	×3	DOUBLE IT	÷3	−2/3 OF IT	+5/9 OF IT	DOUBLE IT	−1/2 OF IT

Numerical ladder 7

EASY	15	DOUBLE IT	÷6	−1/5 OF IT	+180	1/2 OF IT	+18	1/2 OF IT	÷5	×2
MEDIUM	82	1/2 OF IT	×8	−1/8 OF IT	DOUBLE IT	÷14	×4	−3/4 OF IT	×8	÷24
HARDER	168	−5/8 OF IT	DOUBLE IT	1/5 OF IT	TRIPLE IT	×2	÷12	−1/7 OF IT	−1/6 OF IT	×2

Numerical ladder 8

EASY	15	÷3	×8	1/2 OF IT	+80	÷10	×4	1/2 OF IT	÷5	DOUBLE IT

MEDIUM	100	25% OF IT	+100	÷25	×8	+1/2 OF IT	–32	÷4	×7	–32

HARDER	18	TIMES ITSELF	–64	÷13	TREBLE IT	+2/3 OF IT	+3/5 OF IT	÷4	+88	9/16 OF IT

PROPELLERS

Can you propel yourself to a higher level? Remember, there may be more than one way to hit the target in the middle.

Propeller 1

Use all the numbers in the outer triangles to make the target number. You can use +, –, × or ÷ to reach your solution. Target 30 seconds.

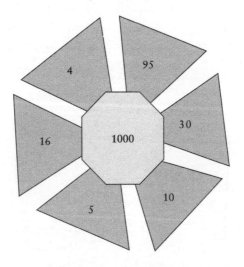

Propeller 2

Use all the numbers in the outer triangles to make the target number. You can use +, –, × or ÷ to reach your solution. Target 30 seconds.

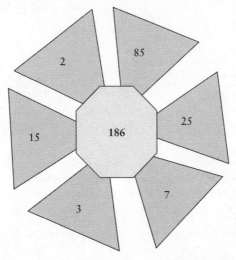

Propeller 3

Use all the numbers in the outer triangles to make the target number. You can use +, –, × or ÷ to reach your solution. Target 30 seconds.

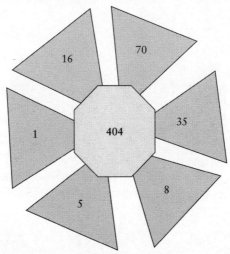

Propeller 4

Use all the numbers in the outer triangles to make the target number. You can use +, −, × or ÷ to reach your solution. Target 30 seconds.

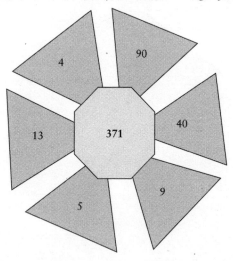

Propeller 5

Use all the numbers in the outer triangles to make the target number. You can use +, −, × or ÷ to reach your solution. Target 30 seconds.

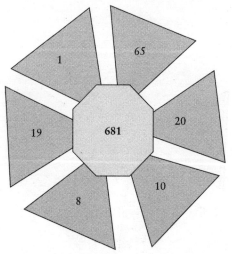

Propeller 6

Use all the numbers in the outer triangles to make the target number. You can use +, −, × or ÷ to reach your solution. Target 30 seconds.

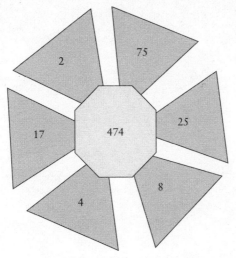

Propeller 7

Use all the numbers in the outer triangles to make the target number. You can use +, −, × or ÷ to reach your solution. Target 30 seconds.

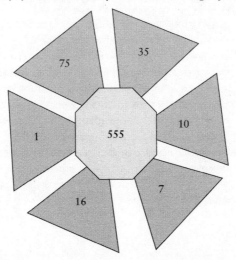

Propeller 8

Use all the numbers in the outer triangles to make the target number. You can use +, −, × or ÷ to reach your solution. Target 30 seconds.

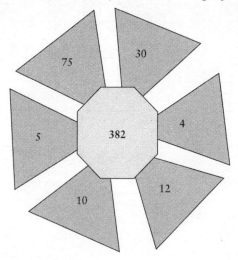

CRYPTIC CROSSWORDS

Now try some cryptic crosswords. Solving a cryptic crossword simultaneously involves traffic between many different areas of your brain as you try to use logic; recollect obscure bits of general knowledge; make creative associations between the bits you remember; count letters and spaces; hold several possibilities in your short-term memory; decide most likely possibilities; analyse the best way to cross check your decision and finally to manage your motivation and frustration! All these separate aspects of your brain development are intensified if you do the puzzle, or discuss the puzzle, with another person. Cryptic crosswords don't just test your brain power; more importantly the attempts you make to solve the cryptic clues leave new neural traces and connections in your brain. These new neural connections create new cognitive capacity that improves your performance on other thinking tasks and also helps to protect your improved performance against disease by creating reserve cognitive capacity.

Crossword 1

Across

3. Staying power of soldiers during Amin's breakdown (7)
6. Blushes about studies involving daughter (7)
8. Concern at hint of snow by those keeping watch (8)
10. Claimed compound is intense, say (7)
11. Non-believer's home life wrecked over daughter (7)
13. Natural to include a bishop's story (9)
14. Letters from the Athenian describe an uncivilized person (7)
15. See plans laid out in fairness (8)
17. Counsel various aides around five (6)
18. He deals with Tom in London (8)

Down

1. Shred all management of aggressive marketing (4,4)
2. Development area (8)
4. It is illegal for boxers to talk too much over a drink (6,5)
5. Where the Queen sometimes hangs out in a woollen cap (8)
7. Withdraw from competition with superficial skin wound (7)
9. Don't notice so much when pure (8)
12. Send out English academic before Etna erupts (7)
16. Impressive element of tone picture (4)

Crossword 2

Across

1. One is far and wide,
   mysteriously fade away (6)
3. Waltz around an old city
   after a measure of stamina (9)
6. Setter worked Wednesday's
   dayshift as a banker (6)
8. Holds back books (8)
9. Dying for father and son to
   perform a song (7)
10. Three-pronged spear I'd
    found in river (7)
12. Good material for
    underwear (7)
13. Dishonest trick involving
    Oxford University Press
    Voucher (6)
15. Equally, a story about a
    thousand (5)
16. I collected rent in Bury (5)
17. Arrive with no concealed
    weapons and confess (4, 5)
18. Son upset by termination of
    allowance (7)

Down

1. Digs Dutch fairies (6)
2. Ireland's premier seaside
   town is perfect (5)
4. Computer virus used in
   warfare (6, 5)
5. Free from worry after
   Penny's promise (6)
6. Dismissal from employment
   received by bandsmen (8,6)
7. Short game interrupted
   sailors' exercise (6)
11. It is enjoyed before
    retirement (8)
14. Change of dress (5)

Crossword 3

Across

2. Fortune in bottle with no top (4)
5. Subdue prisoner with heartless eccentric (7)
6. Joker with broken leg getting to move unsteadily (6)
7. Elsa was cocooned in happiness, born free (7)
11. I've learnt resistance, unfortunately, is immaterial (10)
15. By the sound of it, regret rubbish bread from abroad (6)
16. Market to recommend restricting of private sector investment (9)
18. To maintain contact in Australia is easy (6)
19. Trains get endlessly busy in port (8)
20. Burying treasure in an insecure country (8)

Down

1. Possible reason why blinking international organization involved in snub (8)
3. Appear to have Mercedes stuck in traffic? (8)
4. Wing patterns, variegated (8)
8. Second male trips badly in wake of moving vehicle? (10)
9. Dashing knight, one found in unwelcome spots (6)
10. Attitude found among oldest ancestors (6)
12. How to pay back blackleg (4)
13. Inn, where clergyman reclines in the shade (6)
14. Don't start shutting down (6)
17. More unlikely to have speaking part (5)

Crossword 4

Across

2. Giving out prizes in a random drawing (8)
6. Rough as a dropout from a certain type of Swiss school (10)
7. Type of footballer to remove mudguard from US car (8)
12. Sat awkwardly on mount with a leg either side (7)
15. Copper in interior of skin blemish and kidney stone (8)
16. Chance of coming clean is, unfortunately about nil (8)
17. Spell of shopping in Paris, pre-Eiffel? (5)

Down

1. I dig all operas in which a horse is running (6)
3. In two: equals one second below (7)
4. Verify said European? (5)
5. Like a ranked system, car hire is arranged with drunken outburst? (10)
8. Maybe pirate radio drops one after speed charge (9)
9. Let first of eggs get trapped inside hen – to treat is one option at this time (9)
10. Bacon not quite done – sibling gets sick with bacterial infection (10)
11. Great – attic fan's broken (9)
13. Utter chaos is being blamed, unfortunately (6)
14. Topped salad including topping of lite spicy ranch featured here (6)

Crossword 5

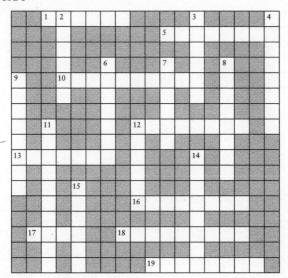

Across

1. Irritate the French after a row (6)
5. Paul's crashed in automobile, to be brief (8)
10. Cheer given by banker entertaining noted batsman amid success (10)
12. Record holder's first in dash, time one never forgets? (8)
13. Ready in Kuala Lumpur to call nasty person (7)
16. Gobstopper (8)
17. Obey the scumbag (4)
18. Bird changes colour (9)
19. Instrument Mike brought up inside, it has a piercing feature (8)

Down

2. Astonished by a confusing mass of information on Germany (6)
3. Sleeps over with editor but rejected by him (6)
4. In first form exam swallowed one drink (8)
6. Awfully bad night, hard going for Aussie fool (7)
7. Look at this bird (6)
8. Characters from sides of divine garden cultivated bananas (8)
9. Plum line? (8)
11. Soprano performing with good accent (10)
12. English model hugs bishop to raise some relief (6)
14. Dogsbody in trade union enthralled by award introduced by account in paper (8)
15. Star's unfashionable hairstyle (6)

Crossword 6

Across

3. Relatively large pawnbroker? (5,5)
5. Note by a bower's front a good container for leaves? (6)
6. Drink and travel regularly, showing flexibility (6)
8. Short song about bairn initially (7)
9. Source of blazing wood gathered by a good one (7)
10. Wide opening showing fruit right away (4)
12. Supreme batting to break duck (6)
16. Age 100, besieged by lost hope (5)
18. Wine in toast imbibed (4)
19. West leading this tricky card game (5)
20. Stranger in favour of accepting Rule 'E' (9)

Down

1. I don't believe its name at all (5)
2. Dairy ingredient, shortening put in purplish cookie (8)
4. Stellar group keeping, say island plant (9)
7. Not working this evening, get drunk (5)
11. So, likely to be offended by page on the smutty side? (7)
13. Object I bumped into when reversing (4)
14. Belongings that have theatrical use (7)
15. Drunk tears around end of corridor bar (8)
17. Rough edged, impure jade. Around two thousand dollars (6)

Crossword 7

Across

3. Gather a builder's not working (5)
6. To cheat people from that which is charitably given (8)
7. Leading Irish art magazine gets around (5)
10. Dramatist with drive to feature in upcoming opening (8)
11. Judge's anger follows start of untruths by politician (6)
17. Scheming female in ultra creation (6)
18. Fashionable thing that could be drawn about element that's rousing (8)
19. Academic girl sculpted a lion by a tree (8)
20. Model engaged to pretty person (4)

Down

1. South American gets consumption from ground meat (7)
2. Not able to eat a bit of sausage before a game (7)
4. Put an end to college books in school (6)
5. Gather one variety of fern (5)
8. Author knocking over tree (5)
9. Tough tactics used by cricketers (8)
12. Strategist said to nail Renaissance painter (9)
13. One who doesn't believe in field sports (7)
14. Refusing to be perusaded by article on the first man to model (7)
15. Carbon and copper backing in rail's redesign is vital (7)
16. Married person who has an affair does this (7)

Crossword 8

Across

2. Little-known doctor's remedy (7)
4. Wandering around in Rome: six stray collegiate athletes (7)
6. Cast in the midst of blaze – a lot stricter for fanatics (7)
8. It's on the Arabian Peninsula, you guys (5)
10. Witch wears red French fibre (8)
12. Heart of palm in unpleasant appetizer (5)
15. Some literature shows all ovens malfunction (8)
16. Piece of peach pie's swallowed by some dogs (7)
18. Youngest decapitated when playing mouth organs (7)
19. Textual representation of language (7)
20. This ground won't support weight of pound container of snack mix (9)

Down

1. Recording group cutting back on old recording (8)
3. Crazy glue in Sis's nose and rear end creates unpleasant scene (8)
5. Turtle egg is seized by mischievous otter (8)
7. One of two asthmatics sometimes not using heroin – they're plucky! (8)
9. 'Hazy Ulster Dawn' is showing. Want to go? (10)
11. They preach non-violence; I put on cap backwards, and they're all set to fight (9)
13. Cattle thief king crosses street (7)
14. Plot summary: Dad's other daughter gets on horse's back (8)
17. It makes tooting sounds within a bathtub audible (4)

Crossword 9

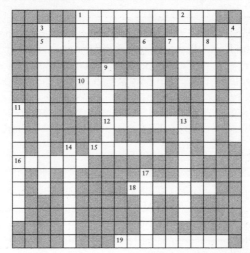

Across

1. The little devil mashed taters? Show me! (11)
5. Try to be like a bird that can't fly after 10 p.m. (7)
7. In somewhat of a panic, I cleared the path of freezing water (6)
10. Joy of infected toenail (7)
12. Stuck with a ditzy redhead (7)
15. A pint and three doubles gets Al Long drunk (6)
16. Portions of crab egg are for one who pleads (6)
18. Some geese foul gardens (7)
19. American football player goes to hospital unit with broken hip – head nurse gives something to dull pain (9)

Down

1. Sandwich shop really bringing food to customers (8)
2. Make outstanding air conditioning unit that's less than a dollar (6)
3. Fat girl putting on weight, then getting empty, becoming a small person (13)
4. Possessed, Beth winced in pain, losing last of million (9)
6. Pardon … stomach muscles love to be exercised (7)
8. Film crew arrived with noodles (9)
9. Greek pastry made using partially baked volcanic rock (7)
11. Check measurement of bacterial waste (9)
13. In front of ship, cavorting naked with roommate beginning when lights go out (8)
14. Extremely hungry, ate something with plain liver in it? (8)
17. Computer adding five-eighths of seventeen thousand divided by two (6)

CROSSWORD CHALLENGE – IS THIS THE WORLD'S MOST DIFFICULT CROSSWORD?

Ross Beresford of the *Times* thinks this crossword is among the hardest in the world. Puzzles like this often attract fewer than ten entries when set in public competitions, whereas a daily newspaper crossword competition commonly attracts many thousands of correct entries. If you think that this challenge crossword is not the world's hardest crossword, please send the solution to the authors (c/o Hodder Education), plus a crossword puzzle that you think is harder.

Challengers are asked to enter numbers, not letters, into the solution matrix given below. There are at least two reasons for this:

1 Firstly, this puzzle will not disadvantage readers whose first language is not English. It will be an international measure of Applied Thinking.
2 Secondly, for reason outlined at the beginning of section 2.1, numerical puzzles and thinking about them is the most rapid warm-up and myelination of the brain. The part of the brain that benefits strongly from numerical or mathematical activity is also associated with the learning of new languages, and the learning of music and musical instruments and with dance. These are all, in turn, closely correlated with expansions in cognitive capacity and in turn with its preservation and protection against the effects of degenerative brain disease.

Is this the world's hardest crossword?

1	2	3	4	5	6	7	8	9	10
11	12			13		14			
15					16		17		
18		19	20		21	22	23		24
25	26		27	28	29				
30						31			
32				33	34	35	36		37
38	39	40	41	42		43	44	45	
46				47					
48			49			50			

All you need to know is that:

▶ 1, 4, 9, 16, 25, 36 and 49 are each perfect squares.
▶ 1, 8 and 27 are each perfect cubes.
▶ 2, 3, 5, 7, 11, 13, 17, 19, 23, 29, 31, 37, 41, 43, 47 are each prime numbers.
▶ 11, 22, 33 and 44 are palindromes.
▶ 7 is less than 20 is less that 24.
▶ 7 is a factor of 14, 21 and 35.
▶ 8 is a factor of 48.
▶ 9 is a factor of 45.
▶ 11 is a factor of 44.
▶ 12 equals 8 plus 9.
▶ 15 is 10 plus 5.
▶ 16 is less than 25, is less than 36.
▶ 22 is 11 plus 11.
▶ 23 is a factor of 46.
▶ 27 is 18 plus 9.
▶ 28's digit sum is the digit's sum of 19.
▶ 28 is 7 plus three 7.
▶ 30's digit sum is the digit sum of 12.
▶ 31's digit sum is the digit sum of 13.
▶ 32 is 26 plus 6.
▶ 32's digit sum is 23.
▶ 33 equals 31 plus 2.
▶ 33's digit sum is one less that the digit sum of 16.
▶ 34's digit sum is the digit sum of 25.
▶ 35's digit sum is the digit sum of 17.
▶ 36 is 9 plus thrice 9.
▶ 38's digit sum is the digit sum of 29.
▶ 38 is less than 39 is less than 40.
▶ 41 is less than 42.
▶ 42's digit sum is less than the digit sum of 36.
▶ 46's digit sum is the digit sum of 37 (which is twice the digit sum of 23).
▶ 49 is 25 plus 24.
▶ 50's digit sum is less than the digit sum of 24.

N.B All the number entries in the matrix are different from one another. No number begins with zero.

Hint: You will often find that the answer entries to clues have similar properties to the clue number.

And to finish the Fiendish Workout …

SIX STINKERS

The six stinkers are problems that have puzzled the world's best problem-solving minds since the eighteenth century. If you cannot solve these, you are in good company, and if you can, well … respect!

Six stinkers 1: Draw two touching circles sharing the same diameter leaving space for a isosceles triangle on the diameter, whose apex also touches the outer and inner circumference of the circle (as shown). A small circle is then dropped in to touch all three shapes – the inner circle, the outer circle and the isosceles triangle at a tangent. A line is then drawn through the centre of the last dropped in circle to the point where the inner circle axis and the corner of the triangle touch. At what angle does the line hit the diameter?

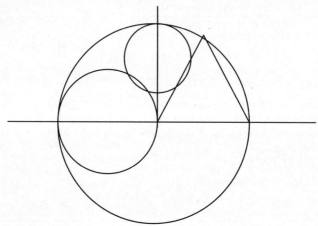

Six stinkers 2: Draw any two intersecting circles. What angle does the longest line that you can draw, which passes through a point of intersection on the circles and which cuts the circumference of both circles make with the line that joins two points of intersection of the two circles. (This line is called a common chord.)

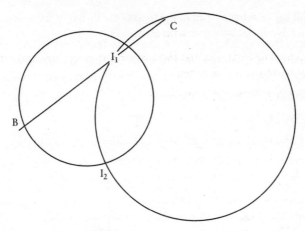

Six stinkers 3: How to fit it in

Create three identical equilateral triangles, T1, T2, T3.

T1: This triangle has the largest circle inside it you can draw, i.e. the three sides touch the circle tangentially. It also has two more circles that touch but do not intersect the triangle sides or the big inserted circle.

T2: This triangle contains three identical circles of the largest size possible. The circles touch (but do not intersect) the other circles and the walls of the triangle.

T3: This triangle contains one big circle and two small circles. All circles touch (but do not intersect) the other circles or walls of the triangle.

Which triangle, T1, T2 or T3, contains circles of the greatest area?

Six stinkers 4: Heartfelt relationships

This is an amicable puzzle.

Six stinkers 5: Are they telling the truth?

Everyone from Lieland lies. Everyone from Truthtown tells the truth. At a fork in the road, you want to know the way to Truthtown. There is a local at the crossroads. If you only had time to ask one question, what question would you ask?

Six stinkers 6: Design the shortest route

What is the shortest route that will link cities C1, C2 and C3?

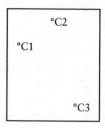

What is the shortest route that will link towns T1, T2, T3 and T4?

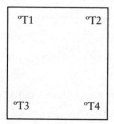

What is the shortest route that will link villages V1, V2, V3, V4 and V5?

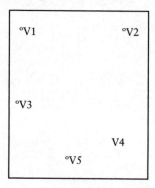

Games people play 1: Dice darts

How many different die could you make by using for each face the four orthogonally possible ways to orient the arrows? (Symmetrical duplicates don't count.)

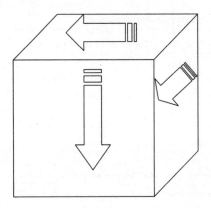

Games people play 2: How to raise money – for charity

Arrange 13 objects (stones, coins, matches) in a touching circle as shown. Two players alternate their turns at removing either a single object or two touching objects from the circle. The one who takes the last object wins the stake. You can donate your winnings! What tactic will ensure that your charity benefits?

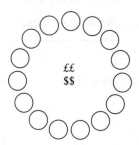

Games people play 3: Good guess chess

Place black's five pieces on the board such that the squares A7, D1 and G5 (marked X) are attacked by at least two black pieces.

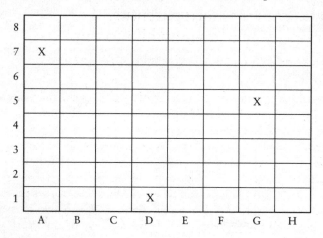

Black's five pieces are:

| Queen | King | Bishop | Knight | Rook |

Games people play 4: The last game, set and match

What shapes can you create using the fewest matches, in which every match end is touching two more match ends?

How many matches would you need if four match ends were required to meet at every match end? Does anyone know the answer to this? Answers c/o Hodder Education please!

Final thoughts

Bright from the start: parenting the brain – teaching your child to think

BANKERS ARE OFF BALANCE AND KIDS ARE ON THE STREETS

Ecologists used to talk of 'the balance of nature' – small fluctuations in one area counter-balanced by compensatory fluctuations in another. Nature has since been shown to be 'off balanced' (*New Scientist* 8 August 2011, p 2825). Economists seem not to have realized this. Bankers are still talking of the survival of the fattest – the need for big fat banks that can spread their risks in diverse ways, so that a bust in some assets can be rescued by a boom in others. If bankers used metaphoric thinking (section 2.3), they would see that these big, supposedly safe, banks are the equivalent of biological 'super spreaders' of contagious diseases. Super spreaders wreak havoc on everything they touch. Hitherto, an unhelpful separation between thinkers and doers, between ideas and actions, has led G7 bankers to talk of 'calming' markets.

Yet applied systems thinking (section 2.3) would likely say that markets are unstable systems and that tactical attempts to 'calm markets' could not have predictable consequences. What is needed here is some practical Applied Thinking.

Children need to develop Applied Thinking in which theory and practice interact to improve the other.

> *'There is nothing so practical as a good theory.'*
>
> Kurt Lewin

It was Applied Thinking that put men on the moon – that was very practical. Applied Thinking would be a more helpful approach to solving the problem of fat cat bankers and kids on the streets than a current superstitious belief in an 'invisible hand' that will 'calm the markets'.

Applied Thinking combines theory with streetwise experience, 'capta' with creativity, imagination with empathic thinking, to solve real world problems (section 1.3), make real world decisions (section 2.3) and take real world practical steps to get things done (section 3.1). Applied Thinking needs to be the basis of your child's parenting at home and their education at school. Your children need to learn to think for themselves as individuals and to learn to think for themselves as another.

THE IMPACT OF THE MIRROR NEURON

Children (and adults) have neurons in their brains called 'mirror neurons'. Mirror neurons allow you, or your child, to learn just by watching others. Mirror neurons appear to act in the same way whether you perform an act yourself, or watch someone else performing the same act, or watch a self-imagined image of yourself performing the same act. Mirror neurons connect people in pairs, and groups, and crowds and communities.

In *Keep Your Brain Sharp* (Wootton and Horne, 2010b), we reported how muscle builders could build as much muscle as others doing heavy lifting circuits, just by sitting on a couch imagining themselves doing it. The illustration below shows the results of brain scans of the progressive increase, after five days, in areas of the brain allocated to practising a piano piece for a music examination. One group did the physical piano practice for real on the piano, and they developed the areas of their brains associated with both the finger muscle flexing and the finger muscle extensions needed. The astonishing finding, as you can see, was that the corresponding brain functional areas developed by the group that only thought about practising, was just as extensive as that in the group that did the physically hard piano practice!

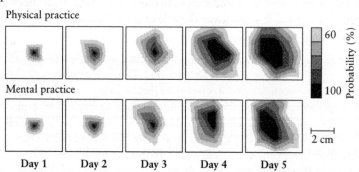

(*Adapted from data on page 29 of ID (Susan Greenfield 2008)*).

Clearly children's brains are very plastic. This makes your children very susceptible and vulnerable to what they see, how they think, and what they imagine. Knowing this, what might be the impact on their brains of digi-disease?

DIGI-DISEASE – THE DISEASE THREATENING YOUR CHILDREN

Professor Susan Greenfield is worried that your great grandchildren may never think for themselves, or of themselves, as individuals.

Your children and grandchildren already live in a swirlstream of socially networked soundbites and half-baked reactions to a flux of gossip, breaking news and senseless first impressions. They feed from a plankton stream of half truths and often do not know how to decide which half is true. Some do not even know that one half is not true, or knowing this, do not believe it matters. The only thing that often seems to matter to your children is how what they think compares with what other young people think, even when what other young people think is externally contradicted, or internally inconsistent. What choice do they have, if they are never helped to discern truth from lies or reliable from unreliable sources? They are not used to the idea of approaching truth via the distillation of thoughtful consideration. Considered opinion finds itself left beached and speechless by a fast-moving tide of audience participation. Audience participation often becomes 'truth for a day'. Your children and grandchildren are then invited to email, text or phone their instant reactions to these audience-generated half truths. Thus they feed a vortex which sucks away the role of carefully considered opinion (section 3.2).

Your children may have already been recruited as 'two-dimensional children of the screen' (Kevin Kelly, 2011). They are already donating between 6.5 and 8.5 hours of their waking hours to their screen gods. Often they are simultaneously in hock to several electronic media at a time. Clearly they will find it hard to think well about the content on any of them. In the UK, 30 per cent of 7-year-olds and 90 per cent of 11-year-olds have their own phones. 90 per cent of 9- to 19-year-olds check their screens every day. This being so, it is imperative that your child is taught how to think and to swim in this sea of data, or your child's sense of self, self-confidence and potential self-reliance will drown. An ever-streaming vortex of information may suck your child into addictive dependency.

The impact of digi-disease on your children
You do not need to wait another 20 years to find out what impact a digi world will have on the brains of your children. A small decline in overall IQ (0.8 IQ points) has already been recorded. This overall decline masks a gain in visual IQ and conceals a serious decline in numerical IQ and memory scores. These declines will have serious implications for your children's ability to learn about science and mathematics, at a time when the world is looking for a technological fix to many of its problems. More important than a decline in traditional IQ measures is diminished capacity for independent thought and learning, for curiosity, proactivity and practicality, and for empathy, thoughtfulness and consideration. If you do not protect your children from hours of passive TV, or from hours of computer games that provide high distraction and stimulation, but little empathy, and if you do not teach your children to think and consider, then you should not be surprised if they grow into adolescents and adults who are thoughtless and inconsiderate and who will perhaps be capable of acts of 'mindless violence' and 'self destruction'. More positively, your children have stronger visual IQs and better strategies for acquiring information. Susan Greenfield, however, is concerned that children are 'information rich and question poor'. By the time your children need higher education: 'answers have they many, but questions have they few' (Horne, 2003).

The impact of Internet addiction on your child's brain
Digi-disease is already producing micro-structural changes in the brains of adolescents suffering from internet addiction. Some of these changes seem to be associated with an increased incidence of autism. Neuroscientist Daphne Bavelier has reviewed evidence that links digi-disease to lack of concentration, violence and addiction in children. It is clear from her review that the digi world does not develop emotional intelligence and the capacity for empathy. Yet this book shows the important role played by Empathic Thinking in creativity and creative intelligence and in Applied Thinking generally. Children need Empathic Thinking skills in order to learn to hold conversations with others and with themselves. Empathic Thinking is central to ethical Thinking (sections 2.2 and 2.3). Social isolation and youth alienation can be the consequences of long hours spent alone with a

screen. Your children are vulnerable. Your children need to become self-reliant individuals who can think for themselves as themselves, and as another.

Children must learn to think in ways that start with questions, not information. This will help them to kick their addiction to 'data' and to operate instead with 'capta' – information that they can learn to 'capture' in relation to their 'specific' individual needs, and in relation to the 'specific' problems that they, as individuals, need to solve. Parents and teachers need to give children the skills, confidence and courage to stand out, and to stand up for those 'specific' ideas that they can learn to think out for themselves as self-reliant individuals. They need to use Applied Thinking to move competently from the general to the specific; from theoretical ideas to practical performance.

You need to parent their brains and help them to think.

Appendix 1

Answers, hints and explanations

1.2.3 REASON AND IMAGINATION – CREATIVE INTELLIGENCE

HINTS ON HOW TO THINK ABOUT THOUGHT EXPERIMENT 2
Consider the actions and attitudes of the whites in South Africa under apartheid, the middle class in the USA and Europe during the slave trade, and the attitudes and actions of men towards women before they were given the vote and equal rights.

HINTS ON HOW TO THINK ABOUT THOUGHT EXPERIMENT 3
'If I don't, someone else will' is a weak argument. Trying to minimize a gross harm is hardly better. (Remember in a thought experiment you are not allowed to think up additional options.) Sometimes there is no right way, only the least worse – damned if you do, damned if you don't. If you do the best you can (and it's still bad) should you be punished, especially when you had no choice? Can the action you do be wrong but you be blameless? Refuse to do wrong? This may preserve your honour and give you a place in heaven. Is this nobler that minimizing the suffering of this innocent woman?

HINTS ON HOW TO THINK ABOUT THOUGHT EXPERIMENT 4
If they both act in their own interests – like two tied donkeys that collaborate to eat two bales of hay that are separated by a distance greater than their shared tether – they will each be better off. Only the fear that they each have that the other might take advantage prevents them from going for the best deal for each of them. This dilemma reveals the limitations of the individual, of rational pursuit of self-interest. Trust can enable you to get more out of life. Less time, resources and anxiety are required for defensiveness and self-protection. But trust is not rational. Scepticism and distrust are based on a rational assessment of the way people behave in a modern western marriage. If you trust others you irrationally leave yourself open to exploitation. If you don't trust others, you deny yourself the possibility of what is best in life.

HINTS ON HOW TO THINK ABOUT THOUGHT EXPERIMENT 5

Not many people would return the money. You have not deliberately taken it with the intention to deprive the owner. You have been given it – unsolicited. It is a gift. No other person has been robbed. Banks are insured (so are shops for that matter, but is shoplifting acceptable?). It was a stroke of luck. If it was a small business, you would point out the error in your favour. But a big corporation? The corporation will hardly suffer, but you (and others!) will benefit greatly. Greater good and happiness result. Stealing by finding is still theft. The accidental acquisition does not excuse a deliberate decision later to keep what is not yours. How would you feel if someone accidently got your $100,000 by picking up the wrong case at an airport and did not report it?

HINTS ON HOW TO THINK ABOUT THOUGHT EXPERIMENT 6

You play while your neighbour pays. This seems unfair. But no one suffers. It is no different from benefiting from the shade of your neighbour's tree, listening to a busker in the street without putting coins into his cap, or enjoying for free a song that you would not otherwise buy. If these are crimes, they are victimless crimes. It's just give and take. However, you are all take and no give. You have no intention of returning the favour. You are a benefit scrounger. How do you feel about that? Would you get uptight about harmless squatters sharing your garden, or gypsies wild camping in your field or local park?

HINTS ON HOW TO THINK ABOUT THOUGHT EXPERIMENT 7

Do you find it hard to admit you are wrong, or at fault? Others find it hard to accept praise or appreciation. Do you hide your personal responsibility behind the advice of solicitors, parents or fellow bureaucrats or managers? Do you keep seeking advisors till you find an advisor who externally validates what you want to do? If the advice you follow is faulty, you are at fault in your choice of advisor. Should your poor judgement justifiably beget harsh judgement from the judiciary? Can you be expected to make good judgements about technical matters, like law or computing? Does ignorance mean it's not your fault?

HINTS ON HOW TO THINK ABOUT THOUGHT EXPERIMENT 8

If you stop flying, it won't stop global warming (the effect of a few flights is infinitesimal). What is needed is international action. It is needed urgently. That is why you need to fly. It is not always true that 'every little helps'. But, if everyone thought that way, charities would raise nothing and the suffering of many would go unrelieved. Telling individuals that their contribution will make a difference is often lying. Is that so wrong? Unless individuals are each made to think their contribution matters, they won't contribute as individuals and the collective project will fail with bad consequences for many. The fact that you are not doing what you ask others to do, does not mean that you do not have good enough reasons for what you ask. In this case, do as I say, not as I do, is a reasonable request, isn't it?

HINTS ON HOW TO THINK ABOUT THOUGHT EXPERIMENT 9

The Kyoto Agreement, which was not implemented, might have delayed the global warming tipping point by about six years. But the loss of wealth generation in the EU alone could have provided the rest of the world with clean drinking water. Which was preferable? (But the EU didn't do that with the money they saved, anyway). Is it right to impair present-day economic development in order to try to delay the inevitable problems of climate change and thereby leave our grandchildren with insufficient wealth and technological development to be able to repair the damage that we have in train already? That is not to say we should ignore the risks of global warming, rather that in our actions we should be simultaneously aware of the consequences of the warming and the economic capacity of our descendants to deal with those consequences. Might it be better under some circumstances to let the Earth get more polluted in the short term? What are those circumstances? The Green Party might resist your ideas, but that does not mean they should.

HINTS ON HOW TO THINK ABOUT THOUGHT EXPERIMENT 10

None of your children will get a worse phone than they would have had before the discovery of the promotional 2-for-1 offer. Two are better off. If you ignore the promotion, two of your children will be worse off. The overall average quality of the children's phones will be higher if the unequal option is pursued. It seems perverse to achieve equality by levelling down or creating equal levels of pain or deprivation. We could make everyone equal by making everyone poor or equally deprived. The poor will remain the same and everyone else will be harmed for no overall gain. When is some inequality acceptable? Even if your reasoning is logical, the perception of unequal treatment might affect the attitude, self-esteem or relationships of one or more of your children, just as it often affects social cohesion, envy and crime levels among the poor (and corruption levels, defensiveness and self-serving among the wealthy). Might not thinking about equality solely in money and material terms be a terrible mistake in groups, families and relationships?

HINTS ON HOW TO THINK ABOUT THOUGHT EXPERIMENT 11

What is lost if you betray trust? Nothing, if no one knows? Ignorance of trust leaves trust intact. No one gets hurt, so why not? Do more happiness points mean more morality, or does more misery equate to more immoral behaviour? Mutual trust is at the heart of most intimate relationships and many people can detect immediately if this has been betrayed. Can you be sure that this would not be the case for you? Some infidelities go to the grave undetected. Do you want to spend the rest of your life anxious about it, guilty even? Did you make a vow – a sacred or religious promise even – that you would never do this under any circumstances? (Even under undetectable circumstances). Does your word count for anything? Even if your partner never finds out, will you risk damage to a trust that goes deeper than detection?

HINTS ON HOW TO THINK ABOUT THOUGHT EXPERIMENT 12

Are you more like Christine than Claire? Do people describe you as good, kind and generous? The probability is that you are more like Claire. After all, you are interested in thinking. You are more likely to be thought of by others as thoughtful, considerate and reasonable. You can think, consider and reason. Wouldn't you rather be thought of as a person who thinks and who considers what to do? Your actions have more moral merit and intentions if for no other reason than they are intentional and not a spontaneous reflex, like Christine's. But if morality is doing what is right, Christine is as moral as Claire, and is warmer and more inspiring of warm feeling into the bargain. However, being less thought out and less well planned and calculated, she places her fugitives at greater risk of her mistakes. She has probably had a generous personality since she was a child. Why should someone be more praiseworthy for having the right genes? What is more moral about that? That credit might need to go to Claire, whose kind actions are the same, but which involve Claire in greater sacrifice and effort, to overcome her natural lack of empathy. Claire does not have the help of instinctive compassion or effortless altruism. When Claire decides to shelter a fugitive, it is a laudable triumph of human will over her natural inclination. Is thinking with your head more moral than responding to the promptings of your heart?

HINTS ON HOW TO THINK ABOUT THOUGHT EXPERIMENT 13

Civilized societies do not officially permit torture under any circumstances. Will you hide behind that? If so, how will you justify your decision to the relatives of the victims? Hasn't the war on terror changed civil expectations of the work of security forces? There are precedents from Guantanamo – can they help you to take this decision now? If so, how? How could you permit something much worse than 9/11, Chernobyl or Hiroshima, for the sake of torturing two innocent young girls, in front of each other and their terrorist father? How can you justify moral self-indulgence, keeping yourself pure, clean and legal, when faced with the imminent grief and suffering of the parents who will lose their children, and the children who will lose their parents? Surely a charge that you were indifferent to the lives of millions of people whom you abandoned to die would be hard for you to live with? Even though torture might be morally justifiable in the special case of this thought experiment, maybe you should still refuse to give this order because of the existence of special pleading precedents which always weaken the application of moral prohibitions. Is it not better to fail to torture when you rarely should, than to torture when you should not have? Perhaps these lines of thinking do not help when you are faced with such a clear opportunity to save the lives of millions of people.

This experiment is not about whether torture should in general be permitted. You probably hold it to be self-evident that it should not. This experiment asks you to decide with good reason that in this case, it is good to torture. Do you agree? If so, why; if not, why not? How will you dispatch the counter-arguments that will be raised at your trial?

HINTS ON HOW TO THINK ABOUT THOUGHT EXPERIMENT 14

This is a utilitarian no brainer. Of course you should nominate and benefit the great number of families in Africa. The minor cost of this great benefit is the relatively minor irritation of yourself and others at the smell of cash for honours. But this smell is and will be around anyway, whether you nominate or not. On the other hand, won't civil society collapse if agreed due processes are disregarded when it suits? A country should award its honours on the basis of merit and not wealth enough to pay. Aren't due processes and the rule of law the luxury of the well padded? Would a destitute African family understand your preoccupation with procedures? Surely rules are for the guidance of the wise and the obedience of fools when children are dying? Do you want to keep your own hands clean while many others are dying? Would your self-indulgence be moral? Might others be corrupted in this way? When net consequences are all that matter to you, can you ever hold up your head as an honest politician?

HINTS ON HOW TO THINK ABOUT THOUGHT EXPERIMENT 15
Surely liberty, freedom of thought and freedom of speech, human dignity and the right to choose are all weasel words when talked about in relation to people who have freely chosen to repeatedly steal, deceive and deprive others of their health and liberty by creating anxiety and fear of violence, rape or robbery? Don't you agree? If not, why not? Is your affront at this use of neuroscience any different from Luddite resistance to technical advances down the centuries? Surely it is no reason not to proceed in this case, which has been extensively and scientifically trialled without side-effects. Everybody wins, don't they? In-vitro fertilization was rejected when it was new. Would you want to withdraw it now? What about chemical contraception – perhaps you think that its withdrawal would harm the freedom of choice of many women? By choosing to reoffend, these criminals are knowingly choosing to risk the chemical cosh. Is this free choice fair enough? They had a choice. They have made their beds and in future will lie in them peacefully, instead of being out on the streets causing mayhem. You are giving them a second chance of having civilized values installed, after society has failed them the first time. Wasn't bromide used by the British Army in the first and second world wars to quell the sexual frustration of soldiers serving overseas?

HINTS ON HOW TO THINK ABOUT THOUGHT EXPERIMENT 16
Be aware that you can be in trouble with the international court even for suggesting that suicide bombing might, under some circumstances, be an understandable act of desperation – a last resort even. You may be instantly guilty of sponsoring or encouraging terrorism. As a terrorist suspect, many of your rights will be abrogated. A British Member of Parliament was sacked by her party for admitting that

she would be tempted to volunteer as a suicide bomber if she lived in Palestine. Why do you think suicide is so reprehensible? Surely for you to deny that you would have feelings approaching those of a suicide bomber under occupation, isn't it just denial? The Palestinians are not another race. They belong to the human race, like you, don't they? What are the implications of your mutual belonging? There is no evidence that there is something inherently more evil, or wicked, or more violent, in Palestinian genes. Wouldn't any claim to the contrary be as racist as anti-Semitic myths about centuries of malevolence on the part of all Jews. But just because something is understandable, do you think it is justified or right? And it would be nothing new – even for the British, whose Second World War RAF pilots were often as suicidal as the Kamikaze pilots from Japan. But none of this makes suicide bombing acceptable, even as a last resort – or does it? Why should different rules of law on how you treat members of the human race vary, if you change their labels from soldier to civilian or from freedom fighter to terrorist?

HINTS ON HOW TO THINK ABOUT THOUGHT EXPERIMENT 17
The dictator thought that you would take the utilitarian moral choice of reducing pain for millions of the population you are responsible for. How can you refuse? What do you imagine will be the consequences for others if you allow the dictator to pursue his final solution unhindered by you? Surely people who have lost relatives in concentration camps, or in Rwanda, would be appalled that you are even considering such appeasement. Does altruism have no place here? How can you buy peace just because the victims will be strangers to you? You will want to be careful what signals you send out. Logic seems to be if a war saves more lives than it costs then it is moral. Do you agree? If so, why? If you agree with the argument, will you accept this dictator's offer and sacrifice your neighbours? Is the principle of humane treatment not more important than numerical lives? Even if it costs more lives to end genocide than allow it, should an ongoing genocide ever be ignored? Can it ever be tolerable for you to allow wickedness and crime to go unchecked, thereby allowing states to become bases for piracy and terrorism and the streets in your town to become unsafe for your citizens? Is it not better to die a free man than to live a slave? Surely you cannot calculate what is right – more lives lost or more lives saved? Perhaps you should not, in this case, give peace a chance?

HINTS ON HOW TO THINK ABOUT THOUGHT EXPERIMENT 18

Okay, so you make a mistake, anyone can. You can be misinformed, tricked, or confused by alcohol. One way or another you can become connected to the life of another for nine months. Does your mistake give you the right to end that life? Your predicament mirrors an unplanned pregnancy. How you think about what to do about the writer has implications for how you would think about an abortion. The doctor thinks that if you disconnect at this stage, you will be guilty of murder. Is the doctor's threat to call the police the only reason you would put up with your personal discomforts and see out your time as a life support for the writer? When abortion was illegal it was still widely practised – often dangerously. If you do your own disconnection from the writer, it could be dangerous for you as well as fatal for them. The foetus is more helpless than your articulate writer who can plead with you and the doctors. Surely that is more, not less, reason why the foetus needs and deserves your protection? A pregnant mother is not so imprisoned and limited as severely as you are, so should she strive more assiduously for her baby to remain alive?

HINTS ON HOW TO THINK ABOUT THOUGHT EXPERIMENT 19

It is not clear what constitutes free speech. Surely free speech is more than being free to speak your mind to another? Isn't it also about to whom, where and when you want to speak? To anyone, wherever, whenever could imply the right to cause dangerous panic in crowded public places by shouting 'bomb' or 'gas', or 'he's got a gun', regardless of whether the speeches were true. Likewise, would you allow groundless public slander or accusations of child abuse? Are racist or sexist remarks to be tolerated? If not, does that mean you approve of censorship? How are you to draw a line? If no clear line can be drawn, then isn't absolutely free speech the only practical alternative, even if that means putting up with pranksters and rousts? Is the price of freedom the irritation of hearing lies? Is it a price worth paying? Do you agree with Voltaire that you must defend to the death the right of even your enemies to say things with which you strongly disagree? An over-simplification? After all, words are not sticks and stones that break your bones – but can they do greater damage than that, if they stir up sectarian hatreds, or riots, or civil disobedience? False accusations can ruin lives and careers. Does this bulletin represent a battle victory for you in your war for free speech? How will you know when you have won the war?

HINTS ON HOW TO THINK ABOUT THOUGHT EXPERIMENT 20

Philosopher Jeremy Bentham said that each person (whether family or not) counts for one. No person counts more than one – not even family. Is your intuition that your own greater duty is to your family members than to others? Surely you would put the welfare of your child above the welfare of other children in their class or street? Does having responsibility for the welfare of your own children mean putting that responsibility above or alongside the welfare of your neighbour's child? In a competition between your child and your neighbour's child for the last place in a good local school, would you act to favour their case unfairly? Would you use money to move house, or to rent a temporary address in the catchment area – or would you think that such family-first motivations are fair and laudable? You will probably not hesitate to turn your back on the drowning ferry passengers. Would you help your family with their homework or assessments, to give them a leg up over their classmates? Your dilemma is more acute because your family's lives are in immediate danger. You know that your partner would understand your professional and moral duty to save the crew who called you first. Does that help you in your difficult decision? Will you still put family first?

HINTS ON HOW TO THINK ABOUT THOUGHT EXPERIMENT 21

There is a difference between killing and letting die. If you could have killed your grandmother had she asked, then presumably you will have no problem ignoring the unplugged life support machine. If both actions are intended to result in Grandma's death, and you carry out either action (killing or ignoring) you are equally culpable. If you kill or let die, you incur the same moral hazard, do you not? The law is little help to you. Doctors can legally starve patients to a slow painful death, but often may not legally give an injection that would hasten a less painful death. The moral superiority of starving your grandmother is not clear. You may not want to appear to sanction deliberate killing – suppose you were to become confused by a head injury and said you wished you were dead – would you want people hearing that to be allowed deliberately to kill you? Even if this results in a few hard cases, isn't it better than opening the door to deliberate killing by doctors who are often on the payroll of the government? Would a better principle be to minimize suffering with respect for a patient's wishes? Are you going to put the plug back in now?

HINTS ON HOW TO THINK ABOUT THOUGHT EXPERIMENT 22

It will be hard for you to think your way round taboos – even when it is in the interest of you and your family to do so. Throughout the world, most people eat meat without qualms. Many eat the flesh of animals kept in cruel and filthy conditions. Many people eat pigs, which are far more intelligent and sensitive than many household pets, so why might you be reluctant to eat your dog or your horse, or your rabbit? Dogs are eaten in Asia, horses in France; rabbits are even reared for meat. So why aren't oysters and mussels more repellent to you? Perhaps you would eat jellied eel but never snake? What is your logic? Is there a moral judgement to be made, or are you willing to condemn some people to starvation rather than permit cannibalism? Is your condemnation of eating a pet or a friend anything more than a culturally conditioned reflex? If you accept that waste is immoral, then surely the case for eating corpses of humans and pets is strong? If your human is a friend, you will have first-hand information on how well your meat has been reared! Author Philip Pullman says that his younger readers have no problem with his characters eating each other, so why should you?

1.3.2 MENTAL CIRCUITS AND PHYSICAL EXERCISES

Mental gymnasium – warm-ups

HINTS FOR HEAVY LIFT 1

Try to think about travelling back to a date before you were born – how could you stand there? Think of a drug that could slow down your metabolism, for example to one heartbeat a week – how fast would the world travel around you? How would that affect you? Einstein correctly predicted that if you travel in a world that is moving close to the speed of light, your watch will slow down! When you get writer's block writing your autobiography, can you fly ahead to a day when it is published and you can plagiarize it to unblock your writer's block? Can Terminator 11 get built as a result of a future nuclear holocaust and then come back to prevent the nuclear holocaust from happening? May be there are parallel universes.

HINTS FOR HEAVY LIFT 2

According to philosopher Rene Descartes (1596–1650), your conscious experience is all in your mind – an entity separate from your body and brain. Few neuroscientists would agree with Descartes. In her BBC series 'Brain Story', Professor Susan Greenfield insisted that 'you are your brain'. Your conscious experience is not something extra. The mental is chemical – neurochemical.

1.3.3 PARADOXICAL PUZZLES AND DEVILISH DILEMMAS

P1: In the sixth triangle from left on the bottom row.

P2: Insert a circle.

P3: 2

P4: B = 16, G = 18

P5: E is the odd one out.

P6: 15 minutes and 52 seconds past 10 p.m. (22:15:52).

P7: G = 10, P = 8, O = 9, R + 7, ? = 34

P8: Pick up the three sides of triangle A and use them to build a triangle whose base is the top of triangles B and C.

P9: 10

P10: 28

P11: 91

P12: One ton (100)

P13: 49

P14: From top to bottom, octagon–hexagon–pentagon–triangle.

P15: 224

P16: 64

P17: C

P18: 288

P19: O

P20: 7

P21: 3

P22: X is in the top left corner.

P23: 458

P24: A

P25: 6 o'clock

P26: 16

P27: 7

P28: 480

P29: 12

P30: 4 = A, 3 = B

Philosophical problems and moral dilemmas – thorns in your brain
Open the Box: If you savour the question and allow your mind to muse, you may find distinctions to be made and caveats that help you to think ethically. Is it right to try to gain something for no effort? To gamble for gain? Thinking empathically, is it likely that the keeper (who knows which box contains the key), would have offered to open another box for you, unless the keeper knew that it was in that box? If you take this cynical view of the keeper, you would never swap.

Thinking verbally, does the title 'keeper' imply a duty to protect, preserve and indeed 'keep' the treasure? Might the keeper be a gamekeeper? Assuming you could discern, with some certainty, the gender of the keeper, would it affect your judgement if you thought the keeper was a man, or a woman? In what way, and why? Do you believe in altruism, or evolutionary Darwinism? Thinking reflectively, could even altruism have survival value in a battle for survival? Thinking critically and self critically, watch out for your own slippery sleights of mind (and those of your authors, who may sometimes exaggerate to illustrate, pretending perhaps to more conviction than they feel!)

2.1.1 SOME DIAGNOSTIC QUESTIONS

Diagnostic test
A1: 80 per cent chance, i.e. 8 times out of 10, you will end up in the canal and likely drown! The chances for your brother are the same.

A2: 5 metres by 5 metres.

A3: Divide 1 by the number.

A4: No, because 7 is a multiple (×23).

A5: (a) the population

A6: Greater (521×370)

A7: More. Pythagoras' theorem states that if you square the two shorter sides in a right-angled triangle and add them together, you get the same as when you square the longest side (the hypotenuse). In the triangle below, **a** and **b** are the two shorter sides and **c** is the hypotenuse, so if we square **a** and **b** and add them together ($a^2 + b^2$) we *should* get the same as if we square c (c^2). Therefore, $a^2 + b^2 = c^2$.

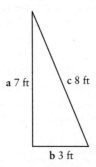

a 7 ft   c 8 ft

b 3 ft

However, in the question, as the wall is **a** and ladder is **c**, a = 49, by calculation the ladder must be above the 7ft wall (i.e. higher, for example, 8 × 8 = 64).

A8: (b) the weight

A9: Time of take off, plus time taken to check in.

A10: 92 canisters

A11: 648 (3×6×6×6)

A12: (e) trapezium

A13: 4b+2d+2e

A14: £50 (Original price is £62.50 minus (50 + 10 + 20)% = sale price)

A15: 1 in 9 (number of possible face combinations is 6×6=36, of which only (1,4), (4,1), (2,3), (3,2) = 5 which = 4/36 or 1 in 9.

A16: 300

A17: 69 (3×23)

A18: 450ml (3/5×750)

2.1.2 THE MENSA CHALLENGE

M19: 61

M20: The three rules are that:

B + C must = E

E − 6 must = D

D + C must = F

The missing number is 12.

M21:

16	18	08	08	02
18	02	14	04	14
08	14	10	06	06
08	04	06	00	12
02	14	06	12	04

M22: In the row next to the trees – one pace in from your right. It is marked 3S.

M23: You can use 10, 16 or 22.

24	6	24	6	20
12	20	22	22	4
22	28	16	4	10
10	10	10	12	38
12	16	8	36	8

M24: Trial and error!

M25: 30

M26: 6 (top + bottom = middle)

M27: 8 (top – bottom = middle)

M28: One solution is each segment totalling 18, each circle totalling 48. For example:

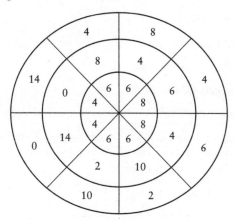

2.1.3 WORKOUT: NUMERICAL THINKING

D29: A=4 and B=304 (separate the digits to discern the series)

D30: 808 (multiply the digit pairs to obtain digit pairs in the next series)

D31: 8×22=176 (centre number ÷ number of sides = bottom)

D32: A=62 ((5×12)+2), B=52 ((5×10)+2), and C=72 ((14×5)+2)

D33: A=0, B=8 (alternate pairs form to intermeshed ascending series; one series ascends in intervals of 2, the other in intervals of 3).

D34: A=2, B=4 (A=Product of tops, B=A×A)

D35: V+30V + 5V +120V = £624. Therefore the valise is worth £4 and the chess set 30×4 = £120.

D36: 16 ((8+22+18) – (14+6+12))

D37: 8 (top left = sum of bottom two squares, Top right = dividend of bottom two squares, etc.)

D38: Blue (the position numbers correspond to the position of the colours in the rainbow spectrum).

D39: 204 (8×8+7×7+6×6+5×5+4×4+3×3+2×2+1×1)

D40: 2 minutes

D41: 6 (start at the top and then keep working left to right down the rows, entering the numbers 63610 in rotation).

D42: 42 (7×6)

D43: 5/18ths (i.e. 18/72)

D44: Only products weighing 10 kg cannot be weighed

D45: 5×16 = 80−9 = 71+19 = 90

D46: 2 twos inserted (22÷22 = 1)

D47: 40 (after any multiples of six moves the original status is restored).

D48: 8 hours, 19 minutes and 52 seconds (ignore the seconds, the hour will be 5+3=8, and the minutes 50+30=20 minus 3½ × 14 + 6 seconds gives the corrected answer).

D49: 3×3=9 × $\sqrt{169}$ = 9×13 = 117

D50: 3/10 × 2/9 = 1 in 15

D51: The northbound trains are time tabled one minute earlier than the southbound trains.

D52: Y (25th letter of alphabet (76=A(1) + E(5) + I(9) + O(15) + U (21) +Y(25) = 76

D53: 222 (sum of the primes is 7+31+23=61 plus sum of the squares = 81+64+36) so 61+181 = 242

D54: 527 (rewrite series as pairs of digits to give ascended series)

D55: 6 clubs (D+2/D + D/2 + 7 − D/2 = 13 (a dealt bridge hand) where D is number of diamonds. Therefore D = 2 therefore S = 1, therefore C = 7−1 = 6)

D56: 12.6 ((7×2×9) ÷ (4+6) = 12.6

D57: 3 and 64 (top row numbers are all odd, bottom row numbers are all even)

D58: Their combined age in one year will be 50 (which is half 100).

D59: 17 squares

D60: Start in bottom left square (number = number squares to move, U = Up, etc.).

D61: 73, TX

D62: 14 (12×4 + 16×2 = 12×2 + 14×4)

D63: One chance in 110 apples (10/100 × 9/99 = 1/110)

D64: 6 (same shapes total 14)

D65: 6

D66: 48 (series ascends omitting primes)

D67: 121 (series alternates ×2 with +1, +2, +3, +4, etc.)

D68: John

D69: 100ml (100×115/100 = 115ml)

D70: 132,600 (52×51×50)

D71: 33 (you cannot have a fraction of a pot)

D72: 8 (all rows total 16)

D73: 55 mph (next milometer palindrome is 16061)

D74: 1 hour (80 miles at 80 mph = same time as friend's 120 miles at 120 mph)

D75: 40 (number of lines ×5)

D76: What is the sum of the products of the terminal numbers at the ends of each of the four lines?

D77: 128976.73 (5×1/3×3/5 = 1)

D78: $61 (1+1+2+1 = you began last day with $5 etc)

D79: 5 minutes to fill and maximum of 40 minutes in the bath.

D80: 33 (1+7+1+6+1+5+1+4+1+3+1+2)

D81:

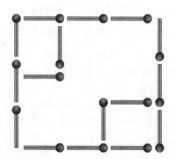

D82:

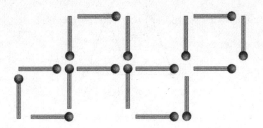

D83:

D84:

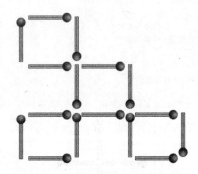

D85:

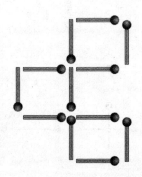

D86:

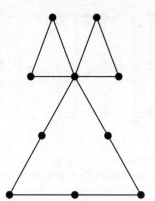

D87:

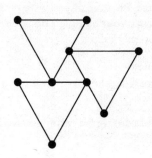

D88:

D89:

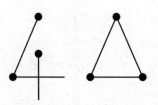

D90:

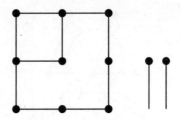

2.2.3 WORKOUT: LATERAL THINKING

Answer to 'Name a vegetable': When tested like this 98 per cent of people give carrot as the name of the vegetable they thought of – did you? Do not be surprised. The tasks you were given take you round your brain in a predetermined way that leads 98 per cent of people to the same predetermined outcome. If you were part of the normal 98 per cent you can improve your ability to think outside the box. You can become a more lateral thinker.

Lateral training workshop
LT1: None of them are what they say they are, e.g. a Koala bear is not a bear.

LT2: They were a band paid by the casino to provide background music for the gamblers.

LT3: Apollo 11. Sea of Tranquillity.

LT4: The tomatoes were still in the tin.

LT5: Task 1

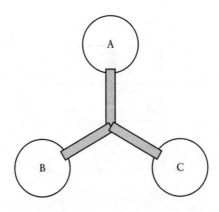

LT5: Task 2

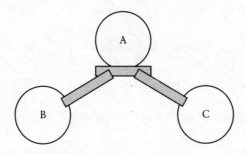

LT6:

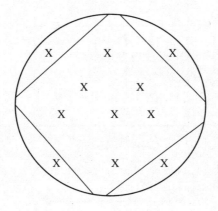

There may be other ways.

LT7:

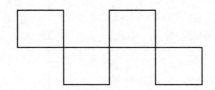

LT8:

LT9: She sawed the table (as in A below) and cut out the hole (if you do this with paper/card you can see this more easily!) She then glued the two pieces back together and covered the table top in dark wax to hide the join (as in B below).

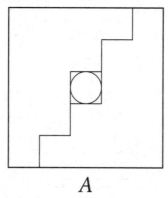

A

She then glued the two pieces back together and covered table top in dark wax to hide the join (B).

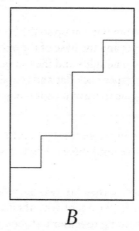

B

LT10: Prince Masoky said to Princess Sadie, 'You will feed me to your lions.' Princess Sadie is still, to this day, trying to decide what she should do next!

LT11:

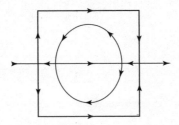

LT12:

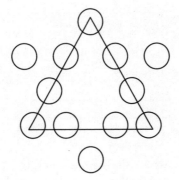

LT13: 128 / 64 / 16 / 4 / 2 / 1

LT14: Fold the paper from bottom up so the bottom edge is tangential to the noughts and the base of the one. Draw down the one and loop the two noughts and the top outer circumference in one sweep. Fold the paper back flat and complete the outer circumference of the circle to leave it containing the 100 speed limit.

LT15: Give the strip a single twist and join the ends. You can now keep drawing on one side until there is a line down through the centre of both sides.

LT16: Lay one coin down, then lay two more on top touching each other. Arrange two more like a tent with their bases touching the three base coins and leaning together to touch at their top edges.

LT17:

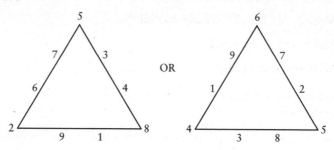

LT18: Tie using a shoelace bow. When cutting twice, cut each loop. The cup will stay put.

LT19:

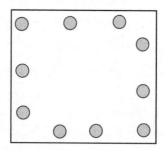

LT20: Crush the cloth into the bottom of the glass. Invert and check it does not fall out. Plunge the glass under the water, open side down. Air will protect the cloth.

LT21: Just one word

3.1.3 MATCH YOUR MIND AGAINST MENSA

The 'Match Your Mind' against Mensa challenge
MM1: Henry (Ford)

MM2: Fluffful

MM3: Time limit. Goals

MM4: Column A is made from anagrams of capital cities.

MM5: Column A words transform by prefixing man ...

MM6: Column A words can retain their meaning when G is replaced with C.

MM7: Q – chess pieces in ascending value.

MM8: e.g. add R and L to make accrual.

MM9: Pro pane (Propane)

MM10: Formaldehydes

Ten cunning conundrums
CC1: Saturday

CC2: 18 days (on this day, it is out and therefore cannot slide backwards)

CC3: T (the initial letter of 10 – it is a series of integers)

CC4: £5

CC5: 45 miles (the fly is flying at one mile per minute)

CC6: Point the Lancaster sign towards the back of your car.

CC7: There is no difference to account for.

CC8: Small, obviously, but give yourself a tick if you wrote, e.g. milli (metre) etc.

CC9: You don't bury survivors

CC10: Halfway (after that it will be coming out).

20 analytic analogies
AA1: Any fruit that grows in trees, e.g. peaches, pears.

AA2: Any Portuguese speaking ex-colonial country, e.g Brazil.

AA3: $32°$ (freezing point on the Fahrenheit scale).

AA4: Warts (word made by reversing letter order).

AA5: 125 ($2×2×2 = 8$, $5×5×5 = 125$)

AA6: C (A and E are the first two vowels, B and C are the first two consonants).

AA7: Dog

AA8: Potter

AA9: Istanbul

AA10: Galaxy (second word refers to larger grouping of first).

AA11: Any plant in the same family as crocus (e.g. lily).

AA12: Roosevelt (he preceded Truman as US President).

AA13: Brain (broca is part of the brain).

AA14: US (Liederkranz is an American cheese).

AA15: Anna (the word reversed).

AA16: Potatoes

AA17: Pod (this is the collective noun, but it can also be school or herd).

AA18: Africa (the southern Capes of each).

AA19: Unorthodox (or heterodox).

AA20: Fraudulent

3.3.1 WARM-UPS

Triangular warm-ups

FW1: 28. Obviously (6+4+18=28), the rest are less obvious unless you are a genius in progress.

FW2: 26 (6+4+16)

FW3: 18 (add corresponding corners and put in centre).

FW4: N (completing the name Mark Twain, read anticlockwise).

FW5: A (the initial and name of Albert Einstein read clockwise).

Circular warm-ups

FW6: 20 (add outer numbers and place sum in next but one segment).

FW7: 12 (8+2+2. Add all outer digits in segment individually, and place in centre of same segment).

Lateral warm-ups

FW8: They recognized each others' habits – monks' habits. Their new father – the Abbot – will take them to their new monastery.

FW9: Grandma has died. The electric clock was on the same circuit as her life support machine.

FW10: The ball was a snowball. By the time they get home, the central heating has dried the water from the melted snow.

FW11: The car's handbrake had not been secure when the driver parked it at the top of the hill. He had scrambled down to retrieve his briefcase from the back seat.

FW12: Serial (an anagram of Israel – 'pains' is an anagram of Spain, and 'a go' is an anagram of Goa).

FW13: Holes.

Pyramid warm-ups
FW14: P (moving on two positions in the English alphabet each time).

FW15: H (in numerical sequence shown go through English alphabet skipping four letters each time. Start with E, go clockwise and back across the centres).

FW16: I (working triangles from left to right, go clockwise and to the centre round each triangle in turn, skipping two letters).

FW17: W (the initial of William Shakespeare seen by proceeding clockwise to centre of each triangle, moving from left to right).

FW18: C (the Roman numeral letters in sequence, spiral each triangle anticlockwise moving left to right).

Four square warm-ups
FW19: 21 (top left × top left + bottom left – top right – bottom right).

FW20: 14 (sum of diagonals square – sum of diagonals square).

FW21: 14 (add three corners clockwise from left, minus remaining corner)

FW22: 31 (from top left clockwise: square of first – square of second + square of third – fourth and put result in next square but one, left to right).

FW23: Spades £300, Clubs £400, Hearts £700, Diamonds £100.

Four-star warm-ups
FW24: N (for Nixon – anticlockwise sequence is Carter, Reagan, Bush, Clinton, Bush), Nixon.

FW25: L for Lenin (Stalin, Khrushchev, Brezhnev).

FW26: A (the second letter in Saturday; O is the second letter in Monday, U is the second letter in Tuesday, etc).

FW27: M for megabyte (they are all units of computing).

FW28: R (last letters of alternate months of the year).

FW29: R (the last letter of Jupiter; the rest are the last letters of planets in our solar system).

3.3.2 HEAVY LATERAL LIFTS

FW30: The clean-faced friend saw his friend's dirty face and assumed his own must be dirty too. His dirty-faced friend had seen his friend's clean face and was thereby not alerted that his own might be dirty.

FW31: One child had 10 coins of value 25 units each. The next child had 16 coins of value 10 units each, and the third child had 26 coins of value 5 units each.

FW32: When 13 (8+5) is the time on a 24-hour clock.

FW33: The judge decreed that the proceeds of the widow's estate be put in trust for the benefit of the family and that the trustees issue a cheque to the total value of the estate payable to the widow. The cheque was cremated with her.

FW34: Put your family at positions 1, 2, 3, 4, 10, 11, 13, 14, 15, 17, 20, 21, 25, 28, 29

FW35: You will receive £330.

FW36: They were the bodies of the two tropical fish.

FW37: The exploring couple were astronauts and so they couldn't light a fire as there is no oxygen to burn in space.

FW38: The other twin is a girl. He was the only male child (constitutionally the king must be the oldest male).

FW39: The factory was located on the west coast.

FW40: Mr Drake was a duck and his mates were all ducks and his party was a flight of migrating ducks that flew over a UK airport as the plane was taking off. Many of Drake's mates died in the bird strike, which disabled two of the jet engines on the plane.

FW41: Jean was the French son of the newly appointed French Ambassador to the USA. At the point the family moved him from Paris to Washington, Jean spoke only French.

FW42: It took 50 per cent longer than he expected, i.e. three minutes, instead of two – with 500 students jeering. In the one-hole case, the rate of running out of oil was 15 globes an hour (a globe is four minutes). In the two-hole case, the running out of oil is initially twice as fast, i.e. 30 globes an hour = 1 minute for half a globe, after which the oil is only running out of one hole, at a rate of 15 globes an hour, so it takes a further two minutes to empty the remaining half globe: 1+2=3 minutes altogether.

FW43: The walkers complained about being asked to pay to cross the field, by the field's owner, Mr Bull.

FW44: Bill was a lighthouse keeper. His fog alarm was faulty.

FW45: She was picked out of the water by a helicopter water scoop that was used to put out the fire but the fall from the sky killed the scuba diver.

FW46: Joan is the teacher.

3.3.3 SUDOKU, LADDERS, PROPELLERS – AND THE WORLD'S HARDEST CROSSWORD?

SUDOKU 1

9	8	6	7	2	5	3	4	1
5	1	3	4	9	6	8	7	2
7	2	4	1	3	8	5	9	6
2	9	7	5	4	3	6	1	8
4	5	8	6	7	1	2	3	9
6	3	1	9	8	2	4	5	7
3	7	9	8	6	4	1	2	5
8	4	5	2	1	9	7	6	3
1	6	2	3	5	7	9	8	4

SUDOKU 2

6	8	3	7	2	1	9	5	4
5	7	4	3	9	8	2	6	1
2	1	9	5	6	4	3	8	7
4	2	8	6	5	9	1	7	3
1	6	7	8	4	3	5	2	9
3	9	5	2	1	7	8	4	6
9	5	2	4	3	6	7	1	8
8	4	1	9	7	2	6	3	5
7	3	6	1	8	5	4	9	2

SUDOKU 3

5	2	4	7	9	8	3	1	6
6	3	1	5	2	4	9	8	7
9	8	7	3	6	1	4	5	2
8	7	9	2	1	5	6	4	3
4	5	6	9	7	3	8	2	1
3	1	2	8	4	6	7	9	5
2	6	3	4	5	9	1	7	8
7	9	8	1	3	2	5	6	4
1	4	5	6	8	7	2	3	9

SUDOKU 4

8	1	5	6	4	9	3	7	2
9	2	3	8	7	1	5	6	4
6	7	4	5	2	3	8	1	9
1	4	8	9	6	7	2	3	5
5	3	9	4	1	2	7	8	6
2	6	7	3	8	5	9	4	1
7	5	1	2	3	4	6	9	8
3	8	2	1	9	6	4	5	7
4	9	6	7	5	8	1	2	3

SUDOKU 5

7	2	6	4	9	8	1	3	5
9	5	3	6	2	1	4	7	8
4	1	8	3	5	7	9	6	2
1	8	9	7	4	2	3	5	6
5	3	4	8	1	6	7	2	9
6	7	2	5	3	9	8	4	1
2	6	7	1	8	4	5	9	3
3	9	1	2	7	5	6	8	4
8	4	5	9	6	3	2	1	7

SUDOKU 6

6	8	2	1	5	9	7	3	4
5	7	3	4	8	6	9	1	2
4	1	9	7	3	2	5	6	8
3	2	7	9	1	4	8	5	6
8	9	6	5	2	3	1	4	7
1	5	4	6	7	8	3	2	9
9	6	5	8	4	1	2	7	3
7	3	8	2	6	5	4	9	1
2	4	1	3	9	7	6	8	5

SUDOKU 7

4	5	8	3	2	9	1	7	6
9	1	2	7	6	5	8	4	3
3	6	7	4	1	8	9	2	5
2	3	9	8	7	4	5	6	1
6	7	4	5	9	1	2	3	8
5	8	1	2	3	6	7	9	4
1	4	3	9	5	2	6	8	7
7	2	6	1	8	3	4	5	9
8	9	5	6	4	7	3	1	2

SUDOKU 8

4	2	3	7	9	6	8	5	1
5	1	9	3	4	8	2	7	6
6	7	8	2	1	5	4	9	3
9	8	6	4	5	3	7	1	2
7	3	4	1	2	9	5	6	8
2	5	1	8	6	7	3	4	9
3	9	7	6	8	4	1	2	5
1	4	5	9	3	2	6	8	7
8	6	2	5	7	1	9	3	4

SUDOKU 9

5	6	9	8	1	4	7	3	2
8	1	3	2	7	9	6	4	5
2	7	4	6	5	3	8	9	1
9	2	8	3	6	1	5	7	4
3	4	6	7	8	5	1	2	9
1	5	7	9	4	2	3	6	8
6	8	2	1	9	7	4	5	3
4	9	1	5	3	6	2	8	7
7	3	5	4	2	8	9	1	6

Numerical ladders

Numerical ladder 1

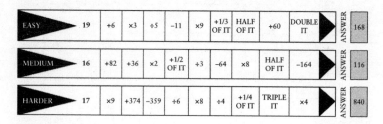

											ANSWER
EASY	36	+3/4 OF IT	÷9	×5	DOUBLE IT	+14	÷7	×4	-1/4 OF IT	TRIPLE IT	108
MEDIUM	28	÷7	CUBE IT	+3/8 OF IT	×2	+32	-1/4 OF IT	TRIPLE IT	-3/4 OF IT	+87	204
HARDER	333	+10	÷49	×16	-3/4 OF IT	-3/7 OF IT	×15	+7/10 OF IT	DOUBLE IT	÷8	102

Numerical ladder 2

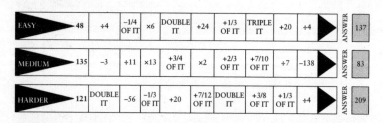

											ANSWER
EASY	19	+6	×3	÷5	-11	×9	+1/3 OF IT	HALF OF IT	+60	DOUBLE IT	168
MEDIUM	16	+82	+36	×2	+1/2 OF IT	÷3	-64	×8	HALF OF IT	-164	116
HARDER	17	×9	+374	-359	÷6	×8	÷4	+1/4 OF IT	TRIPLE IT	×4	840

Numerical ladder 3

											ANSWER
EASY	48	÷4	-1/4 OF IT	×6	DOUBLE IT	+24	+1/3 OF IT	TRIPLE IT	+20	÷4	137
MEDIUM	135	-3	÷11	×13	+3/4 OF IT	×2	+2/3 OF IT	+7/10 OF IT	÷7	-138	83
HARDER	121	DOUBLE IT	-56	-1/3 OF IT	+20	+7/12 OF IT	DOUBLE IT	+3/8 OF IT	+1/3 OF IT	÷4	209

Numerical ladder 4

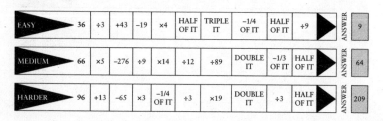

											ANSWER
EASY	36	÷3	+43	-19	×4	HALF OF IT	TRIPLE IT	-1/4 OF IT	HALF OF IT	÷9	9
MEDIUM	66	×5	-276	÷9	×14	÷12	÷89	DOUBLE IT	-1/3 OF IT	HALF OF IT	64
HARDER	96	+13	-65	×3	-1/4 OF IT	÷3	×19	DOUBLE IT	÷3	HALF OF IT	209

Numerical ladder 5

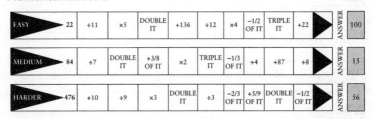

										ANSWER
EASY 22	÷11	×5	DOUBLE IT	+136	÷12	×4	-1/2 OF IT	TRIPLE IT	+22	100
MEDIUM 84	÷7	DOUBLE IT	+3/8 OF IT	×2	TRIPLE IT	-1/3 OF IT	÷4	+87	÷8	15
HARDER 476	+10	÷9	×3	DOUBLE IT	÷3	-2/3 OF IT	+5/9 OF IT	DOUBLE IT	-1/2 OF IT	56

Numerical ladder 6

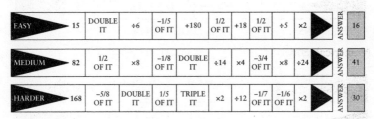

										ANSWER
EASY 22	÷11	×5	DOUBLE IT	+136	÷12	×4	-1/2 OF IT	TRIPLE IT	+22	100
MEDIUM 84	÷7	DOUBLE IT	+3/8 OF IT	×2	TRIPLE IT	-1/3 OF IT	÷4	+87	÷8	15
HARDER 476	+10	÷9	×3	DOUBLE IT	÷3	-2/3 OF IT	+5/9 OF IT	DOUBLE IT	-1/2 OF IT	56

Numerical ladder 7

										ANSWER
EASY 15	DOUBLE IT	÷6	-1/5 OF IT	+180	1/2 OF IT	+18	1/2 OF IT	÷5	×2	16
MEDIUM 82	1/2 OF IT	×8	-1/8 OF IT	DOUBLE IT	÷14	×4	-3/4 OF IT	×8	÷24	41
HARDER 168	-5/8 OF IT	DOUBLE IT	1/5 OF IT	TRIPLE IT	×2	÷12	-1/7 OF IT	-1/6 OF IT	×2	30

Numerical ladder 8

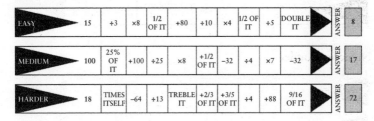

										ANSWER
EASY 15	÷3	×8	1/2 OF IT	+80	÷10	×4	1/2 OF IT	÷5	DOUBLE IT	8
MEDIUM 100	25% OF IT	+100	÷25	×8	+1/2 OF IT	-32	÷4	×7	-32	17
HARDER 18	TIMES ITSELF	-64	÷13	TREBLE IT	+2/3 OF IT	+3/5 OF IT	÷4	+88	9/16 OF IT	72

Propellers

Propeller 1: $(95 + 30) \times (16 \times 10) \div 5 \div 4$

Propeller 2: $(85 - 25) \times 3 + (15 - 2) - 7$

Propeller 3: $(70 + 16) \times 5 - 35 + 8 + 1$

Propeller 4: $4 \times (90 + 9) + 40 - (13 \times 5)$

Propeller 5: $(65 \times 10) + 20 + (19 \times 1) - 8$

Propeller 6: $(75 + 25 + 17) \times 4 + 8 - 2$

Propeller 7: $(35 \times 16) - (75 \times 1) + (7 \times 10)$

Propeller 8: $(75 + 30) \times 4 + 12 - (10 \times 5)$

Cryptic crosswords
CROSSWORD 1

Across	**Down**
3. STAMINA	1. HARD SELL
6. REDDENS	2. DARKROOM
8. LOOKOUTS	4. RABBIT PUNCH
10. DECIMAL	5. BALMORAL
11. INFIDEL	7. SCRATCH
13. NARRATIVE	9. SPOTLESS
14. HEATHEN	12. EMANATE
15. PALENESS	16. EPIC
17. ADVISE	
18. JEWELLER	

CROSSWORD 2

Across	Down
1. DARWIN	1. DELVES
3. ENDURANCE	2. IDEAL
6. MEDWAY	4. TROJAN HORSE
8. RESERVES	5. PLIGHT
9. PASSING	6. MARCHING ORDERS
10. TRIDENT	7. ABRUPT
12. G-STRING	11. NIGHTCAP
13. COUPON	14. SHIFT
15. ALIKE	
16. INTER	
17. COME CLEAN	
18. STIPEND	

CROSSWORD 3

Across	Down
2. LUCK	1. SUNLIGHT
5. CONQUER	3. COMMERCE
6. WAGGLE	4. TRANSEPT
7. LIONESS	8. SLIPSTREAM
11. IRRELEVANT	9. RAKISH
15. ROUBLE	10. STANCE
16. ADVERTISE	12. SCAB
18. LIAISE	13. TAVERN
19. TANGIERS	14. LOSING
20. SLOVENIA	17. EXTRA

CROSSWORD 4

Across

2. AWARDING
6. UNFINISHED
7. DEFENDER
12. ASTRIDE
15. CALCULUS
16. ABLUTION
17. SPREE

Down

1. GALLOP
3. ASUNDER
4. CZECH
5. HIERARCHIC
8. DESPERADO
9. HALLOWEEN
10. BACILLOSIS
11. FANTASTIC
13. BEDLAM
14. DALLAS

CROSSWORD 5

Across

1. RANKLE
5. CAPSULAR
10. EXHILARATE
12. ELEPHANT
13. RINGGIT
16. SPITTOON
17. HEEL
18. TURNSTONE
19. SCIMITAR

Down

2. AMAZED
3. SPIKED
4. ORIGINAL
6. DINGBAT
7. GANDER
8. DERANGED
9. VICTORIA
11. SONGSTRESS
12. EMBOSS
14. FACTOTUM
15. MULLET

CROSSWORD 6

Across	Down
3. GREAT UNCLE	1. NEVER
5. TEABAG	2. MACAROON
6. SUPPLY	4. AQUILEGIA
8. LULLABY	7. TIGHT
9. BONFIRE	11. PRUDISH
10. GAPE	13. ITEM
12. DIVINE	14. EFFECTS
16. EPOCH	15. RESTRAIN
18. ASTI	17. JAGGED
19. WHIST	
20. FOREIGNER	

CROSSWORD 7

Across	Down
3. AMASS	1. SAUSAGE
6. DONATION	2. CANASTA
7. CIRCA	4. SCOTCH
10. TURGENEV	5. INFER
11. UMPIRE	8. CAMUS
17. ARTFUL	9. HARDBALL
18. INCITING	12. TACTICIAN
19. MAGNOLIA	13. INFIDEL
20. TYPE	14. ADAMANT
	15. CRUCIAL
	16. PERFIDY

CROSSWORD 8

Across

2. OBSCURE
4. VARSITY
6. ZEALOTS
8. YEMEN
10. ROUGHAGE
12. SALAD
15. NUMERALS
16. PUPPIES
18. TONGUES
19. WRITING
20. QUICKSAND

Down

1. TAPERING
3. UGLINESS
5. TORTOISE
7. TWEEZERS
9. WANDERLUST
11. PACIFISTS
13. RUSTLER
14. SYNOPSIS
17. TUBA

CROSSWORD 9

Across

1. DEMONSTRATE
5. EMULATE
7. ICICLE
10. ELATION
12. ADHERED
15. GALLON
16. BEGGAR
18. GANDERS
19. ENDORPHIN

Down

1. DELIVERY
2. ACCENT
3. FEATHERWEIGHT
4. BEWITCHED
6. ABSOLVE
8. CAMERAMEN
9. BAKLAVA
11. CALIBRATE
13. DARKNESS
14. FAMISHED
17. HALVED

Six stinkers

SS1: Angle is always 90°. But can you prove it?

SS2: The angle between the longest line and the intersecting chord will always be 90°. You can show this in any case by drawing it and using cotton and pins, but can you prove that it will always be true?

If you make a triangle between the second point of circular intersection and the points where the lines cut the circle circumferences, then when the required line is longest, the other two sides of the triangle will pass through the centres of their respective circles. Does it help you to know this?

SS3: T1 (for proof look up Gian Malfatti, an Italian mathematician in the early eighteenth century).

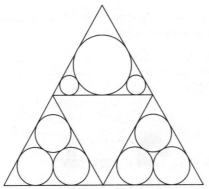

SS4: If you take all the numbers that will divide into 220 and add them together, you get 284 (1, 2, 4, 5, 10, 11, 20, 22, 44, 55,110). You can do the same for 284 and these add together to make 220! These two numbers are called amicable numbers. 220 and 284 are the smallest known pair. The number of amicable pairs found to date is around 5,000. The second smallest pair was discovered by a 12-year-old schoolboy in around 1860. Can you find them? (They are each less than 1500.)

SS5: 'Which is the way to your hometown?' (Think about it!)

SS6: According to Nick Baxter, the shortest route design has no curves or closed loops – only straight line roads with branch points. Each branch leaves a trunk road, or other branch, at angles of 120°.

For example:

Games people might play

GPP1: 192 after eliminating symmetries (there are 4×4×4×4×4×4= 4096 including all the symmetries).

GPP2: If the first player takes 1, you take 1, if he takes 2, you take 1, keep the arrangement on the table symmetrical about an imaginary line drawn through the centre of the circle.

GPP3:

B5   C3   D8

E3   G7

GGP4: For a four match end meeting, 104 matches meeting at 52 points would be required (Yoshigahara). No one has solved the five match ends meeting problem – can you?

For a three match end meeting, a triangular pyramid with six matches would do, with six matches meeting at four points, or you could use 12 matches to create a cube with eight meeting points:

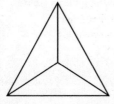 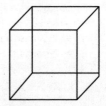

Appendix 2

Do you think like a man (TMB) or like a woman (TFB)?

Men score		Women score
	1. At the end of hard day you prefer to:	
3	▶ Talk to someone about your day	4
2	▶ Listen to other people talking	2
0	▶ Not talk at all	0
2	▶ None of the above	2
Men score	2. Thinking about your spelling and writing:	Women score
3	▶ You find both easy	4
2	▶ One is okay but not the other	2
0	▶ Both are weak	0
2	▶ None of the above	2
Men score	3. In arguments you are most upset by:	Women score
3	▶ A lack of response, silence or sulks	4
2	▶ A refusal to agree with you	2
0	▶ Being contradicted or questioned	0
2	▶ None of the above	2
Men score	4. On the question of routines, you prefer to do things:	Women score
3	▶ Whenever you feel like it	4
2	▶ According to a general but flexible plan	2
0	▶ About the same time every day	0
2	▶ None of the above	2
Men score	5. When shopping you tend to:	Women score
3	▶ Buy special offers, frequently, on impulse	4
2	▶ Sometimes buy, sometimes don't	2
0	▶ Purchase only what you went for	0
2	▶ None of the above	2

Men score	6. You prefer to read:	Women score
3	▶ Fiction	4
2	▶ Newspapers or general magazines	2
0	▶ Specialist magazines or non-fictional information	⓪
2	▶ None of the above	2

Men score	7. You prefer to work:	Women score
3	▶ With a group of people you like	4
2	▶ On your own task but in the company of others	2
0	▶ In solitude	⓪
2	▶ None of the above	2

Men score	8. A friend has a personal problem:	Women score
3	▶ You can generally understand and sympathize	4
2	▶ You can usually explain why it's not so bad after all	2
0	▶ You usually give advice or suggestions on how to solve the problem	⓪
2	▶ None of the above	2

Men score	9. Today you meet more than seven new people. Tomorrow:	Women score
3	▶ You can picture at least seven of the new faces	4
2	▶ You could put some names to some faces	2
0	▶ You could remember names but not many faces	0
2	▶ None of the above	②

Men score	10. You cannot find your keys:	Women score
3	▶ You do something else until they turn up	4
2	▶ You try to do something else, but you're distracted by the loss	2
0	▶ You keep retracing your movements until you find them	⓪
2	▶ None of the above	2

Men score	11. When predicting what is going to happen:	Women score
3	▶ You use your intuition	4
2	▶ You rely on gut feelings to interpret relevant information	2
0	▶ You use trends based on historical statistics or other data	0
2	▶ None of the above	2

Men score	12. When you have heard a song:	Women score
3	▶ You can sing some of the words next time you hear the tune	4
2	▶ You can remember the tune but not the words	2
0	▶ You can vaguely remember the tune	0
2	▶ None of the above	2

Men score	13. You are listening to the radio or TV and the phone rings:	Women score
3	▶ You just take the call and talk	4
2	▶ You turn down the radio /TV and talk	2
0	▶ You turn off the radio/TV, tell others to be quiet and talk	0
2	▶ None of the above	2

Men score	14. You need to reverse a vehicle into a tight spot to park it. Would you:	Women score
3	▶ Look for another parking spot	4
2	▶ Attempt to park, preferably with assistance	2
0	▶ Just try to reverse in	0
2	▶ None of the above	2

Men score	15. In a place you are visiting for the first time:	Women score
3	▶ You would not know which way was north	4
2	▶ You could have a good guess which way was north	2
0	▶ You would know which way was north	0
2	▶ None of the above	2

Men score	16. A child's mechanical toy won't work:	Women score
3	▶ You can sympathize with the child and discuss how they feel about it	4
2	▶ You can find somebody else to fix it	2
0	▶ You will usually try to fix it ✎	0
2	▶ None of the above	(2)

Men score	17. After a good film you prefer:	Women score
3	▶ To picture the scenes in your own mind	4
2	▶ To describe it to someone else	2
0	▶ To relate ideas or themes or lines from the film ✎	(0)
2	▶ None of the above	2

Men score	18. When explaining or defining something:	Women score
3	▶ You often use a pencil, pen, paper or gestures	4
2	▶ You rely on verbal and non-verbal communication only	2
0	▶ You could define it clearly without repeating yourself ✎	(0)
2	▶ None of the above	2

Men score	19. Asked to read a map:	Women score
3	▶ You would prefer some help	4
2	▶ You would have to turn it to face the way you were going	2
0	▶ You find it straightforward ✎	0
2	▶ None of the above	2

Men score	20. When thinking about your forthcoming day:	Women score
3	▶ You often write a list	4
2	▶ You think about what you want to achieve that day	(2)
0	▶ You run through places and activities in your mind ✎	0
2	▶ None of the above	2

....

If you are a man, add up your score under the men score column.

If you are a woman, add up your score under the women score column.

Most men we have tested scored less than 44. Most women we have tested scored more than 40.

People with lower scores tended to use TMB thinking skills. People with low scores were more likely to rely on logic, deduction, analysis and disciplined organization. The closer they were to zero, the more likely it was that they were good at making detailed plans. They tended to be less easily swayed by emotions and more objective when making decisions. Women with low scores were more likely to own their lesbian or bisexual tendencies.

People with high scores tended to make more use of the thinking skills more frequently used by women. People with a higher score were more likely to be creative or artistic. They made greater use of intuition or gut feelings. They could think inductively, recognize patterns and identify and solve problems on the basis of less information. Men with a higher score were more likely to be gay or bisexual. Men who scored closer to zero had great difficulties when in relationships, especially with women who scored nearer 80, and vice versa.

Mid-range scores indicated people who had the ability, under many circumstances, to think either like a TMB man, or like a TFB woman. Such people seemed to perform well when working in groups, or when working as managers, especially where there were multi-factor problems to be solved and where novel solutions were needed.

Since we began our research in 1982, knowledge about the structure and working of the brain has exploded. This has helped us to infer that brain differences might account for the differences in the thinking and behaviour that we encountered. In turn this has allowed us also to examine some implications for the way we might behave more effectively when talking to, relating to, working with, or working for, people of the opposite sex.

Men and women have abilities, to different extents, in a range of thinking skills. The research suggests that many women are better at emotional thinking, verbal thinking, making sense of information and reflective thinking. For many men, the research suggests that they are better at spatial thinking, mathematical thinking and predictive thinking. Hence, whether you are a man or a woman, you may wish to develop skills in those areas in which you feel less skilful.

Appendix 3

References and recommended reading

Ackerman, D. (1991) *A Natural History of Sensations*, US: Vintage

Al-Jajjoka, S. (2001) *Professional Tests*, London: Kogan Page

Amen, D. (2000) *Change Your Brain*, US: Three Rivers

Amen, D. (2004) *Prevent, Delay and Halt Memory Loss*, US: Putnam

Amen, D. (2005) *Sex on the Brain*, US: Three Rivers

Andreasen, N. (2006) *The Creating Brain*, US: Plume

Apperloo, I. (2003) 'The Mood for Sex' in *Journal of Sex Therapy*, 29: 86–103

Archive of Women's Mental Health 7(1) 18–27

Ariety, D. (2008) *Predictable Irrationality – Hidden Forces that Shape Decisions*, UK: HarperCollins

Arnold, A. (2004) 'Sex Chromosomes and Brain Gender' in *Nature Neuroscience* 5: 700–9

Aron, A. (2005) 'Reward Motivation and Romance' in *Journal of Neurophysiology* 94: 326

Aslam, A. (2004) 'Vitamin E deficiency induces neurological disease' in *Clinical Immunology* 112(1) 23–30

Attwood, J. (2007) *The Passion Test*, US: Hudson

Austin, J. (1975) *How to do Things with Words*, UK: Clarendon

Babcock, S. (2004) *Women Don't Ask: Negotiation and Gender*. US: PVP

Bacha, C.S., Wootton S., Horne, T (2011) 'The Neuroscience of Psychopathology' in *Journal of Psychoanalytic Practice* – in print

Baggini, J. (2006) *Do You Think?*, London: Grant

Baghranian, M. (2004) *Relativism*, UK: Routledge

Baron-Cohen, S. (2003) *The Essential Difference*, UK: Allen Lane

Baron-Cohen, S. (2005) *Empathic Thinking and Mind Reading. The Origin of the Social Mind,* NY: Guildford 476–93

Baron-Cohen, S. (2005) 'Sex Difference on the Brain' in *Science* 310:818–24

Barrett, J. (2000) Test Yourself, London: Kogan Page.

Bartels, A. (2004) 'Neural Correlates of Maternal and Romantic Love'.

Becker, J. (2005) 'Sex Difference in Brains and Behavior' in *Endocrinology* 146:1649–74

Belsky, J. (2005) 'Intergenerational Warm Sensitive Stimulatory Parenting' in *Child Development* 76: 383–99

Birk, L. (2001) 'Mirthful laughter modulates immune system' in *Health and Medicine* (2) 61–77

Blackburn, S. (2001) *Being Good,* UK: Oxford University Press

Blakemore, S. (2007) *The Learning Brain*, London: Blackwell

Blanco, I.M. (1999). *Bi-Logic: The Unconscious Mind as Infinite Sets*, UK: Karnal

Bloom, F. (2007) *Mind, Matter, Tomorrow*, US: Dana

Borkowski, J.G. and Muthukrishna, N. (1992) 'Moving metacognition into the classroom: "Working models" and Effective Strategy Teaching' in M. Pressley, K.R. Harris and J.T. Guthrie (Eds.) *Promoting academic competence and literacy in school* (pp. 477–501). San Diego, CA: Academic

Borkowski, J.G., Carr, M., Rellinger, E. and Pressley, M. (1990) 'Self-regulated cognition: Interdependence of metacognition, attributions, and self-esteem' in B.F. Jones and L. Idol (Eds.) *Dimensions of thinking and cognitive instruction* (pp. 53–92). Hillsdale, NJ: Erlbaum

Bortels, A. (2000) 'The Neural Basis of Love' in *Neuro Report* 11: 3828–35

Boyd, A. (2008) *Emergent Maths and Spatial Awareness,* UK: Rosen

Brainstorm, G. (2005) 'Testosterone Patch Treatment of Sexual Desire Disorder in Women' in *Archive International Medicine* 165:1581–90

Bremner, J. (1997) *Mensa Mighty Visual Puzzles,* UK: Carlton

Bridgett, D. (2000) 'Effect of Mozart and Bach on mathematic test results' in *Perception and Motor Skills* 90 (1170–76)

Brizendine, L. (2007) *The Female Brain,* UK: Bantam

Brockman J. (2006) *Dangerous Ideas,* UK: Simon & Schuster

Bryon, M. (2010) *How to Pass Advanced Numeracy Tests,* UK: Kogan Page

Bryon, M. (2011) *How to Pass Graduate Psychometric Tests,* London: Kogan Page

Buchanan, M. (2011) 'Quantum Minds' in *New Scientist* (2828) 3 September 2011, p. 34

Buster, J. (2005) 'Testosterone Patch for Low Sexual Desire Post Hysterectomy' in *Obstetric Gynecology* 105 (Part 1) 943–53.

Butterworth, B. (1999) *The Mathematical Brain,* London: Macmillan

Buzan, T. (1993), *Use Both Sides of Your Brain,* London: Plume

Calder, A. (2002) 'Reading the Mind from Eye Gaze' in *Neuropsychologia* 40 :1128–39

Calhill, L. (2005) 'His Brain Her Brain' in *Scientific American* (2931): 943–48I

Calvin, W. (1997) *Evolving Intelligence,* UK: HarperCollins

Cameron, D (2007) *The Myths of Mars and Venus,* UK: Oxford University Press

Campbell, A. (2002). *A Mind of her Own,* UK: Oxford University Press

Campbell, D. (1997) *The Mozart Effect,* US: Avon

Caral, P. (2008) *Billion Dollar Inexcusable Business Failures,* US: Porfolio

Cavanaugh, J.C. and Perlmutter, M. (1982) 'Metamemory: A critical examination' in *Child Development,* 53, 11–28

Cave, P. (2004) *Thinking about Death*, UK: British Humanist

Cave, P. (2005) *This sentence is false*. BBC Radio 4

Cave, P. (2006) 'Sex without God' in *Think* (12), UK: TPM

Cave, P. (2011) *Humanism,* Oxford: One world

Cave, P. (Ed) (2006) John Stuart Mill and Jeremy Bentham UK: British Humanist

Cave, P. (2007) *Can a Robot be Human?*, Oxford: One World

Chabris, C. (1979) 'Inattentional Blindness' in *Perception* 28, 1058–73

Chabris, C. (2011) *Intuition Deceives*, UK: HarperCollins

Charan, R. (2008) *Leadership and Economic Uncertainty* US: McGraw Hill

Checkland, P. (1981) *Systems Thinking, Systems Practice*, Wiley

Cheng, P.W. (1993), 'Multiple interactive structural representation systems for education', in Cox, R., Petre, M., Bran, P. and Lee, J. (eds), *Proceedings of the Workshop of Graphical Representations, Reasoning and Communication,* at the A1-ED, 1993 World Conference on Artificial Intelligence in Education (pp 25–28), University of Edinburgh

Christakis, D. (2004) 'Early television exposure and attentional problems in children' in *Paediatrics* 113, April 707–14

Clark, M. (2007) *Paradoxes A to Z*, UK: Routledge

Cohen, G. (2000) *Egalitarianism: How come you're so rich?,* US: Harvard University

Cohen, M. (1999) *Philosophy Problems*, London: Routledge

Coren, S. (1996) *Sleep Thieves*, NY: Simon & Schuster

Cornelius G. and Casler J. (1991), 'Enhancing Creativity in Young Children: Strategies for Teachers', *Early Child Development and Care*, 72, pp 96–106

Cousens, G. (2001), *Depression-free for Life: A Physician's All-Natural 5-Step Plan*, Quill, HarperCollins

Daganski, B. (2004) 'Neuroplasticity: Grey matter changes are induced by training' in *Nature* 427 (6972) January 310–313

Dahlen, E. (2004) 'Boredom, anger, aggression and impulsiveness' in *Personality* 37: 1614–28

Davidson, J.E., Deuser, R. and Sternberg, R.J. (1994) 'The role of metacognition in problem solving' in J. Metcalfe and A.P. Shimamura (Eds.) *Metacognition: Knowing about knowing* (pp. 207–226), Cambridge, MA: MIT

Davis, M. (2008) *The Stress Reduction Workbook*, US: New Harbinger

Dawkins, R. (2006) *The God Delusion*, UK: Bantam

Dawkins, R. (2006) *The Selfish Gene*, UK: Oxford University Press

De Bono, E. (2000) *Six Thinking Hats*, UK: Penguin

De Bono, E. (2007) *Creative Ideas*, UK: Vermillion

De Bono, E, (1993) *Six Action Shoes, Six Thinking Hats*, UK: Fontana

Depue, R. (2005) 'A Neuroscience Model of Affiliation' in *Brain Science* 28: 312–51

Dewey, J. (1933) *How We Think*, Boston, Mass: D.C. Heath and Co

Dienstbier, R. (1989) 'Periodic adrenaline rousal boosts health', *Brain-mind Bulletin*, 14 (9)

Dimburg, V. (2000) 'Mirror Neurons' in *Psychological Science* 11:85–90

Doviolio, J. (2007) *Stereotypes*, UK: Cambridge University Press

Duorty, S. (2007) *Liars, Lovers and Heroes: What Brain Science Reveals*, NY: HarperCollins

Ehrlich, S. (2006) *Language and Sexuality,* pp. 195–215, UK: Routledge

Eisenberger, N. (2004) 'Why Reflection Hurts: Neurological Alarm System for Social Pain Trends' in *Cognitive Science* 8 (7): 293–301

Elwes, R. (2010) *Maths 1001*, UK: Quercus

Elwes, R. (2011) *How to Build Brains*, UK: Quercus

Englert, C.S. and Raphael, T.E. (1989) 'Developing successful writers through cognitive strategy instruction' in J. Brophy (Ed.) *Advances in Research on Teaching*, vol. 1. Greenwich, CT: JAI Press

Epstein, R. (2007) *Games that Relieve Stress*, US: McGraw Hill

Epstein, R. (2011) 'The Frazzled Mind' in *Scientific America*, 22(4) October

Everitt, N. (2004) *The Non Existence of God*, UK: Oxford University Press

Finkel, K. (2006) *Stem Cells,*

Fisher, H. (2002) 'The Neural Mechanisms of Mate Choice' in *Neuroendocrinology* 23: 4, 91–98

Fisher, H. (2002) 'Brain Chemistry of Lust Romance Attraction and Attachment' in *Archive of Sexual Behavior* 31(5): 412–20.

Fisher, H. (2004) *Why we love – The Chemistry of Love (from 838)*, NY: Henry Holt

Flavell, J.H. (1963) *The Developmental Psychology of Jean Piaget*, US: Nostrand

Flavell, J.H. (1977) *Cognitive Development*, NJ: Prentice Hall

Flavell, J.H. and Wellman, H.M. (1977) 'Metamemory' in R.V. Kail, Jr. and J.W. Hagen (Eds.) *Perspectives on the Development of Memory and Cognition*, Hillsdale, NJ: Erlbaum

Flavell, J.H., P.H. Miller and S.A. Miller (1993) *Cognitive Development*, third edition, Englewood Cliffs, NJ: Prentice Hall

Fleming, A. (2002) 'Mothering begets Mothering' in *The Neurobiology of Parenting Pharmacological Bio Behavior Rev* 23(5): 672–86

Forger, N. (2006) 'Cell Death in Brains of Men and Women' in *Neuroscience* 138(3): 928–39

Frankish, K. (2005) *Consciousness*, UK: Routledge

Fulton, J. (2006) *Mensa Total Genius,* UK: Carlton

Gardner, H. (1999), *Intelligence Reframed: Multiple Intelligences for the 21st Century*, NY: Basic Books

Gelb, M. (with Tony Buzan) (1994) *Juggling: Business, Learning and Life*, US: Harmony

Gelb, M. (1995) *Alexander Techniques*, US: Holt

Gelb, M. (1996) *Thinking for a change*, US: Harmony

Gelb, M. (1998) *How to Think like Leonardo da Vinci*, UK: HarperCollins

Gelb, M. (2003) *Brain Power: Improve Your Mind as You Age*, New World Library

Gibb, B. (2007) *Rough Guide to the Brain*, UK: Rough Guide

Giedd, J. (2004) *Time* Magazine, May, p. 63

Gigenenger, G. (2007) *Gut Feelings*, US: Viking

Gizewski, E. (2006) 'Gender specific cerebral activity during thinking tasks' in *MRI NeuroRadiology* 47 (1):13–21

Glover, J. (1977) *Causing Death*, UK: Penguin

Goldberg, M. (1998) *The Art of the Question*, US: Wiley

Goldstein, T. (2005) 'Sex difference in frontal cortex during working memory' in *Neuropsychological* 19(4) 508–20

Goleman, D. (2003) *Destructive Emotions*, UK: Bantum

Gordon, P. (2000) *Solving Sudoku*, US: Sterling

Gordon, W.J.J. and Poze T., (1980), *The New Art of the Possible: The Basic Course in Synetics*, Cambridge MA: Porpoise Books

Gray, J. (2003) 'The Neural Mechanisms of Intelligence' in *Nature Neuroscience* 6:315–23

Gray, S. (2003) 'Is vitamin C antioxidant protective of cognitive function?' in *American Journal of Pharmacotherapy* 1 (1) 2–11

Green, H. (2007) *Their Space*, UK: Demos

Greenfield, S. (1997) *Guided Tour of Brain,* UK: Phoenix

Greenfield, S.A. (2002) *The Private Life of the Brain*, UK: Penguin

Greenfield, S.A. (2003) *Tomorrow's People*, UK: Penguin

Greenfield, S.A. (2011) Interviewed by Frank Sevain for *New Scientist* 211(2823), p. 25

Greenfield, S.A. (2008) *ID: The Quest for Meaning in the 21st Century*, UK: Sceptre

Greenleaf, P.K. (1977) *Leadership and Legitimate Power*, NY: Paulist Press

Grewen, K. (2005) 'Effect on Oxytocin and Cortisol Levels in the Brain, following Warm Partner Contact' in *Psychosomatic*: 67(4) 530–39

Haigh, J. (1999) *Taking Chances – Winning with Probability*, UK Oxford University Press

Haier, R. (2005) 'The Neuroanatomy of Intelligence: Why Sex Matters' 25(1) 319–28

Haizink, A. (2004) *Psychological Bulletin*, January.

Halari, R. (2005) 'Inferior Performance by Women in Novel Cognitive Tasks' in *Behavior Brain Research* 158(1) 166–72

Halari, R. (2006) 'fMRI differences in performance between men and women on mental rotation and verbal thinking' in *Experience Brain Research* 169 (1) 1–15

Halbreich, V. (2006) 'Major Depression Diagnosis' in *Psyconeuronocrinology* 31 (1): 15–23

Hanfling, O. (1987) *The Quest for Meaning*, UK: Oxford University Press

Harrison, J. (2010) *Maxing the Brain*, UK: Penguin

Harrison, R. (1993) *Democracy*, UK: Routledge

Harvey, S. (2009) *Acting like a Lady*, NY: HarperCollins

Haselton, M. (2005) 'Sex, Lies and Strategies – Deception between the Sexes' in *Personal Social Psychology Bulletin* 31(1) 2–24

Haworth, A. (1998) *Free Speech*, UK: Routledge

Heilman, K.M (2005), *Creativity and the Brain*, Psychology Press

Herman-Toffler, L.R. and Tuckman, B.W. (1998), The effects of aerobic training on children's creativity, self-perception and aerobic power, *Sports Psychiatry*, 7 (4):773–790

Hinds, P. (2011) *Journal of Applied Experimental Psychology*. (5) p. 204

Hobson, P. (2002) *Cradle of Thought*, UK: Dana

Holyoak K.J. and Thagard P. (1995), Mental Leaps, Mass: MIT Press

Hood, B. (2009) *Why believe the unbelievable*, UK: Harper One

Hood, B. (2012) *The self illusion*, UK: Oxford University Press

Horne, T. and Doherty, A. (2003) *Managing Public Services: A Thoughtful Approach to the Practice of Management*, London: Routledge

Howard, P. (2006) *The Brain*, third edition, Texas: Bard Press

Howard, P. J. (2006) *The Owner's Manual for the Brain – Everyday Applications from Mind and Brain Research*, third edition, Texas: Bard Press

Huttenslocher, P. (2002) *Neural Plasticity*, US: Harvard University

Hyman, S. (2006) 'Neural Addiction' in *Annual Review of Neuroscience* 29, 564–599

Inman, N. (2007) *The Optimists Handbook*, UK: Harrisman

Jansky, J. (2004) 'Orgasmic Aura and the Right Brain' in *Neurology* 58(2) Jan 301–05

Kawashima, D. (2007) *Train Your Brain*, UK: Penguin

Kelly, K. (2011) *What Technology Wants*, US: Penguin.

Kendel, E. (2006) *New Science of Mind*, UK: Norton

Kish, S.J., Furukawa Y., Ang L., Vorce S.P., Kalasinsky K.S., 'Striatal serotonin is depleted in brain of a human MDMA (ecstacy) user', *Neurology* 2000, 55:296–6

Kitzinger, C. (1999) 'Just say No' in *Discourse and Society* 10(3) 291–317

Kodish, S. (1993) *Drive yourself sane using uncommon sense*. US: Engelwood

Koepp, M. (1998) 'Addictive Dopamine Release during Video Games', in *Nature* 393 (6682). May 265–69

Koestler, A. (1970), *The Act of Creation*, London: Pan Books

Kornell, D. (2011) 'Learning Memory Cognition and Behavioral Processes' *Journal of Experimental Psychology* 83, 9206

Lambert, K. (2011) *The Lab Rat Chronicles*, US: Penguin

Lambert, K. (2010) *Clinical Neuroscience – Lifting Depression*, UK: Basic Books

Le Doux, J. (2005) *The Synaptic Self*. NY: Viking

Legato, M. (2005) 'Blood Sweat and Fears – The Neurophysiology of Emotion of Science' in *Annals of Science Academy* 1000: 347–67

Lehr, D. (2009) *The Fence*, US: HarperCollins

Levitin, D. (2008) *Music on the Brain*, US: Atlantic

Li, H. (2005) 'Sex Difference and the Rate of Brain Cell Death' in *Annals of Neurology* 581

Light, K. (2005) 'Partner Hugs increase Oxytocin and Lower Blood Pressure' in *Bio Psychology* 69(1): 4–22

Lim, N. (2004) 'Levels of Vasopressin – The Neurochemical Regulation of Monogamy' in *Journal of Neuroendocrinology* 16(4): 324–33

Lomborg, B. (2001) *The Skeptical Environmentalist*, UK: Cambridge University Press

Luna, B. (2004) 'Algebra and the Adolescent Brain' in *Cognitive Science* 8(10) 436–40

Lunt, M. (2004) 'Caffeine Reduces Brain Blood Flow' in *Physiological Measurement* 25(2) 466–75

Lytle, M. (2004) 'Exercise level and cognitive decline' in *Alzheimer Disease and other disorders* 18(2) April 56–65

Mann, S. (2011) 'Outsmarting Liars. Cognitive Selection' in *Current Directions in Psychological Sciences* 20 (1) 27–33

Manson, N. (2003) *God and Design*, UK: Routledge

Markman, E.M. (1977) 'Realising that you don't understand: A preliminary investigation' in *Child Development*, 48, 986–92

Martin, J. (2006). *The 21st Century*. UK: Eden Project

Mathew, R.J., Wilson, W.H., Coleman R.E., Turkington, T.G., DeGrado, T.R (1997), 'Marijuana intoxication and brain activation in marijuana smokers, *Life Sci*, 60: 2075–2089

Mattson, M. (2003) 'Meal size and frequency affect neuronal plasticity' in *Journal of Neurochemistry* 84 (3) Feb 416–32

McKay, R. and Cameron, H.A. (1999) 'Restoring the production of hippocampal neurons in old age' in *Nature Neuroscience*, October, vol. 2, no. 10, pp. 894–7

McMeel, A. (2009) *Puzzling Numbers*, US: Meel Publishing

Mellor, D. (1998) *Real Time* UK: Routledge

Metcalfe, J. and A.P. Shimamura (Eds.) (1994) *Metacognition: Knowing about Knowing*, Cambridge, MA: MIT Press

Middleton, J. (2006) *Upgrade Your Brain*, London: Infinite Ideas

Midgley, M. (2002) *Evolution as Religion*, UK: Routledge

Miller, G. (2004) 'Brain cells pay the price for Bad Sleep' in *Science* 206, p. 1126 (5699)

Molteni, R. (2002) 'High Fat and Refined Sugar reduce BDNF neuronal plasticity, learning and memory' in *Neuroscience* 112(4) 502–15

Neill, A. (2002) *Arguing about Art – Horror, Tragedy and Suspense*, UK: Routledge

Nelson, E. (2005) 'A Neuroscine Perspective on the Social Re-orientation of Adolescents' in *Psychological Medicine*, 35(2) 163–74

Nelson, T.O. and Narens, L. (1990) 'Metamemory: a theoretical framework and new findings' in G. Bower (Ed.) *The psychology of learning and motivation* (Vol. 26). New York: Academic

Newberg, A. (2006) *Why we believe what we believe*. UK: Free

O'Doherty, J. (2003) 'Beauty in a Smile' in *Neuropsychologia* 41: 146–551

Oppenheimer, D. (2008) 'Fluency Delusions' in *Trends in Cognitive Science* 12, 236–42

Osborn, A.F. (1953) *Imagination: Principles and Procedures of Creative Thinking*, New York: Scribner.

Ostrom, E. (2008) *Governing Commons – Collective Action*, UK: Cambridge University Press

Otten, L. (2006) *Journal of Neuroscience*, February

Paris, S.G. and Winograd, P. (1990) 'How Metacognition Can Promote Academic Learning and Instruction' in B.F. Jones and L. Idol (Eds.) *Dimensions of Thinking and Cognitive Instruction* (pp. 15–51). Hillsdale, NJ: Erlbaum

Pascual-Leone, A. (2007) 'The Brain: How the Brain Rewires Itself', *Time Magazine Science*, 19 January.

Pentland, A. (2010) *International Journal of Organisational Design* (1), p. 69

Perkins, D.N. (1988), 'Creativity and the quest for mechanism', in Srernbert, R.J. and Smith, E.E. (eds), *The Psychology of Human Thought* (pp 309–36), NY: Cambridge University Press

Poidevin, R. (1993) *Philosophy of Time*, UK: Oxford University Press

Poon, H. (2005) 'Neuroprotective effects of alpha lipoic acid; implications for ageing and neurodegenerative disease' in *NeuroImage* 23:1154–67

Posner, M. (2006) *Education and the Brain*, US: American Association Psychological

Poundstone, W. (1992) *Prisoner's Dilemmas*, NY: Doubleday

Priesta, G. (2000) *Logic*, UK: Oxford University Press

Prinker, S. (2002) *If Men Could Talk*, NY: Little Brown

Prior, M. (2006) 'No evidence for Mozart Effect in Children' in *Music and perception* 23 304–18

Rawls, J. (1971) *Theory of Justice*, US: Harvard University

Rescher, N. (2001) *Paradox – Root, Range and Resolution*, US: Opencourt

Restak, R. (2001) *The Secret Life of the Brain*, UK: Dana

Rogoff, B. (1990) *Apprenticeship in Thinking: Cognitive development in cultural context*, NY: Oxford University Press

Rosenblum, L. (1994) 'Adverse early experiences affects neurochemical functions in adult primates' in *Biological Psychiatry* 35(4): 220–28

Rosenzweig, P. (2007) *The Halo Effect and 8 other managerial delusions*, US: Free Press

Ross, H. (2009) 'Oxytocin regulates social cognition and affiliative behavior' in *Frontiers in Neuroendocrinology* 30 533–548

Rubinhow, D. (2002) 'Gonadal hormones Concentration or Context?' in *Hormones Brain and Behavior* Pfaff (Ed) 5:35–75

Rupp, R. (1998) *Committed to Memory*, London: Aurum Press Limited

Ryle, G. (1990) *The Concept of Mind*, UK: Penguin

Schaie, K. (1996) *Intellectual Development in Adults: Seattle Study*, Oxford University

Schellenberg, E. (2005) 'Music and Cognitive Ability in 10 year olds' in *Annals NY Academy of Science* (1060) 210

Schmitt, D. (1996) 'Strategic Self Promotion and Competitor Derogation: Sex Effects on Effectiveness of Mate Attraction Tactics' in *Journal of Personal Social Pschology* 70(6)1184–205

Schwing, J. (2005) *Visual Analysis of Data Mining*, UK: Springer

Scruton, R. (1986) *Sexual Desire*, UK: Weidenfeld & Nicolson

Seligman, M. (1991) *Learned Optimism*, US: Knopf

Sheeney, G. (1999) *Men's Lives – New Directions at Midlife*, London: Simon & Schuster

Shellenbarger, S. (2005) *The Breaking Point Midlife Crisis in Women*, NY: Henry Holt

Shore, B.M. and Kanevsky, L.S. (1993), 'Thinking Processes: Being and Becoming Gifted', in Heller, K.A,, Monks, F.J. and Passow, A.H. (Eds), *International Handbook of Research and Development of Giftedness and Talent*, Oxford: Pergamon Press Ltd

Shutzwohl, A. (2006) 'Assessing the Female Figure: A new approach to the waist hip ratio' in *Biological Psychology* 71(2): 222–30

Skuse, D. (2003) 'The Amygdala and the Social Brain' in *Academy of Science*, 1008:90–102

Sloan, P. (2003) *Colourful Lateral Puzzles*, UK: Sterling

Sloan, P. (2006) *Cunning Lateral Puzzles*, UK: Sterling

Small, G. (2006) 'Lifestyle on cognition and Brain' in *Annual Journal of Psychiatry* 14(6) 538–46

Snowdon, D. (1997) 'Aging and Alzheimer's – the Nun Study' in *Gerontologist* 37(2) 149–57

Sorenson, R. (1999) *Clear and Queer Thinking*, UK: Duckworth

Sorenson, R. (2003) *The History of Paradox*, NY: Oxford University

Speke, E. (2005) 'Sex Differences in Aptitudes for Math and Science' in *AM Psychology* 60(9): 949–59

Stickels, T. (2006) *Mind Bending Puzzles by Mensa*, UK: Sterling

Swartz, R.J. (1989) 'Making Good Thinking Stick: The role of metacognition, extended practice, and teacher modelling in the teaching of thinking' in D.M. Topping, D.C. Crowell and V.N. Kobayashi (Eds.) *Thinking Across Cultures: The third international conference on thinking*, NJ: Erlbaum

Tallis, F. (2004) *Love Sick*, UK: Century

Taylor, K. (2004) *Brainwashing*, UK: Oxford University

Tharp, T. (2004) *The Creative Habit*, New York: Simon & Schuster

Thompson, A. (1999) *Critical Reasoning*, New York: Routledge

Treffinger, D.J. and Feldhusen, J.F. (1986) *Creative Thinking and Problem Solving in Gifted Education*, Iowa: Kendall/Hunt Publishing Co

Tuller, D. (2006) *Mensa Maths and Logic*, UK: Sterling

Umilta, C. (2011) *Neuromania: The Limits of Brain Scan*, UK: Oxford University Press

Valbergs, J. (2007) *Dream, Death and the Self*, US: Princeton Univesity

Vygotsky, L.S. (1963) *Thought and Language*, Cambridge MA: Harvard University

Watson, G. (2003) *Free Will*, UK: OUP

Weir, D. (1999) 'Brain Function – the role of vitamin B12 and Folic acid' in *British Medical Bulletin* 55 (668–85)

Wesnes, K. (2000) 'Memory Enhancement of Gingko Biloba and Ginseng in Middle age Volunteers' in *Psychopharmacology* 152(4) 353–62

Whalley, L. (2001) 'Childhood IQ and Longevity' in *British Medical Journal* 322:819

Whalley, L. (2001) *The ageing brain*, UK: Weidenfeld & Nicolson

Whitehouse, H. (2004) *Cognitive Theory of Religion*, UK: Altaminra

Williams, L. (1986), *Teaching for the Two-Sided Mind*, Touchstone Books

Winston, R. (2003) *The Human Mind*, UK: Bantam

Wiseman, R. (2003) *Change luck - change life*, UK: Century

Wiseman, J. (2007) *Quirkology*, London: Macmillan

Witchells, C. (2007) 'Join the Blub' in The *Independent*, 10 April, p. 8

Wootton, S and Horne, T. (2010a) *Train Your Brain*, UK: Hodder Education

Wootton, S. and Horne, T. (2010b) *Keep Your Brain Sharp*, UK: Hodder Education

Wootton, S. and Horne, T. (2010c) *Strategic Thinking*, UK: Kogan Page

Appendix 4

---

20 brain-friendly family days out (or days in)

1 **Make a rainbow:** hang old CDs on a washing line; face a garden hose upwards with the sun behind you; put water in a jar, preferably a square jar on a window sill; put a small mirror in a bowl of water near a window.

2 **Museums to check out:** Natural History and Science Museums, London; Pitt Rivers Museum, Oxford; Kelvingrove Museum, Glasgow; museums in Dorchester, Dorset, Torrington, Devon; Manchester, Liverpool and Lancaster.

3 **Build a tree house:** tree trunk and platform 1.8 metres off the ground. Rope ladder and trap door to get onto the platform. Rope from a branch to slither down or to swing on. Pulley over a branch to pull up supplies. Safer without rails. Ensure soft landing.

4 **Pick fruit** – wild blackberries, bilberries, damsons, elderberries, grow your own gooseberries in pots. Look up more than 1000 Pick-Your-Own farms in telephone directories or on the internet.

5 **Play cards**, for example, Cheat, Patience, Newmarket, Brag, Whist, Uno, Go Fish, Hearts, Contract, Two-Hand Whist.

6 **Water Games:** drop sticks into a river from a bridge and see whose come out the other side first; build a dam; row a boat; play with water.

7 **Put on a show:** invite friends or neighbours round. Children like to sing, dance, dress up, face paint, tell jokes, anything that adults can cheer and applaud at the end.

8 **Read a story** while children colour, trace, thread beads, knit, do a jigsaw, sort or arrange toys. Try stories by Spike Milligan, Dr Seuss, Michael Rosen, A.A. Milne, Lewis Carroll, Rudyard Kipling.

9 **Find and read** (and maybe memorize) a verse of a poem, beginning for example.

   a Tyger! Tyger burning bright...

   b The Owl and the Pussycat went to sea...

   c 'You are old Father William,' the young man said...

   d She walks in beauty, like the night...

    e How do I love thee? Let me count the ways...

    f If you can keep your head, when all about you are...

10 **Keep a diary** but only one sentence a day – to share.

11 **Ask a child for advice** about how to solve a problem.

12 **Plot a random secret act of kindness.**

13 **Become a secret friend.**

14 **Climb something:** slope, hill, mountain.

15 **Think of a friend** to contact.

16 **Volunteer for something:** go to the volunteers' bureau.

17 **Write down a story:** from a parent's or a grandparent's life.

18 **Memorize things:** trays of objects, cards, poems.

19 **Teach a child** to ride a bike, swim, make boiled eggs, do a card trick, play with a yo-yo, make a map of hidden dark chocolates.

20 **Do a thank you card** for a checkout assistant, or a post person, or a refuse collector, or a school crossing warden, or someone else the children think deserve one.